The Dangerous Passion

Why Jealousy Is as Necessary as Love and Sex

DAVID M. BUSS, Ph.D.

THE FREE PRESS

New York London Sydney Singapore

THE FREE PRESS
A Division of Simon & Schuster Inc.
1230 Avenue of the Americas
New York, NY 10020

THE FREE PRESS and colophon are trademarks of Simon & Schuster Inc.

Designed by Anne Scatto / PIXEL PRESS

Manufactured in the United States of America

10 9 8 7 6 5 4 3 2 1

Library of Congress Cataloging-in-Publication Data

Buss, David M.
    The dangerous passion: why jealousy is as necessary as love and sex /
            David M. Buss. p. cm.
    Includes bibliographical references and index.
    ISBN 978-1-4516-7313-5
    1. Jealousy. I. Title.
BF575.J4 B87 2000
15.2.4'8—dc21

For Cindy

Acknowledgements

THOSE WHO DEVOTE THEIR LIVES to penetrating the mysteries of human nature face an unusual circumstance, one in which the targets of study happen to include their own minds. Sometimes it's a personal insight that leads to a scientific discovery, but in my case, it was a scientific finding that led to a personal revelation. In one of my first formal studies of jealousy, we asked women and men to imagine their partner having sex with someone else. Some people displayed intense sexual jealousy, shaking with rage when these disturbing images filled their heads. Others seemed less upset, at least on the surface. I wanted to find out why. One critical factor turned out to be whether or not a person had already experienced a committed sexual relationship. Those who were either in love or who had loved and lost, displayed far more florid sexual jealousy than those who merely longed for love but had never experienced it.

As these results rolled off the computer printer, memories flooded my head of previously buried events of my past. As a youth of 17, influenced no doubt by the prevailing cultural ideologies of the time, I publicly proclaimed that my girlfriend's body was her own, that she could have sex with anyone she wanted, and that jealousy was an immature emotion of up-tight, hung-up, unliberated individuals. I, of course, was above all that. There was only one problem—I didn't have a girlfriend! A year later, when I became involved for the first time, my feelings about the matter suddenly reversed. It was as though a jealousy switch in my brain, previously on the "off" setting, suddenly got flipped to "on." I found myself glaring at other men who seemed a bit too friendly to my partner at parties, calling her up unexpectedly just to see whether she was where she said she would be, and thinking that every man harbored secret desires for her. I became aware of a deep dimension of my own psychology that had previously lain dormant.

Over the past decade, together with many talented colleagues, my scientific research has focused on the dangerous passion of jealousy and its tethered soul mate, the specter of infidelity. In the course of this work I discovered that some private demons are surprisingly widespread afflictions. This book represents a synthesis of that work, as well as of studies conducted by hundreds of scientists from around the world. I owe a deep debt to many who contributed directly or indirectly to its content and form. The first thanks goes to Don Symons, who helped me through friendship, published writings, dozens of discussions, and generous feedback on my work. Next, I owe special gratitude to Leda Cosmides and John Tooby, whose seminal writings and hours of lively discussion now spanning nearly two decades have greatly influenced my thinking. Martin Daly and Margo Wilson pioneered the exploration of the perilous passion, illuminated its special danger to women, and have generously helped to clarify my thinking over the years.

My direct-research collaborators deserve special thanks. I've had the good fortune to work with Alois Angleitner, Armen Asherian, Mike Barnes, Kevin Bennett, April Bleske, Mike Botwin, Bram Buunk, Jae Choe, Ken Craik, Lisa Dedden, Todd DeKay, Josh Duntley, Bruce Ellis, Barry Friedman, Steve Gangestad, Arlette Greer, Heidi Greiling, Mariko Hasegawa, Toshikazu Hasegawa, Martie Haselton, Doug Kenrick, Lee Kirkpatrick, Randy Larsen, Neil Malamuth, Victor Oubaid, David Schmitt, Jennifer Semmelroth, Todd Shackelford, and Drew Westen.

The incomparable Todd Shackelford must be singled out, since one could not ask for a more superlative collaborator. He has been co-author with me on more than a dozen publications on topics ranging from signals of infidelity to tactics men and women use to keep mates. Heidi Greiling helped to get me out of my male mind enough to collaborate on a raft of studies on the hidden dimensions of women's sexual psychology. Martie Haselton, primary author of *Error Management Theory,* brought insight to the signal detection problem and the importance of women's ovulation cycles. Josh Duntley contributed to understanding the extreme violence that jealous men sometime direct against women. April Bleske helped me to understand why friends are sometimes rivals and why men and women have so much difficulty being "just friends." Barry Friedman helped to explore how men and women "test" mating bonds.

Discussions with many other colleagues also influenced the ideas expressed in this book: Dick Alexander, Rosalind Arden, Robin Baker, Jerry Barkow, Laura Betzig, Nap Chagnon, Helena Cronin, Richard Dawkins, Irv DeVore, Randy Diehl, Paul Ekman, Steve Gangestad, Bill Hamilton, Kim Hill, Sarah Hrdy, Bill Jankowiak, Doug Jones, Doug Kenrick, Lee Kirkpatrick, Kevin MacDonald, Neil Malamuth, Geoffrey Miller, Randy Nesse, Dick Nisbett, Laura Nitzberg, Steve Pinker, David Rowe, Jeff Simpson, Dev Singh, Barb Smuts, Frank Sulloway, Del Thiessen, Nancy Thornhill, Randy Thornhill, Bill Tooke, John Townsend, Robert Trivers, Jerry Wakefield, Lee Willerman, George Williams, D.S. Wilson, E.O. Wilson, and Richard Wrangham.

My agents, Katinka Matson and John Brockman, were instrumental in helping me to shape the vision for this book. Philip Rappaport, of The Free Press, trained his fine editorial eye on an early draft of this book and brought a unique sensibility to its final tone. Rosemary Davidson, of Bloomsbury Publishers, April Bleske, Joshua Duntley, Barry Friedman, Martie Haselton, and Todd Shackelford all offered insightful comments on the entire book.

Finally, I owe special thanks to the thousands of women and men who generously opened their lives to reveal some of the darker secrets of the dangerous passion.

Contents

THE DANGEROUS PASSION

CHAPTER 1

The Dangerous Passion

Jealousy is not only inbred in human nature, but it is the most basic, all-pervasive emotion which touches man in all aspects of every human relationship.
—*Boris Sokoloff, 1947,* Jealousy: A Psychological Study

EVERY HUMAN ALIVE IS AN evolutionary success story. If any of our ancestors had failed to survive an ice age, a drought, a predator, or a plague, they would not be our ancestors. If any had failed to cooperate with at least some others in the group or dropped below a minimal position in the social hierarchy, they would have met certain death by being cast out from the group. If even one had failed to succeed in choosing, courting, and keeping a mate, the previously inviolate chain of descent would have irreparably broken, and we would not be alive to tell the tale. Each of us owes our existence to thousands of generations of successful ancestors. As their descendants, we have inherited the passions that led to their success—passions that drive us, often blindly, through a lifelong journey in the struggle for survival, the pursuit of position, and the search for relationships.

We usually think of passion as restricted to sex or love, the burning embrace or constant craving. But it has a broader meaning, referring to the drives and emotional fires that propel us in our quests through life. They sometimes glow quietly, but at other times they burst into full flame. They range from tranquil devotion to violent eruption. Their expression yields life's deepest joys, but also the cruelest suffering. And

1

although we commonly think of passion as a force opposed to reason and rationality, something to be tamed or overcome, passions when properly understood have a crystalline logic, precise purpose, and supreme sensibility.

The drives that stir us out of bed at dawn and hurl us headlong into our daily struggles have two sides. On the positive side, passions inspire us to achieve life's goals. They impel us to satisfy our desire for sex, our yearning for prestige, and our quest for love. The dazzling plays of Shakespeare, the mezmerizing art of Georgia O'Keeffe, and the brilliant inventions of Thomas Edison would not exist if passion had not stirred them from repose and impelled creation. Without passion, we would lie listless in bed, for there would be no motivation to do anything at all.

But passions carry a darker, more sinister side. The same passions that inspire us with love can lead to the disastrous choice of a mate, the desperation of unrequited obsession, or the terror of stalking. Jealousy can keep a couple committed or drive a man to savagely beat his wife. An attraction to a neighbor's spouse can generate intoxicating sexual euphoria while destroying two marriages. The yearning for prestige can produce exhilarating peaks of power while evoking the corrosive envy of a rival and a fall from a greater height. *The Dangerous Passion* explores both the destructive and triumphant sides of human desires.

Together with many colleagues, my research over the past decade has centered on exploring the nature, origins, and consequences of the passions of men and women, with a special focus on jealousy, infidelity, love, sex, and status. Our goal has been to seek a deeper understanding of what makes men and women tick, the desires that drive people to heights of success or depths of despair, and the evolved mechanisms of mind that define who we are. This book illuminates the dark side of sexual treachery, the mysterious puzzle of romantic love, and the central role of jealousy in our intimate relationships.

Some argue that these mysteries should be left alone, pristine and untrammeled, shielded from the harsh glare of scientific scrutiny. But is the woman who has her freedom and sense of safety crushed by a jealous husband better off unequipped with the knowledge of how to prevent her torment? Is the man obsessed by unrequited love better off failing to

2

understand the underlying reasons for his rejection? Ignorance may sometimes be bliss, but it can also cause needless anguish. My hope is that revealing the underlying logic of dangerous passions will be intellectually illuminating, provide one path for understanding the distress we experience at the hands of our lovers and rivals, and just possibly improve in some small measure the tools for coping with the untamed demons in our lives.

At the center of *The Dangerous Passion* is an exploration of a hazardous region of human sexuality—the desires people experience for those who are not their regular partners and the jealous shield designed to combat its treacherous consequences.

The Green-Eyed Monster

Think of a committed romantic relationship that you have now, or that you had in the past. Now imagine that your romantic partner becomes interested in someone else. What would upset or distress you more: (*a*) discovering that your partner is forming a deep emotional attachment, confiding and sharing confidences with another? or (*b*) discovering that your partner is enjoying passionate sex with the other person, trying out different sexual positions you had only dreamed about? Both scenarios are distressing, of course, but which one is more distressing? If you are like the majority of women we surveyed recently in the United States, the Netherlands, Germany, Japan, Korea, and Zimbabwe, you will find the emotional infidelity more upsetting. The answer seems obvious, at least to women. The majority of men, however, find the prospect of a partner's sexual infidelity more agonizing. The gulf between the sexes in emotional reactions to infidelity reveals something profound about human mating strategies.

The explanation for sex differences in jealousy lies deep in the evolutionary past of the human species. Consider first a fundamental sex difference in our reproductive biology: fertilization takes place inside women's bodies, not men's. Now, internal female fertilization is not universal in the biological world. In some species, such as the Mormon crickets, fertilization occurs internally within the male. The female takes her egg and literally implants it within the male, who then incubates it until birth. In other species, fertilization occurs externally to both sexes. The female salmon, for example, drops her collection of eggs after swimming upstream. The male follows and deposits his sperm on top, and then they die, having fulfilled the only mission in life that evolution gave them. But humans are not like salmon. Nor are we like Mormon crickets. In all 4,000 species of mammals, of which we are one, and in all 257 species of primates, of which we are also one, fertilization occurs internally within the female, not the male. This posed a grave problem for ancestral men—the problem of uncertainty in paternity.

From an ancestral man's perspective, the single most damaging form of infidelity his partner could commit, in the currency of reproduction, would have been a sexual infidelity. A woman's sexual infidelity jeopardizes a man's confidence that he is the genetic father of her children. A cuckolded man risks investing years, or even decades, in another man's children. Lost would be all the effort he expended in selecting and attracting his partner. Moreover, he would lose his partner's labors, now channeled to a rival's children rather than his own.

Women, on the other hand, have always been 100 percent sure that they are the mothers of their children (internal fertilization guarantees that their children are genetically their own). No woman ever gave birth and, watching the child emerge from her womb, wondered whether the child was really hers. One African culture captures this sex difference with a phrase more telling than any technical summary: "Mama's baby, papa's maybe." Biology has granted women a confidence in genetic parenthood that no man can share with absolute certainty.

Our ancestral mothers confronted a different problem, the loss of a partner's commitment to a rival woman and her children. Because emotional involvement is the most reliable signal of this disastrous loss, women key in on cues to a partner's feelings for other women. A husband's one-night sexual stand is agonizing, of course, but most women want to know: "Do you love her?" Most women find a singular lapse in fidelity without emotional involvement easier to forgive than the nightmare of another woman capturing her partner's tenderness, time, and affection. We evolved from ancestral mothers whose jealousy erupted at signals of the loss of love, mothers who acted to ensure the man's commitment.

But who cares who fathers a child or where a man's commitments get channeled? Shouldn't we love all children equally? Perhaps in some utopian future, we might, but that is not how the human mind is designed. Husbands in our evolutionary past who failed to care whether a wife succumbed to sex with other men and wives who remained stoic when confronted with their husband's emotional infidelity may be admirable in a certain light. Perhaps these self-possessed men and women were more mature. Some theories, in fact, propose that jealousy is an immature emotion, a sign of insecurity, neurosis, or flawed character. Nonjealous men and women, however, are not our ancestors, having been left in the evolutionary dust by rivals with different passionate sensibilities. We all come from a long lineage of ancestors who possessed the dangerous passion.

Jealousy, according to this theory, is an adaptation. An adaptation, in the parlance of evolutionary psychology, is an evolved solution to a recurrent problem of survival or reproduction. Humans, for example, have evolved food preferences for sugar, fat, and protein that are adaptive solutions to the survival problem of food selection. We have evolved specialized fears of snakes, spiders, and strangers that are adaptive solutions to ancestral problems inflicted by dangerous species, including ourselves. We have evolved specialized preferences for certain qualities in potential mates, which helped to solve the problems posed by reproduction. Adaptations, in short, exist in modern humans today because they helped our ancestors to combat all of the many "hostile forces of nature," enabling them to successfully survive and reproduce. Adaptations are coping devices passed down over millennia because they worked—not perfectly, of course, but they helped ancestral humans to struggle through the evolutionary bottlenecks of survival and reproduction.

Jealousy, according to this perspective, is not a sign of immaturity, but rather a supremely important passion that helped our ancestors, and most likely continues to help us today, to cope with a host of real reproductive threats. Jealousy, for example, motivates us to ward off rivals with verbal threats and cold primate stares. It drives us to keep partners from straying with tactics such as escalating vigilance or showering a partner with affection. And it communicates commitment to a partner who may be wavering, serving an important purpose in the maintenance of love. Sexual jealousy is often a successful, although sometimes explosive, solution to persistent predicaments that each one of our ancestors was forced to confront.

We are typically not conscious of these reproductive quandaries. Nor are we usually aware of the evolutionary logic that led to this dangerous passion. A man does not think, "Oh, if my wife has sex with someone else, then my certainty that I'm the genetic father will be jeopardized, and this will endanger the replication of my genes; I'm really mad." Or if his partner takes birth-control pills, "Well, because Joan is taking the pill, it doesn't really matter whether she has sex with other men; after all, my certainty in paternity is secure." Nor does a woman think, "It's really upsetting that Dennis is in love with that other woman; this jeopardizes my hold on his emotional commitments to me and my children, and hence hurts my reproductive success." Instead, jealousy is a blind passion, just as our hunger for sweets and craving for companionship are blind. Jealousy is emotional wisdom, not consciously articulated, passed down to us over millions of years by our successful forebears. One goal of *The Dangerous Passion* is to bring to the surface the deep roots of the inherited emotional wisdom we possess.

The Othello Syndrome

Despite its value for people past and present, jealousy is an emotion that exposes partners to extreme danger. The dark side of jealousy causes men to explode violently to reduce the odds that their partners will stray. Women seeking refuge at shelters for battered women almost invariably report that their husbands seethe with jealousy. In one study of battered women, many of whom required medical attention, the typical woman reported that her husband "tries to limit my contact with friends and family" (the tactic of concealment), "insists on knowing where I am at all times" (the tactic of vigilance), and "calls me names to put me down and make me feel bad about myself" (the tactic of undermining self-esteem).

Jealousy is the leading cause of spousal battering, but it's even worse than that. Men's jealousy puts women at risk of being killed.

Consider the following remarks made to police by a 31-year-old man who stabbed his 20-year-old wife to death, after they had been reunited following a six-month separation.

> Then she said that since she came back in April she had fucked this other man about ten times. I told her how can you talk about love and marriage and you been fucking this other man. I was really mad. I went to the kitchen and got the knife. I went back to our room and asked: Were you serious when you told me that? She said yes. We fought on the bed, I was stabbing her. Her grandfather came up and tried to take the knife out of my hand. I told him to go and call the cops for me. I don't know why I killed the woman, I loved her.

Jealousy can be emotional acid that corrodes marriages, undermines self-esteem, triggers battering, and leads to the ultimate crime of murder. Despite its dangerous manifestations, jealousy helped to solve a critical reproductive quandary for ancestral men. Jealous men were more likely to preserve their valuable commitments for their own children rather than squandering them on the children of their rivals. As descendants of a long line of men who acted to ensure their paternity, modern men carry with them the dangerous passion that led to their forebears' reproductive success.

A professional couple therapist I know related to me the following story. A young couple, Joan and Richard, came to her with a complaint of irrational jealousy. Without provocation, Richard would burst into jealous tirades and accuse Joan of sleeping with another man. His uncontrollable jealousy was destroying their marriage. Richard and Joan both agreed on this point. Could the therapist help cure Richard of irrational jealousy? A common practice in couple therapy is to have at least one session with each member of the couple individually. The first question the therapist posed to Joan during this individual interview was: Are you having an affair? She burst into tears and confessed that, indeed, she had been carrying on an affair for the past six months. Richard's jealousy, it turned out, had not been irrational after all. He had been picking up on subtle cues of his wife's infidelity that triggered his jealousy. Since he trusted Joan and she had assured him of her fidelity, however, he believed that his jealousy had been irrational. In a sense, Richard had failed to listen to his internal emotional whisperings. He came to the wrong conclusion because he overrode his feelings with "rationality."

This episode gave me the first hint that jealousy represented a form of ancestral wisdom that can have useful as well as destructive consequences. Despite the possible hazards of conducting research on jealousy, its potency convinced me that it could not be ignored by science. In surveys we discovered that nearly all men and women have experienced at least one episode of intense jealousy. Thirty-one percent say that their personal jealousy has sometimes been difficult to control. And among those who admit to being jealous, 38 percent say that their jealousy has led them to want to hurt someone.

Extreme jealousy has been given many names—the Othello syndrome, morbid jealousy, psychotic jealousy, pathological jealousy, conjugal paranoia, and erotic jealousy syndrome. Jealousy, of course, can be pathological. It can destroy previously harmonious relationships, rendering them hellish nightmares of daily existence. Trust slowly built from years of mutual reliance can be torn asunder in a crashing moment. As we will explore in a later chapter, jealousy leads more women to flee in terror to shelters than any other cause. A full 13 percent of all homicides are spousal murders, and jealousy is overwhelmingly the leading cause.

But destruction does not necessarily equal pathology. The pathological aspect of extreme jealousy, according to the mainstream wisdom, is not the jealousy itself. It is the delusion that a loved one has committed an infidelity when none has occurred. The rage itself upon the actual discovery of an infidelity is something people everywhere intuitively understand. In Texas until 1974, a husband who killed a wife and her lover when he caught them *in flagrante delicto* was not judged a criminal. In fact, the law held that a "reasonable man" would respond to such extreme provocation with acts of violence. Similar laws have been on the books worldwide. Extreme rage upon discovering a wife naked in the arms of another man is something that people everywhere find intuitively comprehensible. Criminal acts that would normally receive harsh prison sentences routinely get reduced when the victim's infidelity is the extenuating circumstance.

The view of jealousy as pathological ignores a profound fact about an important defense designed to combat a real threat. Jealousy is not always a reaction to an infidelity that has already been discovered. It can be an anticipatory response, a preemptive strike to prevent an infidelity that might occur. Labeling jealousy as pathological simply because a spouse has not yet strayed ignores the fact that jealousy can head off an infidelity that might be lurking on the horizon of a relationship.

Excessive jealousy can be extraordinarily destructive. But moderate jealousy, not an excess or an absence, signals commitment. This book explores both sides of this double-edged defense mechanism.

To understand the power of this extraordinary emotion, we must trace it to its origin, long before capitalism, long before agriculture and cash economies, long before writing and recorded history, and long before humans fanned out and colonized every habitable continent. We must trace its roots to the evolution of one of the most unusual adaptations in primate history, yet one that we take so much for granted that its existence is hardly questioned: the emergence of long-term love.

The Evolution of Love

Our closest primate cousins, the chimpanzees, lack exclusive sexual bonds. Most mating takes place within the narrow window of female estrus. When a female chimpanzee is in heat, a variety of physiological changes take place. Her genitals become swollen and pink for four to six days. The swellings peak just before ovulation when she is most likely to conceive. She emits pheromonal signals, hormone-saturated substances that males find especially attractive, sometimes driving them into a sexual frenzy. Sarah Hrdy of the University of California at Davis notes that males sometimes touch the vagina of the estrous female, gathering her secretions on their fingers to smell or taste. Males use these signals to monitor the female's reproductive state.

A male chimpanzee's position in the social hierarchy strongly determines his sexual access to estrous females. Among the chimpanzees at a large zoo colony in Arnham, the Netherlands, for example, the dominant male achieves as many as 75 percent of the matings with estrous females. The relationships between male and female chimps are complex and can extend over time, but chimps do not form the long-term committed relationships that most humans desire.

Men and women have always depended on each other for survival and reproduction. Love was not invented a few hundred years ago by European poets, contrary to conventional wisdom in this century. Love is a human universal, occurring in societies ranging from the !Kung San of Botswana to the Ache of Paraguay. In my study of 10,041 individuals from 37 different cultures, men and women rated love as the single most important quality in selecting a spouse. Across the globe, people sing love songs and pine for lost lovers. They elope with loved ones against the wishes of parents. They recount personal tales of anguish, longing, and unrequited love. And they narrate great love stories of romantic entanglements down through the generations. The German writer Herman Hesse summed it up best: Life is "the struggle for position and the search for love." Love is the universal human emotion that bonds the sexes, the evolutionary meeting ground where men and women lay down their arms.

The universal existence of love, however, poses a puzzle. From an evolutionary perspective, no single decision is more important than the choice of a mate. That single fork in the road determines one's ultimate reproductive fate. More than in any other domain, therefore, we expect evolution to produce supremely rational mechanisms of mate choice, rational in the sense that they lead to wise decisions rather than impetuous mistakes. How could a blind passion like love—a form of dementia that consumes the mind, crowds out all other thoughts, creates emotional dependency, and produces a delusional idealization of a partner— possibly evolve to solve a problem that might be better solved by cool rationality?

To penetrate this mystery, we must start with the scientific evidence for mate preferences. Worldwide, from the coastal dwelling Australians to the South African Zulu, women desire qualities such as ambition, industriousness, intelligence, dependability, creativity, exciting personality, and sense of humor—characteristics that augur well for a man's success in acquiring resources and achieving status. Given the tremendous investment women undertake to produce a single child, the nine months of costly internal fertilization and gestation, it is perfectly reasonable for women to want men who can invest in return. A woman's children will survive and thrive better if she selects a resourceful man. Children suffer when their mothers choose "slackers." Men, in contrast, place a greater premium on qualities linked with fertility, such as a woman's youth, health, and physical appearance—clear skin, smooth skin, bright eyes, full lips, symmetrical features, and a slim waist. These preferences are also perfectly sensible. We descended from ancestral mothers and fathers who chose fertile and resourceful partners. Those who failed to choose on these bases risked reproductive oblivion.

Although these rational desires set minimum thresholds on who qualifies as an acceptable mate, rationality profoundly fails to predict the final choice of a mate. As the psychologist Steven Pinker of the Massachusetts Institute of Technology observes, "Murmuring that your lover's looks, earning power, and IQ meet your minimal standards would probably kill the romantic mood, even if statistically true. The way to a person's heart is to declare the opposite—that you're in love because you can't help it."

One key to the mystery of love is found in the psychology of commitment. If a partner chooses you for rational reasons, he or she might leave you for the same rational reasons: finding someone slightly more desirable on all of the "rational" criteria. But if the person is blinded by an uncontrollable love that cannot be helped and cannot be chosen, a love for only you and no other, then commitment will not waver when you are in sickness rather than in health, when you are poorer rather than richer. Love overrides rationality. It's the emotion that ensures that you won't leave when someone slightly more desirable comes along or when a perfect "10" moves in next door. It ensures that a partner will stick by you through the struggles of survival and the hazards of childbirth.

Love, however, has a tragic side. The stories of great lovers of the past, in fiction and in history, are often marked by disaster. Juliet died of poison. Romeo chose to kill himself rather than live without her. Love suicides have pervaded Japanese culture for centuries, a final vindication of the intensity of a person's commitment. When parents and society conspire to keep lovers apart, lovers sometimes tie themselves together and jump off a cliff or hurl themselves into a well. The most perilous side of love, however, comes not from a *folie à deux*, but from a *folie à un*—the demonic possession that consumes a person when love is not reciprocated. Unrequited love is the foundation for fatal attraction.

Consider the case of John W. Hinckley, Jr., who scrawled a final letter to the actress Jodie Foster on March 30, 1981, shortly before attempting to assassinate President Ronald Reagan:

> *Dear Jodie:*
>
> *There is a definite possibility that I will be killed in my attempt to get Reagan. It is for this very reason I am writing you this letter now.*
>
> *As you well know by now I love you very much. Over the past seven months I've left you dozens of poems, letters and love messages in the faint hope that you could develop an interest in me . . . I know the many messages left at your door and in your mailbox were a nuisance, but I felt that it was the most painless way for me to express my love for you . . .*
>
> *Jodie, I would abandon this idea of getting Reagan in a second if I could only win your heart and live out the rest of my life with you . . . I will admit to you that the reason I'm going ahead with this attempt now is because I just cannot wait any longer to impress you. I've got to do something now to make you understand, in no uncertain terms, that I am doing this for your sake! By sacrificing my freedom and possibly my life, I hope to change your mind about me. This letter is being written only an hour before I leave for the Hilton Hotel. Jodie, I'm asking you to please look into your heart and at least give me the chance, with this historic deed, to gain your respect and love.*
>
> *I love you forever.*
> *John Hinckley*

Cases as extreme as John Hinckley are rare, but the experience of unrequited love is quite common. In one recent survey, 95 percent of men and women indicated that, by the age of 25, they had experienced unrequited love at least once, either as a would-be lover whose passions were rejected or as the object of someone's unwanted desires. Only one person in 20 has never experienced unrequited love of any kind.

Although unrequited love is a perilous passion, producing fatal attractions and unwanted stalking, the dogged persistence it produces sometimes pays off. One of the great love stories in history is that of Nicholas and Alexandra. Nicholas inherited the Russian throne at the end of the 19th century. During his adolescence his parents started looking for a suitable mate for him. At age 16, contrary to his parent's wishes, he became obsessed with Alexandra, a beautiful princess then living in England with her grandmother, Queen Victoria. Despite parental objections, cultural chasms, and a separation spanning thousands of miles, Nicholas was determined to capture Alexandra's love. Alexandra, however, found him a bit dull and did not relish the thought of moving to the harsh climate of Moscow. She spurned his advances. In 1892, Nicholas turned 24 and, having loved Alexandra for nearly eight years, resolved to make one final effort to win her heart. Given this state of mind, he was devastated when she wrote saying that she had definitely decided not to wed him. She asked him not to contact her again. All seemed lost.

Nicholas left his beloved Moscow immediately. He traveled across Europe, suffering rough terrain and treacherous weather in the journey to London. Although exhausted from travel, Nicholas immediately began to persue Alexandra with great passion. After two months, she finally relented and agreed to marry him. The young couple thus became man and wife, rulers of the Russian empire.

Although Nicholas's love was initially unrequited, their marriage proved a joyful one. Diary entries from each revealed sublime happiness, the great joy of their union, and the depth of their love for each other. They produced five children. Nicholas so enjoyed spending time with Alexandra and their children that the Russian empire apparently suffered from his neglect. When forced to be apart, they pined for each other, wrote often, and endured great psychological pain until their reunions. Their mutual love lasted throughout their lives, until the Russian Revolution brought down the czarist rule and they were executed. They died on the same day, their lifelong love never having diminished. Had Nicholas given up when initially spurned, their great love would have been lost forever.

The same passion that led John Hinckley to pursue Jodie Foster with desperate measures led Nicholas to succeed in turning an unrequited obsession into lifelong love. In retrospect, one seems irrational and unbalanced, the other logical and normal. One we call pathological, the other a love story. But what if Hinckley had succeeded in winning Jodie Foster's love and Nicholas had failed in his quest for Alexandra? Love is a dangerous passion that cuts both ways. There's a rationality to the irrationality.

Once humans evolved love, the bonds they created required protection. It would be extraordinarily unlikely that evolution would fail to defend these fragile and fruitful unions against interlopers. In the insect world, there is a species known as the "lovebug." Male lovebugs venture out in a swarm of other males each morning in search of a chance to mate with a female. When one succeeds, the couple departs from the swarm and glides to the ground to copulate. Because other males sometimes attempt to copulate with her, even after the pair has begun mating, the couple maintains a continuous copulatory embrace for as long as three days, hence the nickname "the lovebug." This strategy guards the union against outside intruders.

In humans, guarding a bond must last more than days, months, or even years because love can last a lifetime. The dangerous emotion of jealousy evolved to fill this void. Love and jealousy are intertwined passions. They depend on each other and feed on each other. But just as the prolonged embrace of the lovebug tells us that their bonds can be threatened, the power of jealousy reveals the ever-present possibility that our love bonds can be broken. The centrality of jealousy in human love reveals a hidden side of our desires, one that we typically go to great lengths to conceal—a passion for other partners.

Hidden Desires

One Sunday morning William burst into the living room and said, "Dad! Mom! I have some great news for you! I'm getting married to the most beautiful girl in town. She lives a block away and her name is Susan." After dinner, William's dad took him aside. "Son, I have to talk with you. Your mother and I have been married 30 years. She's a wonderful wife, but has never offered much excitement in the bedroom, so I used to fool around with women a lot. Susan is actually your half-sister, and I'm afraid you can't marry her."

William was heartbroken. After eight months he eventually started dating again. A year later he came home and proudly announced, "Dianne said yes! We're getting married in June." Again, his father insisted on a private conversation and broke the sad news. "Dianne is your half-sister too, William. I'm awfully sorry about this."

William was furious. He finally decided to go to his mother with the news. "Dad has done so much harm. I guess I'm never going to get married," he complained. "Every time I fall in love, Dad tells me the girl is my half-sister."

His mother just shook her head. "Don't pay any attention to what he says, dear. He's not really your father."

We find this story funny not simply because the ending carries a surprise. It's amusing because the mother ultimately gets payback for the "father's" philandering. Cuckolds are universal objects of laughter and derision, and a constant source of engaging tales from the tragedy of William Shakespeare's *Othello* to the middle-class marital dramas portrayed in the novels of John Updike.

To understand the origins of sexual passion we must introduce a disturbing difference between the sexes. Everyday observation tells us that men are more promiscuously inclined than women. "Men found to desire more sex partners than women desire" would be no more likely to make the headlines than "Dog bites man." But scientific verification is always useful, since common sense, which tells us that the earth is flat, sometimes turns out to be wrong. Science, in this case, has verified the everyday knowledge that men do display a greater passion for playing around. In one of our recent studies of more than 1,000 men and women, men reported desiring eight sex partners over the next three years, whereas women reported desiring only one or two. In another study, men were four times more likely than women to say that they have imagined having sex with 1,000 or more partners.

Observing that men and women differ, however, is not the same as explaining *why* they differ. There are compelling evolutionary reasons for the fact that this difference in desire for sexual variety is universal, found not just in cultures saturated with media images of seductive models, not just among Hugh Hefner's generation of *Playboy* readers, and not just in studies conducted by male scientists. To explain this desire, we must introduce another key fact about human reproductive biology.

To produce a single child, women bear the burdens and pleasures of nine months of pregnancy—an obligatory form of parental investment that men cannot share. Men, to produce the same child, need only devote a few hours, a few minutes, or even a few seconds. Wide is the gulf between men and women in the effort needed to bring forth new life. Over time, therefore, a strategy of casual mating proved to be more reproductively successful for men than for women. Men who succeeded in the arms of many women out-reproduced men who succeeded with fewer. An ancestral woman, in contrast, could have had sex with hundreds of partners in the course of a single year and still have produced only a single child. Unless a woman's regular partner proved to be infertile, additional sex partners did not translate into additional children. As a consequence, men evolved a more powerful craving for sex with a variety of women.

This sex difference in desire creates an intriguing puzzle. Sexual encounters require two people. Mathematically, the number of heterosexual encounters must be identical for the sexes. Men cannot satisfy their lust for sex partners without willing women. Indeed, men's passion for multiple partners could never have evolved unless there were some women who shared that desire. Is casual sex a recent phenomenon, perhaps created by the widespread prevalence of birth control devices that liberated women from the previous risks of pregnancy? Or did ancestral women do it too?

Three scientific clues, when taken together, provide a compelling answer. Men's sexual jealousy provides the first clue, the ominous passion that led us to this mystery. If ancestral women were naturally inclined to be flawlessly faithful, men would have had no evolutionary catalyst for jealousy. Men's jealousy is an evolutionary response to something alarming: the threat of a loved one's infidelity. The intensity of men's jealousy provides a psychological clue that betrays women's desire for men other than their regular partners.

Second, affairs are known in all cultures, including tribal societies, pointing to the universal prevalence of infidelity. Prevalence rates vary from culture to culture (high in Sweden and low in China), but affairs occur everywhere. Sexual infidelity causes divorce worldwide more than any other marital violation, being closely rivaled only by the infertility of the union. The fact that women have affairs in cultures from the Tiwi of northern Australia to the suburbs of Los Angeles reveals that some women refuse to limit themselves to a single partner despite men's attempts to control them and despite the risk of divorce if discovered.

A third line of evidence comes from new research on human sperm competition. Sperm competition occurs when the sperm from two different men inhabit a woman's reproductive tract at the same time. Human sperm remain viable within the woman's tract for up to seven days, not merely one or two days as scientists previously believed. Indeed, my colleagues have discovered hundreds of "crypts" recessed within the vaginal walls of women in which they store a man's sperm and then release it several days later to enter a marathon race to her egg. If a woman has sex with two men within the course of a week, sperm competition can ensue, as the sperm from different men scramble and battle for the prize of fertilizing the egg. Research on sperm competition reveals that men's sperm volume, relative to their body weight, is twice that which occurs in primate species known to be monogamous, a clue that hints at a long evolutionary history of human sperm competition.

Human sperm, moreover, come in different "morphs," or shapes, designed for different functions. Most common are the "egg getters," the standard government-issue sperm with conical heads and sinewy tails designed for swimming speed—the Mark Spitzes of the sperm world. But a substantial minority of sperm have coiled tails. These so-called kamikaze sperm are poorly designed for swimming speed. But that's not their function. When the sperm from two different men are mixed in the laboratory, kamikaze sperm wrap themselves around the egg getters and destroy them, committing suicide in the process. These physiological clues reveal a long evolutionary history in which men battled with other men, literally within the woman's reproductive tract, for access to the vital egg needed for transporting their genes into the next generation. Without a long history of sperm competition, evolution would have favored neither the magnitude of human sperm volume nor the specialized sperm shapes designed for battle.

All these clues—the universality of infidelity, men's sexual jealousy, and the hallmarks of sperm competition—point to a disturbing answer to the question of ancestral women's sexual strategies. They reveal the persistent expression of women's passion for men other than their husbands, a phenomenon that must have occurred repeatedly over the long course of human evolution. Modern women have inherited this passion from their ancestral mothers.

Why Women Have Affairs

Because scientists have focused primarily on the obvious reproductive benefits of men's desire for sexual variety, the potential benefits to women of short-term sexual passion languished for years unstudied. The puzzle is compounded by the fact that a woman's infatuation with another man comes laden with danger. An unfaithful woman, if discovered, risks damage to her social reputation, the loss of her partner's commitment, physical injury, and occasionally death at the hands of a jealous man. Undoubtedly, many women weigh these risks, and choose not to act on their sexual desires. The benefits to women who do act on their passion for other men, given the possibility of catastrophic costs, must be perceived as sufficiently great to make it worth the risk.

For the past seven years, Heidi Greiling and I have been studying why women have affairs. Our lab has focused on the benefits that are so alluring that women from all walks of life are willing to take great risks to pursue sex and love outside of marriage. Our research centered on three questions: What *benefits* do women reap from affairs? What *circumstances* are most likely to drive a woman into another man's arms? And *which women* are most prone to affairs?

Historically, women may have benefited from an affair in countless ways. The first and most obvious benefit comes from the direct resources that an affair partner may provide. A few expensive dinners may not seem like much today, but an extra supply of meat from the hunt would have made the difference between starving and surviving during ancestral winters when the land lay bare, or between merely surviving and robustly thriving during more plentiful times.

Women also can benefit from affairs in the currency of quality genes. The puzzle of the peacock's tail provided the telltale clue to this benefit. A peahen's preference for peacocks with brilliant plumage may signal selection for genes for good health. When peacocks carry a high load of parasites, their diminished health is revealed in duller displays. By selecting for luminescence, peahens secure good genes for health that benefit their offspring. Research by Steve Gangestad and Randy Thornhill of the University of New Mexico reveals that women may be choosing affair partners with especially healthy genes. Women who have sex with different men can also produce more genetically diverse children, providing a sort of "hedge" against environmental change.

Although genetic and resource benefits may flow to women who express their hidden sexual side, our studies uncovered one benefit that overshadowed the others in importance, a benefit we call "mate insurance." During ancestral times, disease, warfare, and food shortages made survival a precarious proposition. The odds were not trivial that a husband would succumb to a disease, become debilitated by a parasite, or incur injury during a risky hunt or a tribal battle. The paleontological and cross-cultural records reveal this clue—the skulls and skeletons show injuries mostly on males. A woman's husband, in short, stood a significant chance of suffering a debilitating or lethal wound.

Ancestral women who failed to have mate insurance, a backup

replacement in the event that something happened to her regular partner, would have suffered greatly compared to women who cultivated potential replacements. Modern women have inherited the desires of their ancestral mothers for replacement mates. In the words of one woman in our study, "Men are like soup—you always want to have one on the back burner." Mate insurance provides a safeguard against reasonable risks of losing a partner.

And mate insurance remains relevant today, even though we've conquered many of the hazards that felled our forebears. American divorce rates now approach 67 percent for those currently getting married, up from the mere 50 percent figure that alarmed many over the past two decades. Remarriage is rapidly becoming the norm. *The Dangerous Passion* explores how women's desire for additional partners is ancestral wisdom that, however alarming to husbands, continues to serve a critical insurance function for women today.

Urges of Ovulation

Women's attraction to lovers has another mysterious ingredient: the puzzle of concealed ovulation. Unlike chimpanzees, women's genitals do not become engorged when they ovulate. Women have "lost estrus" and engage in sex throughout their ovulatory cycle. Conventional scientific wisdom has declared that a woman's ovulation is cryptic, concealed even from the woman herself. But have the urges associated with ovulation totally vanished?

In the most extensive study of ovulation and women's sexuality, several thousand married women were asked to record their sexual desires every day for a period of twenty-four months. The methods were crude but straightforward: women simply placed an *X* on the recording sheet on each day that they experienced sexual desire. Basal body temperature was recorded to determine the phase of the menstrual cycle. These thousands of data points yielded a startling pattern. On the first day of a woman's period, practically no women reported experiencing sexual desire. The numbers rose dramatically across the ovarian cycle, peaking precisely at the point of maximum fertility, and then declining rapidly during the luteal phase after ovulation. Women, of course, can experience sexual desire at any phase of their cycle. Nonetheless, they are five times more likely to experience sexual desire when they are ovulating than when they are not.

Women sometimes act on their passions. A recent survey of 1,152 women, many of whom were having affairs, revealed a startling finding. Women who stray tend to time their sexual liaisons with their affair partners to coincide with the peak of their sexual desire, when they are most likely to conceive. Sex with husbands, in sharp contrast, is more likely to occur when women are *not* ovulating, a strategy that may be aimed at keeping a man rather than conceiving with him. None of this is conscious, of course. Women do not think "I'll try to time sex with my affair partner when I'm ovulating so that I'll bear his child and not my husband's." Psychologically, women simply experience sexual desire more when they are ovulating, and if they have an affair partner, have urges to have sex with him during this phase. Ovulation may seem concealed to outside observers, but women appear to act on the impulses that spring from it. And when that desire for men other than their husbands occurs, it's difficult for most men to tell when their mates are straying or may be likely to stray. I call this the signal detection problem.

The Signal Detection Problem

Across cultures, people have affairs that are specifically designed to avoid detection. In Arizona, one motel marquee boasts that it is the "No-Tell Motel." In states across America, you can rent some hotel rooms at an hourly rate. The woman returning from a business trip does not make her brief fling on the road the first topic of conversation. The husband who conceals his finances from his wife may be funneling resources to support a mistress on the side.

Spouses experience a signal detection problem. Consider camping in the woods at night and hearing a sound somewhere in the dark. Was that the sound of a twig snapping, merely the wind blowing, or the unfamiliar night sounds playing tricks on your ears? Assuming that you have correctly detected the signal as a twig snap, the possible causes of this event are many, but they are not infinite. It could be a rock that somehow got dislodged. But it could also be a dangerous animal or a hostile human. The signal detection problem is not merely about picking up accurate signals in the face of an uncertain and ambiguous welter of information. It is also about making correct inferences about the cause of the signal.

Since sexual infidelities are almost invariably secret, the signals they might emit are intentionally muted. An unfamiliar scent, the purchase of a sharp new jacket, the running of a yellow light, a new interest in Beethoven or the Beastie Boys, an unexplained absence—all of these can be signals, but they can originate from many causes other than infidelity. The jealous person experiences an elevated sensitivity to signals of infidelity: "He may see a red flush on his wife's cheek, she may appear to be standing awkwardly, or sitting sideways on a chair, she has put on a clean dress, there is a cigarette-end in the fireplace . . . the jealous man sees a handkerchief on the floor, a wet cloth in the bathroom, newspapers in a ditch, and attaches to all the same import."

Consider the case of a European psychiatrist who counseled many couples referred to him in which one of the spouses experienced "morbid jealousy." Most cases were husbands who had delusions that their wives were sexually unfaithful, and these delusions destroyed the fabric of trust required for harmonious marriage. Because he believed that extreme jealousy was a psychiatric illness that could not be cured, his most common recommendation was that the couples separate or divorce. Many couples followed his recommendations. Because he was keenly interested in the subsequent fate of his patients, he routinely contacted them after a number of months had passed. To his astonishment, he discovered that many of the wives of his patients had subsequently become sexually involved with the very men about whom their husbands had been jealous! Some of these women actually married the men who were the objects of their husbands' suspicions. In many cases, the husbands must have been sensing signs of infidelity. But because the wives proclaimed innocence and declared that their husbands' jealousy was irrational, the husbands ended up believing that the problem was in their heads. The problem of signal detection is how to identify and correctly interpret a partner's betrayal in an uncertain social world containing a chaos of conflicting clues.

Jealousy is often triggered by circumstances that signal a real threat to a relationship, such as differences in the desirability of the partners, as illustrated by the following case. The man was 35 years old, working as a foreman, when he was referred to a psychiatrist and diagnosed with "morbid jealousy." He had married at age 20 to a woman of 16 whom he deeply loved. During their first two years of marriage, he was stationed in military service in England. During this two-year separation, he received several anonymous letters saying that his wife was carrying on an affair. When he returned to America to rejoin her, he questioned her intensely about the allegations, but she denied them. Their own sexual relations proved disappointing. He became obsessed with the earlier time in their marriage, repeatedly accused his wife of infidelity, and hit her from time to time, especially after a bout of drinking. He tried to strangle her twice, and several times he threatened to kill himself.

He openly admitted his problems to the psychiatrist: "I'm so jealous that when I see anyone near her I want to hurt her. I have always loved her but do not think she has returned my affection. This jealousy is something I feel in my stomach and when it comes out of me there is nothing I can do about it. That is why I behave so madly. . . . My wife is always telling me that other men are stronger and can beat me. . . . I'm not a big chap or a handsome chap but my wife is so pretty and I don't think I come up to her high standards." In other words, he perceived a difference in their level of desirability; she was attractive and alluring, and he saw himself as beneath her. When the psychiatrist questioned the wife in private, she admitted to meeting and having an affair with a married man. The affair was carried on in secret, and throughout the duration of her affair she insisted that her husband's jealousy was delusional. The affair began roughly one year before the husband was referred to the psychiatrist to treat "his problem."

Differences in desirability—when an "8" is married to a "10"—can heighten sensitivity to signals of infidelity in the partner who has fewer outside mating options. Elaine Hatfield and her colleagues at the University of Hawaii discovered that the more desirable partner in the couple in fact is more likely to stray. Those who have been in relationships with both more attractive and less attractive partners have an acute awareness of how jealousy is attuned to these differences. These differences represent one among many signs of actual or impending infidelity explored in depth later in the book.

Emotional Wisdom

Jealousy is necessary because of the real threat of sexual treachery. In a hazardous world where rivals lurk, partners harbor passions for other people, and infidelity threatens to destroy what could have been a lifelong love, it would be surprising if evolution had not forged elaborate defenses to detect and fend off these threats. Exposing these threats, and the psychological arms we have to combat them, is a first step toward comprehending the wisdom of passions that sometimes seem so destructive.

The Dangerous Passion takes us on a journey through the rationality of these seemingly irrational emotions, examining the fundamental desires of what men and women want, and why these longings so often produce conflict. Chapter 2 introduces the jealousy paradox—why an emotion that evolved to protect love can rip a relationship apart. It explores the evolution of conflict between men and women, why painful emotions are necessary in resolving conflicts, and why men and women are locked in a never-ending spiral of love and strife.

Chapter 3 focuses on why men and women differ in their underlying psychology of jealousy. It reveals that men and women are neither unisex equivalents nor aliens from different planets. When it comes to adaptive problems that differ for men and women, passions diverge; for adaptive problems that are the same, their emotions joyfully commingle.

Chapter 4, "The Othello Syndrome," investigates seemingly bizarre clinical cases in which a jealous person becomes untethered, resulting in delusional suspicions about a partner's infidelity. We explore why our minds are designed not merely to pick up on infidelities that have already occurred, but also to detect circumstances that signal an increased likelihood that a partner will stray in the future. Chapter 5 delves into the frightening abuses produced by the dangerous passion—battering, stalking, and killing—and identifies when women are most vulnerable to these violations.

Although I call jealousy the dangerous passion, it cannot be disentangled from the risky cravings that men and women harbor for other lovers. Chapter 6 examines the qualities of relationships that make a person susceptible to infidelity, the personality characteristics that predict who's likely to cheat, and why some people unwittingly drive their partners into the arms of a paramour. Chapter 7 explores why women have affairs, and why modern women have inherited from their ancestral mothers a roving eye.

Chapter 8 identifies the strategies we use to cope with jealousy and infidelity and why some therapeutic efforts to eradicate jealousy are often misguided. The final chapter reveals the positive uses of jealousy for enhancing sexual passion and life-long love, and examines how we can harness emotional wisdom to enrich our relationships.

CHAPTER 2

The Jealousy Paradox

[Men] originally lived in small communities, each with a single wife, or if powerful with several, whom he jealousy guarded against all other men.
— *Charles Darwin, 1871,* The Descent of Man
and Selection in Relation to Sex

WHEN I BEGAN TO EXPLORE sexual jealousy in my research, a colleague warnéd me to stay away from the topic. He related the following experience. He wanted to elicit jealousy in a laboratory setting to examine the various emotional expressions and behaviors that followed. So to pilot the study, he brought a married couple into the lab and put the husband in a room containing a speaker through which he could listen to the conversation in the next room. Then the researcher took the wife into the adjoining room and instructed her to answer his questions using an intimate and seductive tone of voice. After two minutes of the interview, which the husband could hear through the speaker, he burst into the room and punched my colleague in the nose. The husband had listened to his wife talking to another man in a tone of voice reserved only for him. The jealousy induction was too strong. My colleague had to stop the experiment due to the ethical problems of evoking such an intense emotion, hence his warning to me to stay away from this volatile topic.

I was deterred only briefly, for soon I came to realize that jealousy was a deeply rooted human emotion largely neglected by social scientists. When I questioned my colleagues about the neglect of jealousy by the scientific community, some told me that jealousy was not a "primary" emotion, but rather merely a blend of other more "basic" emotions such as anger, fear, and sadness. As a derivative of other emotions, it simply did not deserve the attention usually reserved for the more basic emotions. Others dismissed jealousy as a symptom of other problems, such as immaturity or neurosis. Mere symptoms, they argued, did not deserve study like the more fundamental problems.

The more I probed, however, the more I came to believe that these dismissals were premature. Jealousy turned out not to be merely a mark of some character defect. It is expressed in perfectly normal people who show no signs of neurosis or immaturity. Moreover, jealousy has deep evolutionary roots that were critical to the success and proliferation of our ancestors. By uncovering the origins of this emotion, we can better understand its modern manifestations and learn how to grapple with them. Jealousy, I was forced to conclude, is no less basic than fear or rage, its expression no less important than flight or fight.

The Jealousy Paradox

Jealousy poses a paradox. Consider these findings: 46 percent of a community sample stated that jealousy was an *inevitable* consequence of true love. St. Augustine noted this link when he declared that "He that is not jealous, is not in love." Shakespeare's tormented Othello "dotes, yet doubts, suspects, yet strongly loves." Women and men typically interpret a partner's jealousy as a sign of the depth of their love, a partner's absence of jealousy as lack of love.

The psychologist Eugene Mathes of Western Illinois University asked a sample of unmarried, but romantically involved, men and women to complete a jealousy test. Seven years later, he contacted the participants again and asked them about the current status of their relationship. Roughly 25 percent of the participants had married, while 75 percent had broken up. The jealousy scores from seven years earlier for those who married averaged 168, whereas the scores for those who broke up registered significantly lower at 142. These results must be interpreted cautiously; it's just one study with a small sample. Nonetheless, it points to the possibility that jealousy might be inexorably linked with long-term love.

Contrast this with another finding: In a sample of 651 university students who were actively dating, more than 33 percent reported that jealousy posed a significant problem in their current relationship. The problems ranged from the loss of self-esteem to verbal abuse, from rage-ridden arguments to the terror of being stalked.

Jealousy, paradoxically, flows from deep and abiding love, but can shatter the most harmonious relationships. The paradox was reflected in O. J. Simpson's statement: "Let's say I committed this crime [the slaying of his ex-wife, Nicole Brown Simpson]. Even if I did do this, it would have to have been because I loved her very much, right?" The emotion of jealousy, designed to shelter a relationship from intruders, "turns homes that might be sanctuaries of love into hells of discord and hate." This book attempts to resolve the paradox.

The Meaning of Jealousy

The word *jealousy* came into the English language through the French language. Comparable words in French are *jaloux* and *jalousie*, both of which derive from the Latin word *zelosus*. The Latin, in turn, was borrowed from the Greek work *zelos*, which meant fervor, warmth, ardor, or intense desire. The French word *jalousie*, however, has a dual meaning. One meaning is similar to the English *jealous*, but *jalousie* also refers to a Venetian blind, the kind with numerous horizontal slats suspended one above the other. The Norwegian psychiatrist Nils Retterstol at the University of Oslo speculates that this meaning arose from a situation in which a husband suspicious of his wife could observe her undetected from behind the *jalousie*, presumably to catch her in the act of intercourse with another man.

The psychologist Gordon Clanton of San Diego State University defines jealousy as "a feeling of displeasure which expresses itself either as a fear of loss of the partner or as discomfort over a real or imagined experience the partner has had with a third party." This definition captures two central ingredients of jealousy: the threat of losing a partner and the presence of a third party. Indeed, the jealous situation is sometimes described as "the eternal triangle," referring to the fact that three parties are involved: the jealous party, the mate, and the rival. The definition, however, leaves open precisely what sort of "real or imagined experience" the partner has had with someone else—time, attention, sharing a cup of tea, oral sex, or intercourse. As we will discover later in this book, different imagined experiences evoke different facets of jealousy. It also leaves out the complex array of emotions that characterize the jealous experience, including anger, rage, humiliation, fear, anxiety, sadness, and depression. Finally, this definition omits the behavior that people exhibit when jealous; jealousy is not merely an emotion that rattles around in people's heads, lacking expression in action.

Evolutionary psychologists Martin Daly and Margo Wilson of McMaster University in Ontario define jealousy as "a *state* that is aroused by a perceived threat to a valued relationship or position and motivates behavior aimed at countering the threat. Jealousy is 'sexual' if the valued relationship is sexual." This definition highlights three additional facets of jealousy. First, jealousy is a state, which means that it is a temporary or episodic experience, not a permanent affliction. Unlike qualities such as height or hair color, no one can remain in a state of jealousy constantly. Second, jealousy is a response to a threat to a valued relationship in which a person is heavily invested. People rarely experience jealousy by threats to a casual acquaintanceship, a brief affair, or a temporary alliance. Third, jealousy motivates action designed to deal with the threat.

But even this definition fails to identify all the layers of this complex human emotion. To take one example, there are many different forms of threats to romantic relationships, such as sexual threats, emotional threats, economic threats, and even intellectual threats. To penetrate the jealousy paradox, we must understand the precise nature of the threats it is designed to combat.

Some writers fail to distinguish *jealousy* from another term that is sometimes used in its stead: *envy*. Envy appears to come from the Latin word *invidere*, which means to look upon with malice. The Oxford English Dictionary defines envy this way: "To feel displeasure and ill-will at the superiority of (another person) in happiness, success, reputation, or the possession of anything desirable." A concrete example illustrates the difference between jealousy and envy. A man might experience envy of another man who has a beautiful wife. The envy is directed at the man who possesses what he wants, but lacks. The husband, however, may be jealous of his beautiful wife if he suspects she is developing an interest in another man. Envy implies covetousness, malice, and ill-will directed at someone who has what you lack; jealousy, in contrast, implies the fear of losing to a rival a valuable partner that you already have.

Myths About Jealousy

Although jealousy has been largely neglected by social scientists, it has not been entirely ignored. Several authors have proposed theories to explain the origins and existence of jealousy. According to psychologist Ralph Hupka of California State University at Long Beach, jealousy is a social construction: "It is unlikely . . . that human beings come 'prewired,' so to speak, into the world to be emotional about anything other than the requirements for their immediate survival . . . the desire to control the sexual behavior of mates is the consequence of the social construction of the gender system. Social construction refers in this context to the arbitrary assignment of activities and qualities to each gender (e.g., the desire for honor, beauty, masculinity, femininity, etc.)." According to this argument, society or culture assigns men and women roles and activities, and presumably assigns men the role of controlling the sexuality of their partners. Since social constructions are arbitrary, they should vary widely from culture to culture. We should find cultures where men are jealous but women are not. Others where women are jealous and men are not. And in cultures that do not make these arbitrary assignments, there should be a total absence of jealousy.

The psychiatrist Dinesh Bhugra at the Institute of Psychiatry in London argues that jealousy is a result of "capitalist society." According to this argument, capitalist societies place a premium on personal possessions and property, which extend to possessing other people. Capitalist society encourages "treating the love object in a literal object manner, taking the partner to be the individual's personal possession or property." If this theory is correct, then several implications follow. First, men and women living in capitalist societies should be equally jealous and jealous about the same things. Second, men and women living in socialist, anarchist, or dictatorship societies should be entirely free of jealousy. Third, since "motives for jealousy are a product of the culture," then there should be wide variability across cultures in motives for jealousy.

Another explanation of jealousy invokes low self-esteem, immaturity, or character defects. According to this line of thinking, adults who enjoy high self-esteem, maturity, and psychological soundness should not experience jealousy. If personality defects create jealousy, then curing those defects should eliminate it.

The fourth type of explanation proposes that jealousy is a form of pathology. The core assumption behind this explanation is that extreme jealousy results from a major malfunction of the human mind, so curing the malfunction should eliminate jealousy. Normal people, according to this account, simply do not experience extreme or intense jealousy.

Some of these explanations contain grains of truth. Sometimes jealousy is indeed pathological, a product of brain injury from boxing or warfare. Expressions of jealousy do vary somewhat from culture to culture. Among the Ache of Paraguay, jealous rivals settle disputes through ritual club fights, whereas among the Kipsigis in Kenya, the offended husband might demand a refund on the bride-price he paid for his wife.

None of these explanations, however, squares with all the known facts about jealousy. Even among the Ammassalik Eskimos in Greenland, sometimes held up as a culture lacking jealousy, it is not unusual for a husband to kill an interloper who sleeps with his wife. And contrary to Margaret Mead's assertion that Samoans are entirely lacking in jealousy and "laugh incredulously at tales of passionate jealousy," jealousy on Samoa is a prominent cause of violence against rivals and mates; they even have a word for it, *fua*. To cite one example, "after Mata, the wife of Tavita, had accused his older brother, Tule, of making sexual approaches to her during his absence, Tavita attacked his brother, stabbing him five times in the back and neck." Samoan women also succumb to fits of jealousy. In one case the husband of a 29-year-old woman named Mele left her for another woman, so Mele sought them out and "attacked them with a bush knife while they were sleeping together." Cultures in tropical paradises that are entirely free of jealousy exist only in the romantic minds of optimistic anthropologists, and in fact have never been found.

Women labeled as suffering from "pathological jealousy" sometimes turn out to have husbands who have been romancing other women for years. To understand jealousy, we must peer deep into our evolutionary past to a time before computers, before capitalism, and even before the advent of agriculture.

The Evolution of Conflict Between the Sexes

The process of evolution is extraordinarily simple at heart, but unraveling its implications yields subtle and profound insights into human nature. Evolution refers to change over time in organic design. Characteristics, or "design features," that help an organism to survive and reproduce, relative to other organisms with different design features, get represented in future generations more than characteristics that are neutral or that impede survival and reproduction. At any one slice in time, organisms can be viewed as collections of characteristics that owe their existence to this process of evolution by selection, operating repeatedly over thousands or millions of years. All modern humans come from a long and literally unbroken line of ancestors who succeeded in the tasks needed to survive and reproduce. As their descendants, we have inherited collections of characteristics that led to their success. These characteristics are called adaptations.

The evolutionary process is inherently competitive. If there is not enough food to feed all members of a group, for example, then some survive while others perish. If two women desire the same man, to take another example, one woman's success in attracting him is the other woman's loss. If a rival tries to lure a man's mate, then the two men collide in conflicting interests. In an important sense, therefore, all men and all women are in competition with one another to contribute to the ancestry of future generations. The evolutionary contest is a zero-sum game, with the victors winning at the expense of losers. The conclusion is obvious but profound: Each person's primary competitors are members of the same sex within the same species.

This evolutionary logic raises an intriguing puzzle. If our primary competitors are members of our own sex, why would men and women ever get into conflict with one another? In fact, since men and women need each other, and can't reproduce without each other, shouldn't we expect true cooperation between men and women? On one level, the answer must be yes. Men cannot reproduce without women, nor can women reproduce without men. Furthermore, the children of these unions represent the "shared vehicles" by which both the mother's and father's genes get transported to future generations. A mother and father are fundamentally united in their interest in the well-being of their mutually produced children. The emotion of love has evolved partly for this purpose, for there can be no greater alliance producer than a child that melds the genetic fates of two individuals. A spouse is the one person on a planet of billions who has as much interest in the fate of the children as the mate does. If that were all there is to say on this issue, there would be no justification for this book. But as anyone who has ever experienced a committed romantic relationship knows, there are sometimes snakes in the garden of love.

Battles between the sexes can occur in an astonishing variety of forms. When I started to conduct my research, I asked several hundred people to write down anything a member of the opposite sex had done that had irritated, angered, annoyed, or upset them. People were very articulate on the subject, and I was able to identify 149 distinct sources of conflict between the sexes, ranging from seemingly small irritations such as leaving the toilet seat up to more traumatic events like emotional abuse and physical violence. Some of these I explored in my previous book, *The Evolution of Desire: Strategies of Human Mating*. For predictable evolutionary reasons, women get far more upset than men by acts of sexual aggression, such as uninvited touching, unwanted sexual advances, and forced acts of sex. Sexual aggression interferes with a woman's free choice of when she wants sex and with whom she wants sex, jeopardizing her valuable reproductive resources. Also for predictable evolutionary reasons, men tend to get far more upset than women when someone they seek withholds sex. A withholding woman deprives a man of access to the reproductive resources that he has devoted so much effort to attaining. Some men feel "led on" by a woman who subsequently changes her mind.

The sources of conflict that concern us here, however, are those that occur within relationships. The union of a man and a woman can be fragile; evolutionary logic reveals why. Consider the movie *It Could Happen to You,* featuring a policeman played by Nicholas Cage, his wife played by Rosie Perez, and a waitress played by Bridget Fonda. In the movie, when Cage goes to pay for his breakfast at a cafe, he realizes that he does not have any cash to leave a tip. Instead, he offers Bridget Fonda half of his lottery ticket as the tip, in the unlikely event that he wins. But win he does, and being an honorable man, Cage lives up to his promise and gives half of the multimillion-dollar jackpot to Fonda. Cage's wife, however, is furious, for she wants to keep the entire sum. Their conflict over the jackpot leads to their divorce, and by the end of the movie, Nicholas Cage and Bridget Fonda have fallen in love. This movie points out a pervasive source of strife between husband and wife: conflict over the use of jointly held resources. In real-life situations, such conflicts abound, and from an evolutionary perspective, spending decisions that are good for one partner might not be good for the other. This is especially true if there are genetic kin on the scene, where joint resources funneled to the woman's family take away from those spent on the man's family.

Conflict over the apportionment of resources, however, is merely the beginning. A deeper danger comes from threats to monogamy. A sexual infidelity by the man can undermine his loyalties to his mate and his children. If a woman fails to guard against her husband's infidelity, she risks losing his energy, commitment, investment, time, and attention—resources that get diverted away from her and her children toward a rival woman and her children.

If a man fails to prevent his wife's infidelity, this lapse can literally threaten his DNA. Consider what happens if his wife gets pregnant with another man's child without his awareness. The reproductive costs are multiple. First, he loses out on the chance to reproduce himself. Second, his wife's motherly love ends up going to the interloper's children. And third, he might devote all of his parenting efforts to the other man's children in the mistaken belief that they are his. It's unlikely that fatherly love could have evolved unless men were successful in guarding against threats of their wife's infidelity, or at least were able to reduce the likelihood of being cuckolded.

Infidelity represents the partial diversion of evolutionarily valuable resources. Desertion, abandonment, and defection from the relationship represent the entire loss of those assets. Breaking up can inflict many costs on the partners, children, and the entire collection of kin. The abandoned partner may be stuck raising children without the aid of the other parent. Divorced status and the existence of children lower a person's desirability to others in the mating market. The children suffer, since it is known that the rates of stepchild physical and sexual abuse are at least 40 times greater than when the children reside with both genetic parents. The alliance of the two sides of the family, brought together by the marriage, may be torn asunder. On nearly all counts, divorce, desertion, or abandonment can be catastrophically costly for all involved. Given these circumstances, it would be spectacularly unlikely that evolution would have failed to fashion defense mechanisms designed to lower the odds of a partner defecting.

The most dramatic threats to the fragile unions between men and women, in short, are the dual specters of infidelity and abandonment. These dangers constituted threats so extreme that, unless they could be successfully combated, or at least partially subdued, long-term romantic bonds of love and marriage could not have emerged at all.

A central argument of this book is that the complex emotion we call jealousy did not arise from capitalism, patriarchy, culture, socialization, media, character defects, or neurosis. Although jealousy sometimes can reach pathological or deadly extremes, the vast majority of jealous episodes are useful expressions of effective coping strategies that are designed to deal with real threats to relationships. To understand how jealousy is an adaptation, not a pathology, we must examine the role of emotions in human psychology.

Emotions as Signals of Strategic Interference

The study of emotions in psychology has a curious history. Many researchers contrast "emotionality" with "rationality." According to this view, rationality causes humans to make sensible decisions. When faced with a problem, we use reason, logic, and deduction to figure out a judicious solution. Emotions, according to this view, only get in the way— anger addles the brain; fear distorts reason; jealousy clouds the mind. Emotions are presumed to be carryovers from our ancestral past, unfortunate relics of an ancient time when human ancestors acted more from instinct than logic. Psychologists have labeled anger, fear, distress, and jealousy the "negative" emotions, which need to be controlled, reigned in, and subdued so that they do not impede rational solutions.

I disagree with all of these experts who take a dim view of the dark side of human emotion. In my view, these "negative" emotions are exquisitely tailored adaptive mechanisms that served the interests of our ancestors well and likely continue to serve our interests today. Specifically, the theory proposes that these emotions are designed to cope with what I call "strategic interference." Strategic interference occurs whenever something or someone impedes, thwarts, or blocks a strategic set of actions. Consider the relatively simple case of encountering a poisonous snake on a path as you walk through the woods. The snake coils, rattles his tail, and hisses at you suddenly, threatening your goal of survival. Because snakes have been a recurrent hostile force of nature for us humans, we have evolved a special proclivity to develop a fear of snakes.

This fear serves several related functions. It focuses our attention laserlike on the source of the threat, simultaneously screening out irrelevant sources of stimuli. It prompts storage of the relevant information in memory, so that future travel through this location can be avoided or traversed with greater caution. It also prompts immediate beneficial actions such as freezing or fleeing. Given the prevalence of snake fears among humans and our closest genetic relatives, chimpanzees, it is reasonable to believe that those who were indifferent to dangerous snakes were more likely to die and less likely to become our ancestors.

The most common human fears fall heavily in a small number of categories: snakes, spiders, heights, darkness, and strangers. Charles Darwin expressed the key insight: "May we not suspect that the . . . fears of children, which are quite independent of experience, are the inherited effects of real dangers . . . during ancient savage time?" We are far more likely to develop fears of dangers that were present in our ancestral environment than to those in our current environment. Snakes, for example, are hardly a problem in Los Angeles or New York City, but automobiles are. Fears of cars or electrical outlets are virtually unknown, since these are evolutionarily novel hazards, too recent for natural selection to have fashioned specific fears. The fact that more city dwellers go to psychiatrists with phobias of snakes and strangers than fears of cars and electrical outlets provides a window into the hazards of our ancestral environment.

The specific array of human fears emerges in development precisely at the time when infants first encounter particular dangers. Fear of heights and strangers, for example, emerges in infants around six months of age, which coincides with the time when they start to crawl away from their mother. In one study, 80 percent of infants who had been crawling for 41 days or more avoided crossing over a "visual cliff," an apparent vertical drop that was in fact covered with a transparent but sturdy glass, to get to their mother. Crawling increases the risk of dangerous falls and encounters with strangers without the protective mother in close proximity, and so the emergence of the fear of heights and strangers at this time coincides with the onset of these dangers. Fear of strangers in human infants has been documented in a variety of different cultures, including the Guatemalans, Zambians, !Kung Bushmen, and Hopi Indians. In fact, the risk of infants being killed by strangers appears to be a common "hostile force of nature" in nonhuman primates as well as in humans.

As the Harvard psychologist Jerome Kagan has documented, separation anxiety is another kind of fear for which there is widespread cross-cultural documentation, peaking between 9 and 13 months. In one cross-cultural study, Kagan recorded the percentage of infants who cried following the departure of their mother from the room. At the peak age of separation anxiety, 62 percent of Guatemalan Indians, 60 percent of Israelis, 82 percent of Antigua Guatemalans, and 100 percent of African Bushmen infants exhibited this overt display of separation anxiety. Animal fears, in contrast, do not emerge until around age two, as the child more expansively explores the environment. Adaptations need not show up at birth. The onset of specific fears, like the onset of puberty, is a developmentally timed psychological emergence.

The conclusion from all of this evidence is clear: far from being an "irrational" or "negative" emotion, fear is patterned in highly adaptive ways that aided the survival of our ancestors. Fears are like physical pain. Although they feel unpleasant, they help us to avoid the events that interfere with our strategies of survival.

Now consider a different type of strategic interference, the blocking of a preferred mating strategy. Abundant evidence documents what any grandmother could have told you—that most women look for long-term love, seeking a committed partner who will be there for the long run. Men also pursue a strategy of committed mating some of the time, but they have another strategy that also looms large in their repertoire, a strategy of casual sex. When a man seeks casual sex from a woman who seeks commitment, the man interferes with the woman's preferred long-term mating strategy. But a woman who refuses to have sex prior to signs of commitment is simultaneously interfering with a man's short-term mating strategy.

My research has consistently shown that the patterns of men's and women's anger correspond precisely to their respective sources of strategic interference. Women, far more than men, become angry and upset by those who seek sex sooner, more frequently, and more persistently than they want. Men, far more than women, become angry and upset by those who delay sex or thwart their sexual advances.

In each of these examples, the anger serves a specific set of adaptive purposes, just as the patterns of fear serve specific purposes. First, anger alerts the person to the source of strategic interference, drawing attention to the interfering events and screening out less relevant information.

Second, anger singles out these events for storage in memory. Third, it motivates action directed toward reducing the strategic interference. A woman's anger at a man's persistent and unwanted sexual advances, for example, functions to stop the man in his tracks and alert others to the man's sexual impropriety. Finally, anger motivates action designed to reduce future episodes of strategic interference. Expressing anger at the man's advances can deter future unwanted advances, as well as cultivating a woman's reputation as someone who is not "easy" or "loose."

These particular examples of fear and anger as emotions designed to solve adaptive problems are relatively straightforward and illustrate the logic of strategic interference theory. Jealousy, however, is a more complicated adaptation, imbued with a complex collage of emotions. Paul Mullen, a psychiatrist at the University of Otago in New Zealand, discovered that men and women experience these emotions when jealous: pain, distress, self-blame, oppression, anxiety, loss, sadness, apprehension, anger, restless distress, humiliation, shame, agitation, sexual arousal toward partner, fear, depression, and betrayal.

Don Sharpsteen, a professor of psychology at the University of Missouri at Rolla, asked 100 people to list all the characteristics of romantic jealousy, including what people who experience jealousy think, feel, and do. This study yielded 86 distinct characteristics. Subsequently, a second group of 25 men and 25 women rated each of the 86 features on its "centrality" or "prototypicality" to the jealous experience. Among the emotions that emerged as highly prototypical were hurt, threatened, broken-hearted, upset, insecure, feeling betrayed, feeling rejected, angry, possessive, envious, unhappy, confused, frustrated, lonely, depressed, resentful, scared, and paranoid.

Despite this complex emotional tapestry, the logic of strategic interference theory applies with equal force to jealousy. Like anger and fear, jealousy serves as a signal that alerts a person to the source of strategic interference, causes the interfering events to be burned into the brain, prompts action designed to eliminate or reduce the source of strategic interference, and motivates behavior designed to avoid similar kinds of interference in the future.

The complexity of emotional reactions subsumed by jealousy mirrors the complexity of threats that must be handled. Since jealousy is triggered by signals of a partner's infidelity, the loss of the partner is one obvious threat. But consider a subtler threat, the loss of status and reputation. The psychiatrist Mary Seeman, a professor at the University of Toronto, examined five women referred to her for extreme jealousy. In all five cases, the woman displayed an obsession for the circumstances of the husband's infidelity, imagined the husband ridiculing her in front of the rival (humiliation), became preoccupied with the fact that others might know about the infidelity and feel sorry for her (shame), and imagined her loss of status and reputation in the eyes of others. All of these women showed more concern for the circumstances surrounding the husband's infidelity and the subsequent damage to their reputations than for the details of the sexual activity itself.

Damage to reputation is merely the beginning of the problems posed by a partner's infidelity. Others include a questioning of one's own desirability as a mate, the loss of trust in the partner, threats to the welfare of the children, the loss of a partner's investment, potential severing of family ties that had been built up gradually over the years, and many more. Jealousy is such a complex emotion because the corresponding problems involve so many distinct components.

The main conclusion is that jealousy is a negative emotion only in the sense that it causes psychological pain. But it is an exquisitely useful coping device when we understand that it is designed to deal with real relationship threats.

Combating Threats: The Design of the Defense

Mechanisms such as jealousy have three essential ingredients: input, information processing procedures, and output. Consider as an analogy the defense mechanism humans have evolved to guard against damage from repeated friction to the skin. Repeated friction is a "hostile force of nature," since it threatens to harm the protective layer of the skin and the bodily mechanisms the skin protects. Humans have evolved an ingenious solution to this problem: calluses. When you walk around on bare feet, for example, your soles and heels grow calluses, which enable you to continue walking around without your skin getting worn down to the bone. Although this seems obvious to us, in a sense we should be amazed, because this phenomenon appears to defy the laws of physics. When you drive around in your car, for example, your tires do not grow thicker as a consequence of the repeated friction. Tires wear down, just like all other objects exposed to these physical forces. Humans, however, possess an adaptation to defend against these hostile forces of physics.

Callus-producing adaptations have three components. The first consists of "input," repeated friction, which signals a threat and activates a suite of physiological procedures. The physiological responses set into motion a chain of events designed to produce new skin cells at precisely the locations that have experienced repeated friction. The "outputs" are the new skin cells, the calluses that then afford protection from further repeated friction. This trio of components—input, procedures, and output—describe at an abstract level the nature of the body's evolved defense against this hostile force of nature.

Threats to romantic relationships pose different sorts of adaptive problems, but the evolved defenses can be thought of in much the same way. First, there are inputs that tell a person that he or she is facing the threat. These inputs can include strange scents you detect on your partner, sudden changes in sexual desire, the introduction of a new sexual technique, mysterious hang-up phone calls, prolonged eye contact between your partner and an attractive member of the opposite sex, and a host of others. Gregory White and Paul Mullen noted a different constellation of cues: "The divining of a changed attitude, a subtle alteration in sexual responsiveness, an unexplained absence, a suspicious hair on the lover's clothing—all these are examples of events that may provide the context for the suspicions." All these "inputs," explored later in greater detail, alert a person to a possible danger.

The next step requires complex information processing and evaluation. Has an infidelity already occurred, or do these signs signal an impending infidelity? Is the rival more or less attractive, more or less successful, more or less charming than you are? As you search your memory, have there been other signals in the past? Or are you just being silly to suspect your partner, who after all vowed never to stray?

Inferences about a mate's infidelity require an array of information processing devices: paying attention to certain classes of cues, making inferences based on them, and linking them with other circumstantial information. This information processing, however, is not cold, rational, and dispassionately calculated. Many emotions accompany jealousy, including rage, humiliation, panic, fear, anxiety, and depression, and they must be understood, for they are essential to the design of this defense mechanism.

Combating a threat requires output or action. Adaptive solutions cannot stop with merely recognizing that a threat exists. As we will see in chapter 8, the coping that comes from jealousy is as complex and varied as the signals it responds to. It ranges from heightened vigilance, the first line of defense, to explosive violence, the last line of defense. It ranges from self-recrimination to a brutal attack on a rival. It ranges from attempts at suicide to attempts to kill a partner.

The design of the defense, in short, has three essential components—input, decision rules, and output—whose nature must be revealed in order to plumb the mystery of jealousy and its explosive manifestations. In subsequent chapters we will explore this design in greater detail. For now, the presence of a poignant defense mechanism implies something to defend against. And that raises the next question: Given that marital vows promise devotion and fidelity "until death do you part," why do more than half of all married couples suffer from an infidelity at some point in their marriages? Why are people tempted by adultery in such great numbers, given that they risk losing so much? And how does jealousy combat these threats?

The Co-Evolutionary Spiral

Most professionals who devote their lives to studying the mysteries of the human mind focus on a single topic or phenomenon. Among the ranks of psychologists we find expert specialists in areas such as aggression, cooperation, attitudes, status, love, language, the ear, the eye, panic disorder, attention deficit disorder, and narcissistic personality disorder. The human mind, however, does not exist in isolated bundles. It contains a complex web of interconnected mechanisms. Furthermore, human minds cannot be understood individually or in isolation. Our minds are designed to deal with the minds of other humans.

One of the most important tools for understanding jealousy is the theory of co-evolution—the reciprocal changes that occur sequentially in interacting species or between the sexes within one species. Predators and prey provide the clearest illustration of the theory of co-evolution. Rabbits are natural prey for foxes, but the two species coexist in a special way. The rabbits captured and eaten by foxes tend to be those who are slower, more preoccupied, less observant, and less attentive to the hostile forces around them. The quicker, more attentive rabbits survive and leave more descendants. Each generation of rabbits, therefore, is slightly more adept at evading foxes than the previous generation.

Now consider things from the foxes' perspective. In each generation, foxes who are more agile and fleet of foot are more successful at catching rabbits. The uncoordinated and sluggish foxes fail to feed and leave fewer descendants. So each generation of foxes is in some slight way better equipped to catch rabbits. Each increment in the speed and agility of rabbits, in essence, imposes selection pressure on foxes, just as each increment in the speed and agility of foxes imposes selection pressure on rabbits. The changes over time in rabbits and foxes, like all predators and prey, are best described as a co-evolutionary spiral that continues indefinitely, or until natural physical limits are reached.

The same logic applies to parasites and their hosts. Humans play host to thousands of parasites that cannot exist without us. Parasites, as a general rule, feed on the host organism, and can destroy it over time. Hosts have evolved defense mechanisms to combat parasites, such as immune systems. The parasites that survive, however, are those that are most skilled at evading the host's defense mechanisms. Parasites and hosts thus co-evolve in a never-ending spiral, with each change in hosts imposing selection pressure on parasites, and each change in parasites imposing selection pressure on the hosts.

The logic of reciprocal changes in interacting species applies with equal force to interacting sexes within a species. Consider as an example the co-evolutionary spiral that occurs between men and women over the linked issues of commitment and sex. As I documented in *The Evolution of Desire,* women have evolved a preference for partners who show reliable indications of the ability and willingness to channel resources to them and their children. Over human evolutionary history, women who succeeded in attracting committed men survived and reproduced more successfully than women who failed to attract such men.

Women's preferences, in turn, can exert co-evolutionary selection pressure on men. Men who display reliable cues to commitment are preferentially chosen by women; men unable to display these cues get banished from mating. Decisions to mate, however, are always made in a shroud of uncertainty, which opens the door to deception. Some men may develop a strategy of providing false cues to commitment, luring the woman into a sexual encounter, and then abandoning her. Men's deceptive strategy is one co-evolved outcome of women's initial preference for commitment.

As a strategy of deception spreads, however, it produces selection pressure on women to screen out the deceivers. Women might begin to insist on a longer period of courtship, for example, before consenting to sex, or look for signs that the man is "playing the field," such as how much his attention is diverted from their conversation when an attractive woman walks by. They might develop tests of a man's commitment, such as asking that he cancel watching the Monday night football game with his friends to attend to her needs.

As women developed the ability to detect deception, they imposed selection pressure on men to become better deceivers. And so the co-evolutionary spiral continues, with each increment in one sex producing reciprocal evolutionary change in the other. Adaptations in one sex lead to counter-adaptations in the other, and those in turn lead to further counter-adaptations and counter-counter-adaptations. As long as the strategies of the sexes are in some degree of conflict, this co-evolutionary spiral will continue unabated. At the current moment in time, we are poised in the middle of this spiral, with women being excellent detectors of deception, as indicated by factors such as their superiority over men in decoding nonverbal signals. Men, in turn, can be notoriously skilled at deceiving women.

Jealousy provides the perfect example of the power of the co-evolutionary spiral, and it starts with the evolution of love. Sustained romantic bonds pose a special problem: how to defend against the possibility that "poachers" lurk in the wings and might succeed in luring a partner away. One popular song captured the essence of the poaching problem, albeit from a man's point of view: "When you're in love with a beautiful woman, watch your friends." The more desirable your partner, the more intently interested potential interlopers will be to intrude.

Jealousy evolved as a primary defense, a co-evolved response to threats of a partner's infidelity and abandonment. It becomes activated whenever a person perceives signs of defection—a strange scent, a sudden change in sexual behavior, a suspicious absence. It gets triggered when a partner holds eye contact with someone else for a split second too long, or when a rival stands a tad too close to your loved one or suddenly seems fascinated by the minutiae of his or her life. These signals do not inevitably mean that a partner will stray, just as the annoying blare of a fire alarm does not inevitably mean that a fire is blazing. Alarms may be false. But these signals alert us to the possibility of infidelity, since they have been statistically linked with relationship loss over the long course of human evolutionary history.

This is where co-evolution kicks in again. Jealousy, which gives us sensitivity to signals of betrayal, produces partners who conceal their defections and would-be poachers who conceal their interest in your mate. A classic case of misdirection occurred in Vladimir Nabokov's novel *Laughter in the Dark*. The central character is a wealthy, respectable businessman named Albinus, who pursues art and cinema as hobbies. After a long period of fantasizing about it, Albinus leaves his wife and starts to live with his young mistress, named Margo Peters. Unbeknownst to Albinus, Margo begins to scheme to fleece him of his money. In time, Albinus hires an artist named Axel Rex to indulge his fantasy for producing a new kind of movie. Albinus remains in the dark about the fact that Rex and Margo had previously been lovers. Before long, Margo and Rex resume their torrid affair. Axel Rex delights in carrying out the deception right under Albinus's nose. When Albinus begins to grow suspicious, Rex uses an interesting ruse—he pretends to be gay. Margo joins Rex in the deception, declaring her contempt for Rex's feminine mannerisms. With these deceptions in place, Margo and Rex succeed in allaying Albinus's suspicions, and Rex is allowed to become a common presence in their household while cuckolding Albinus at every opportunity.

Co-evolution continues. Concealment, which evolved as a response to a partner's jealousy, now produces an increased sensitivity to subtle signs of treachery. Jealousy becomes more easily activated. In *Laughter in the Dark,* a car accident renders Albinus literally blind, a metaphor for his psychological blindness. His inability to "see" Margo and Rex's deception led to his inability to see at all. He moves uneasily with a cane, bumping into objects as he stumbles through the darkness. But over time, his physical blindness improves his psychological sensitivity. He begins to hear the laughter in the dark. And for the first time, psychologically, he begins to "see." Over evolutionary time, those who got duped failed to reproduce as successfully as those with psychological antennae attuned to deception. So humans have become incredibly skillful detectors of deception, just as we are adept at carrying out deception.

The spiral continues unabated, as long as the conflicts of interest between men and women continue. In some cases, the good sleuth wins, the deception is successfully detected, and the threat to the relationship is skillfully vanquished. In other cases, the betrayer wins. And in some cases, there is no clear winner. When Albinus finally hears the laughter in his darkness, Axel Rex and Margo are forced to flee. Although they manage to cheat Albinus sexually and monetarily, his emerging psychological sensitivity to betrayal helps him to staunch the losses. He returns to his wife and seeks revenge on his betrayers. At this moment in the evolution of our species, we are all end products of the co-evolutionary process that has produced an exquisite capacity for romantic deception as well as a great capacity for detecting it.

Now consider another co-evolutionary spiral involving jealousy. Although it is primarily a defense against a partner's defection, the intensity of jealousy also reveals to the partner information about the strength of commitment. People correctly interpret the total absence of jealousy as failure to be sufficiently committed to the relationship. Imagine that you started passionately kissing someone else at a party while your partner looked on, all the while displaying not the slightest sign of being upset. You would almost certainly wonder whether your partner really cared about you, or even had a pulse. Absence of jealousy signals lack of love.

People interpret moderate jealousy, in contrast, as a sign that their partner feels committed to them, but excessive jealousy signals danger. Men and women interpret excessive jealousy as a sign of anxiety about the relationship. They sense correctly that the partner feels perpetually threatened by real or imagined rivals.

How do these signals enter into the co-evolutionary arms race of jealousy? Women have developed a strategy of *intentionally evoking* jealousy by strategically flirting with other men in their partner's presence. Why trip an emotional switch and risk jealous violence? First, by evoking jealousy, women increase the man's perception of their desirability. A man who takes his girlfriend for granted, for example, might come to believe (or be reminded) that she is a real "babe" after rivals start sniffing around. Second, evoking jealousy provides a litmus test for the woman. By gauging the partner's response, she can evaluate the strength of his commitment. If he is indifferent to her flirtations with other men, it signals the lack of commitment; if he gets jealous, it signals the depth of his emotional involvement. Third, evoking jealousy increases a man's commitment. By convincing the partner that he is surrounded by rivals, the man comes to believe that he is extraordinarily lucky to be with his partner, and thus strengthens his commitment to her.

In principle, this should set the stage for yet another spiral in the co-evolutionary process. Men are not merely passive puppets at the hands of women, having their jealousy strings tightened and slackened at women's whim—at least not all the time. They learn to distinguish real threats from false alarms, to separate a mate's casual flirtation from real sexual interest in a rival. But we live in a social world filled with uncertainty. A person's smile may be the most ambiguous signal in the mating universe, so it's often hard to know if it signifies casual flirting, real sexual interest, or merely friendliness.

These examples give some flavor of the co-evolutionary spirals that have evolved over time in the intricate dance of men and women in romantic relationships. The next chapter explores how women and men do this dance differently.

CHAPTER 3

Jealousy on Mars and Venus

The female of the species is more deadly than the male.

—*Rudyard Kipling*

C OUPLE THERAPIST AND AUTHOR John Gray argues that, when it comes to relationships, men seem like they are from Mars, women from Venus. Are men more jealous than women? Or are women more jealous than men? Literature, drama, and movies often depict men as the jealous sex. Shakespeare's Othello was consumed with jealousy, for example, and it is hard to find comparable dramatic cases portraying women. Common lore, on the other hand, notes that "hell hath no fury like a woman scorned," suggesting that women might react more intensely to a betrayal or defection. What do the scientific studies show about which sex is most jealous?

How would you respond to the following questions, rating them on a 7-point scale from *strongly disagree* (1) to *strongly agree* (7)?

_____ 1. It does not bother me when I see my lover flirting with someone else.

_____ 2. When I see my lover kissing someone else my stomach knots up.

_____ 3. When my lover dances with someone else I feel very uneasy.

_____ 4. When somebody hugs my lover I get sick inside.

_____ 5. It would bother me if my partner frequently had satisfying sexual relations with someone else.

_____ 6. It is entertaining to hear the sexual fantasies my partner has about another person.

Bram Buunk, a professor at the University of Groningen in the Netherlands, and his collaborators posed these questions to 2,079 people in Hungary, Ireland, Mexico, the Netherlands, the former Soviet Union, the United States, and Yugoslavia. Yugoslavians expressed the greatest distress at a lover flirting with someone else, whereas Hungarians showed the least distress about flirting. In sharp contrast, Hungarians topped the scale in being upset about a lover kissing someone else, whereas Yugoslavians expressed little distress over a few stolen kisses.

The most important finding, however, was that men and women across all seven nations reported virtually identical levels of jealousy. Dutch men and women, like Russian men and women, scored almost exactly alike in their jealousy over a partner flirting with someone else. Jealousy responses to more extreme forms of infidelity, such as a partner frequently having satisfying sexual relations with someone else, also revealed that the sexes are virtually identical in all cultures.

Other studies on American samples verify the lack of sex differences on global measures of jealousy. In response to the question, "How upset would you get if your boyfriend or girlfriend fantasized about having sex just once with a very attractive person they saw in a magazine?" men judged it to be 3.42 on a 7-point scale and women 3.70, both moderately upsetting and not significantly different. Dozens of other studies verify the conclusion that overall, men and women are equally jealous.

Clinical cases of extreme jealousy are populated with both sexes, contrary to the stereotype that extreme jealousy afflicts only men. Here are two cases, one from each sex. Case 1: "Enid, convinced that her husband was carrying on in his office, paid him a surprise visit intending to catch him 'in the act.' She found the office empty but completely rearranged. There were photographs and paintings on the wall that she did not recognize. She immediately concluded that the lover had redecorated the office. Only later did she realize that she was in fact in someone else's office—an office that was very different in size and shape from her husband's." Case 2: "A middle-aged man began to worry about his wife's infidelity. As he approached the house, he would turn off the car engine and headlights and coast into the driveway. Then he would burst into the house precipitously. One night he went to the back of the house, climbed up the steps on tiptoe and dramatically flung open the rear door, fully expecting to surprise his wife in the arms of another man. His wife was simply standing by the stove . . . cooking dinner and looked at him with considerable curiosity."

The conclusion is clear: women and men alike can be plagued by jealousy, both in its everyday manifestations and in its more florid clinical expressions. If that were all to the story, we could conclude the chapter at this point. It was not until evolutionary psychologists posed a different set of questions, driven by a powerful theory, that sex differences in the psychological components of jealousy began to emerge.

Violations of Desire

Men's and women's mating strategies differ profoundly. Women place a premium on commitment and all of the cues to commitment, most centrally emotional involvement and love. Men have evolved a greater desire for sexual variety, which produces tremendous conflict between the sexes, for it violates women's desire for intimate involvement. Because youth and beauty are so strongly correlated with fertility in women, men have evolved a strong desire for women who embody these qualities. Finally, men value sexual fidelity in a partner, for any infidelity on a woman's part puts her mate's paternity at risk. Men's and women's sexual strategies provide the foundation for the psychological design of jealousy.

To understand the implications, recall the concept of strategic interference, which occurs when someone blocks or impedes the strategies and goals of another person. The so-called negative emotions such as anger, fear, and jealousy are tracking devices, alerting us to strategic interference. Since men and women have evolved different sexual strategies, they should get jealous, angry, and upset about different events. A woman's desire for emotional involvement, for example, will be violated when a potential partner treats her as a one-night stand. A man's desire for a partner's sexual fidelity will be violated when his partner has sex with another man.

In the following sections, we explore the research that tests these ideas. We start with the most fundamental sex difference in the psychology of jealousy, a difference centering on the importance of emotional and sexual involvement with rivals.

Mama's Baby, Papa's Maybe

Compromises in paternity certainty come at a substantial cost to men. In evolutionary currencies, men risk wasting all the mating effort they expended, including the time, energy, and gifts they have invested while courting a woman. The man also incurs what economists call "opportunity costs," the missed opportunities with other women as a result of devoting all their effort to one woman. A cuckolded man also loses the woman's parental effort, which becomes channeled to a rival's genetic children. He risks parenting a rival's genetic children in the mistaken belief that they are his own. Finally, the man risks damage to his reputation, since cuckolds are universally ridiculed in the eyes of others.

In Greece, for example, a man's reputation is threatened when "the wife's infidelity . . . brings disgrace to the husband who is then a Keratas—the worst insult for a Greek man—a shameful epithet with connotations of weakness and inadequacy. . . . While for the wife it is socially acceptable to tolerate her unfaithful husband, it is not socially acceptable for a man to tolerate his unfaithful wife and if he does, he is ridiculed as behaving in an unmanly manner."

Given these potentially catastrophic costs, we expect that evolution would have forged powerful defenses to prevent incurring them. Jealousy is the best candidate. The specific nature of the risk should have left deep grooves on the psychological record that defines male sexual jealousy. Jealousy in men should pivot heavily around the *sexual* aspects of a partner's infidelity. A sexual infidelity by the woman, more than any other form of infidelity, imposed the greatest costs on ancestral men. This may seem obvious, perhaps, but the same logic does not apply to women.

Emotional Currents

No woman ever risked maternity uncertainty as a result of a partner's infidelity. Human reproductive biology guarantees a woman certainty that she is the genetic mother of her children. Certainty in maternity, however, does not exempt women from the costs of a partner's philandering. Ancestral women would have risked the loss of a man's time, energy, resources, and commitment, all of which could get diverted to a rival woman and her children.

In human evolutionary history, there have been at least three situations in which a woman was in danger of losing a man's investment. First, in a monogamous marriage, a woman risked having her mate invest in an alternative woman with whom he was having an affair. This represents a partial loss of the man's investment. Second, in a monogamous marriage, a woman chanced losing her husband to another woman, a large or total loss of his investment. Third, in a polygynous marriage, a woman risked having her husband invest more in other wives and their children at the expense of her and her children.

The most reliable indicator that a man would divert his investment was not in having sex with another woman per se, but rather in becoming *emotionally involved* with another woman. The ability to gauge a man's emotional involvement becomes paramount in gauging commitment. How would you respond these two statements, using a 7-point scale ranging from *strongly disagree* (1) *to strongly agree* (7): "Sex without commitment is very unsatisfying" and "I would find it hard to have sex with someone I was not in love with." If you are like most women, you would tend to agree with these statements, rating them over 5.00. If you are like most men, however, you tend to disagree, rating them around 3.00. People from the United States and Germany give roughly equivalent responses, revealing a large sex difference in the desire for love to accompany sex—a desire that transcends cultures.

What happens when you have sex anyway, without any emotional involvement from your partner? The anthropologist John Marshal Townsend of Syracuse University explored this issue in detail. He interviewed a sample of 50 college students, selected for being highly sexually active. These students were preselected based on their scores on the Sociosexual Orientation Inventory, an instrument that evaluates a person's proclivity toward many short-term sexual encounters versus a preference for one long-term committed partner. The women selected for Townsend's study defied the normal stereotype of women by their unusually high levels of sexual activity with a variety of men. Do these sexually active women respond like sexually active men in their emotional reactions to casual sex?

Townsend asked participants: "Have you ever continued to have sex on a regular basis with someone you did not want to get emotionally involved with?" Only a third of the women (37 percent) answered yes to this question, compared with more than three-fourths (76 percent) of the men. Of those who answered yes, the follow-up question was: "If you answered yes, did you find it difficult to keep from getting emotionally involved with this person?" Again, a large sex difference emerged, with 74 percent of the men, but only 22 percent of the women, saying that they found it easy to keep from getting emotionally involved. Other questions revealed similar sex differences. To the statement, "I feel I should be emotionally involved with a woman/man before having sex with him/her," 72 percent of the men disagreed, whereas only 32 percent of the women disagreed.

Women who have sex without emotional involvement tend to feel vulnerable afterward, expressing the view that they feel used, degraded, and cheapened by the experience. Here is what one woman reported: "I consider myself a very sexual woman. I love sex, but I don't just want sex. I want to make love. Making love is very different. It implies you have a relationship. And you have some control. So about two weeks ago I was really, really sad. I just hated myself for giving in to men as easily as I've done . . . I have been to bed with 24 guys. That's how old I am: 24. Twenty-four guys within the last five years. I think that's sick because not one of them meant anything to me. Or, let's put it this way: I didn't really mean anything to them. This made me feel really cheap." As

Townsend concludes from his studies on women, "attempts to continue regular coitus when they desired more investment than their partners were willing to give produced feelings of distress, degradation, and exploitation despite acceptance of liberal sexual morality."

Men and women, in short, differ in their attitudes about the role of emotional involvement in sex. Most women, even those who end up having a number of casual sexual encounters, want some kind of emotional involvement. Most men, in contrast, have less difficulty having sex without any emotional involvement. For such casual flings, men devote neither much time nor many resources. If a man became emotionally involved with an affair partner, however, it would signal a longer-term threat; increasingly large diversions of resources follow. For these reasons, we predicted that women's jealousy will focus less on the sex act per se, and more on a man's emotional involvement with other women. When a man is emotionally involved with another woman, it's a telltale sign that he might commit to her over the long run. When a woman's regular partner becomes involved with someone else, both sexually and emotionally, it is the emotional involvement that should provoke the strongest feelings of jealousy.

The Sophie's Choice of Jealousy

Our theory of sex differences in jealousy, of course, does not imply that women will be indifferent to a mate's sexual infidelity, nor that men will be indifferent to a woman's emotional involvement with other men. To the contrary, both forms of infidelity are extremely upsetting to both sexes. On a 7-point scale, where 7 is *extremely upsetting*, both sexes score between six and seven when asked to judge how upsetting either form of infidelity would be, when each is evaluated individually.

What happens when you are forced to choose which is more upsetting, a partner's sexual infidelity or a partner's emotional infidelity? The two are correlated in nature, of course, since people tend to become emotionally involved with those they have sex with and sexually involved with those they are emotionally close to. But not always. Sex can occur without emotional involvement, as in a one-night stand or a spring break fling in Cancun. And people can get emotionally involved without any sex, as occurs in some close opposite-sex friendships.

But what if you had a choice—experiencing your partner having sexual intercourse with someone else or becoming emotionally involved with someone else? This is what I call the "Sophie's choice" of the jealousy dilemmas. In the movie *Sophie's Choice,* the female lead, played by Meryl Streep, is forced to choose which of her two children will be killed. Clearly, this dilemma is a horror that no parent should ever face. But when forced, Sophie indeed makes a choice. This dilemma revealed a preference that may never have been revealed by any other situation.

The jealousy dilemma is in some ways analogous to "Sophie's Choice." Although having a partner become sexually or emotionally involved with someone else is a monogamist's nightmare, men and women can determine which one would be more upsetting when asked to imagine the dilemma. Here is what we asked the participants in one study: "Please think of a serious committed relationship that you have had in the past, that you currently have, or that you would like to have. Imagine that you discover that the person with whom you've been seriously involved started seeing a former lover. What action would be *more difficult* for you to *forgive?* (*a*) Your partner rekindles passionate sexual intercourse with the former lover, or (*b*) Your partner rekindles a deep emotional attachment to the former lover." In this study of 530 men and women, 67 percent of the men reported that they would find the sexual involvement of their partner more difficult to forgive, whereas only 44 percent of women reported that the sexual infidelity would be more difficult to forgive.

Verbal reports are reasonable sources of data, but ideally, confirming evidence from other types of tests is more convincing for experts and nonexperts alike, so we brought 60 men and women into our psychophysiological laboratory. To evaluate physiological distress from imagining the two types of infidelity, the experimenters placed electrodes on the corrugator muscle on the brow of the forehead, which contracts when people frown. We also attached electrodes on the first and third fingers of the right hand to measure electrodermal response, or sweating, and on the thumb to measure pulse or heart rate. Then participants were asked to imagine either a sexual infidelity ("imagining your partner having sex with someone else . . . get the feelings and images clearly in mind") or an emotional infidelity ("imagining your partner falling in love with someone else . . . get the feelings and images clearly in mind"). Participants pressed a button when they had the feelings and images clearly in mind, which activated the physiological recording devices for the next 20 seconds.

The men became more physiologically distressed by the sexual infidelity. Their heart rates accelerated by nearly five beats per minute, which is roughly equivalent to drinking three cups of strong coffee at one time. Their skin conductance, also an indication of distress, increased with the thought of sexual infidelity, but showed a smaller change from baseline in response to the thought of emotional infidelity. And their forehead brow muscle began to contract accordion-like in response to sexual infidelity, indicating deep displeasure, as compared with smaller contractions in response to emotional infidelity. When we observed the men in this condition through a one-way mirror, many appeared flushed and so obviously upset that we hardly needed the physiological recording devices to document it.

Women tended to show the opposite pattern. They exhibited greater physiological distress at the thought of emotional infidelity. Women's frowning, for example, increased nearly three times as much in response to a partner's emotional infidelity as compared to sexual infidelity. The convergence of psychological and physiological reactions of distress strongly confirms the predicted sex difference—men and women may be equally jealous, but the events that trigger jealousy differ.

Rival Explanations for Sex Differences

Not every psychologist agrees with our interpretation. David DeSteno and Peter Salovey proposed that men and women differ in their "beliefs" about sexual and emotional involvement. When a man thinks that his partner is becoming sexually involved with a rival, for example, he might also think that his partner will be getting emotionally involved as well—a so-called double shot of infidelity. The reason men get more upset about sexual rather than emotional infidelity, they argue, is not because men are really more jealous about sexual infidelity but because they "believe" that a sexual infidelity will result in the double shot of infidelity, which includes emotional infidelity.

Women, they argue, have different beliefs, although DeSteno and Salovey fail to explain why. Women believe in a reverse double shot, that if their partner becomes emotionally involved with a rival, he will also become sexually involved. It's women's beliefs about this double shot of infidelity that upsets them, DeSteno and Salovey argue, and not that women really are more upset about an emotional betrayal.

Our theory opposes the double-shot theory. Given the large sex differences stemming from fundamental differences in reproductive biology, it would be extremely unlikely for selection to have failed to produce psychological sex differences about the two forms of infidelity. The hard hand of data usually settles scientific disagreements. So my research collaborators and I conducted four studies in three different cultures to pit the predictions from our evolutionary theory against the predictions from the double-shot hypothesis. One study involved 1,122 participants from a liberal arts college in the southeastern United States. We asked them to imagine their partner becoming interested in someone else: "What would upset or distress you more: (*a*) imagining your partner forming a deep emotional (*but not sexual*) relationship with that person, or (*b*) imagining your partner enjoying a sexual (*but not emotional*) relationship with that person?"

Men and women differed by roughly 35 percent in their responses, as predicted by the evolutionary model. Women continued to express greater upset about a partner's emotional infidelity, even if it did not involve sex. Men continued to show more upset than women about a partner's sexual infidelity, even if it did not involve emotional involvement. If the double-shot hypothesis was the correct explanation for the initial sex differences that we found, then the sex difference should have disappeared when we isolated the sexual and emotional components of infidelity. It did not.

In a second study of 234 women and men, we used a different strategy for pitting the competing hypotheses against each other. We asked participants to imagine that their worst nightmare had occurred, that their partner had become both sexually *and* emotionally involved with someone else. We then asked them to state *which aspect* they found more upsetting.

The results were conclusive. We found large sex differences precisely as predicted by our evolutionary theory: 63 percent of the men, but only 13 percent of the women, found the sexual aspect of the infidelity to be most upsetting; in contrast, 87 percent of the women, but only 37 percent of the men, found the emotional aspect of the infidelity to be most upsetting. No matter how the questions were worded, no matter which method we used, we saw the same sex difference in every test.

Together with Jae Choe, at Seoul National University, and Mariko and Toshikazu Hasegawa, at the University of Tokyo, we conducted a final study on Koreans and Japanese. Choe and the Hasegawas found precisely the same sex differences: women reported more distress than men when imagining that their partner was emotionally unfaithful; men reported more distress than women when imagining a partner having sex with a rival.

Several other scientists have now confirmed our results using somewhat different methods. In a study of 392 men and women in Sweden, Michael Wiederman and Erica Kendall of Ball State University posed these dilemmas: "Please read the following two scenarios and circle the one you would find most upsetting: (*a*) Your partner recently made friends with a co-worker of the other gender and has been spending more and more time with that person. You are sure that the two of them have not had sexual intercourse, but they seem to like each other very much. The two of them have many things in common and you suspect that they are falling in love. Or (*b*) You discover that, while your partner was away on vacation, your partner met someone and had sexual intercourse once with that person. You are sure that your partner loves you very much and highly values your relationship together. You also realize that, even though your partner did have sexual intercourse while on vacation, it was a 'one night stand' and your partner would never see that person again."

Wiederman and Kendall found that a majority of the Swedish men (62 percent) found the sexual infidelity of their partners more upsetting, whereas the majority of the Swedish women (63 percent) found the emotional infidelity of their partners more upsetting. They concluded that "contrary to the double-shot explanation, choice of scenario was unrelated to attitudes regarding whether the other gender was capable of satisfying sexual relations outside of a love relationship."

These and similar sex differences have now been replicated in China, Germany, the Netherlands, Korea, Sweden, and Japan. The Swedish and Chinese findings are particularly intriguing because they represent cultures at opposite ends of the spectrum of sexual liberality. Sweden tends to be a sexually open culture, with high rates of premarital and extramarital sex. Swedes stress equality between the sexes in most matters, including sexuality. China, according to David Geary of the University of Missouri-Columbia, strongly frowns on premarital sex and shows low affair rates. The same basic sex differences emerge in all these diverse cultures. Men's jealousy is more sensitive to cues of sexual infidelity, and women's jealousy is more sensitive to cues of emotional infidelity. These cross-cultural findings provide striking support for the theory that these are universal sex differences. The double-shot theory cannot explain why these sex differences would be universal.

The Mars and Venus of Jealousy Episodes

These basic sex differences also emerge in actual reports of jealous episodes. We asked several hundred men and women to describe, in their own words, the details of a specific episode where they experienced jealousy. The following example is one woman's description:

"My boyfriend chose to talk about a problem with a female friend of his instead of me. She happened to be home when he called and I wasn't. His friend doesn't like me and always tells my boyfriend bad things about me. What triggered my jealousy was just the fact that he chose to talk to her instead of me . . . it made me so mad! He doesn't talk about his feelings often, so when he does it's a really special experience. I yelled at him because he felt better after talking to her, and didn't want to talk more about it, even to me. I cried because I was really hurt."

Another woman reported the following episode that triggered her jealousy:

"My boyfriend got a call from a girl that used to like him not that long ago and they were talking up a blast. He was laughing and sounded really interested in what she was saying and cracking jokes with her . . . etc. The fact that we had not had a conversation like that in a really long time and we were supposed to hang out that night, and while he was on the phone, I just sat there waiting for him . . . I yelled at him when he got off and refused to have sex that night."

The emotional aspects of the betrayal pervaded women's descriptions of the situations that triggered their jealousy. Contrast these with a man's description of what triggered his jealousy:

"I had a feeling that my girlfriend was cheating on me. When I got home one evening, I checked the messages and there was some guy who had called for her. I looked up the number on our caller ID, and called the guy. The guy basically admitted that they had been together, having sex. When my girlfriend came home she confessed. I grilled her about every detail of their sexual activity. We tried to make it past this explosion, but I could not get the images out of my mind. I kept picturing her naked underneath this other guy, trying out sexual positions we had tried. She swore that she loved me and that it would never happen again, but it tore me up; I couldn't get the images out of my head. We split up a few weeks later."

Men's sexual jealousy can be triggered even before a full-blown relationship has formed, as illustrated by the following case:

"I've got a smart, cool, attractive neighbor that I've been falling in love with. I had been actively pursuing her for weeks, helped set her up in her apartment, showed her the town, and had fun with her. Then my [male] roommate and I had a big party. He is handsome, I can admit, and he ended up hooking up with [having sex with] the woman I had been falling in love with. Then, last night, while I was at work, my roomie and my attractive neighbor cooked dinner, drank a little, smoked a little pot, and wound up having sex again! The shitty part was that I was wired on caffeine and trying to fall asleep, and I could hear them kissing in his room because the door was open. I had actively pursued this girl for weeks, and my roommate spends one fucking night with her, and bang. I got dressed and left, because when I get jealous I get really hot and flustered and nauseous. I walked the streets for hours alone, cursing the way this cookie had crumbled."

Women also report that the sexual aspects of their involvement with other men provoke their current partner's jealousy more than anything else. Here is what one woman reported:

"My boyfriend and I broke up, but then we decided to rekindle the relationship. He insisted on knowing what I'd been doing since our first break-up, and I told him how many people I'd slept with. He was *very, very, very* upset. He had come to visit for the fourth of July, and I thought we would rekindle what we had. Boy did I ever blow the spark out of that one! When I told him the number of people I'd slept with he nearly jumped through his skin."

Bear in mind that sexual and emotional infidelity upset both men and women. Men are not indifferent to their partners getting emotionally intimate with other men, nor are women indifferent to their partners having sexual intercourse with other women. When asked to describe a specific episode of jealousy, however, men more often recite sexual aspects of infidelity, often with vivid descriptions of their partners in sexual positions with other men. Men have trouble exorcising these images from their minds. Women more often describe emotional aspects of infidelity, including a partner spending time, giving attention, sharing confidences, joking, and laughing with a rival.

The sex differences in events that activate jealousy are so strong that they filter down to the very definition of infidelity. When asked to define infidelity, men tend to focus narrowly on a partner who has had sex with someone else. Women have a broader definition and include a partner spending time with someone else or giving a lot of attention to someone else. As journalist Judith Viorst noted, speaking on behalf of women, "I think the everyday kind of jealousy has less to do with a fear of overt sexual betrayal than it does with a fear of intimacy that excludes us." In these respects, men and women differ in their psychology of jealousy as much as they differ in the size and shapes of their bodies.

Jealousy in Homosexual Relationships

For committed romantic relationships, pretty much everyone, no matter what their sexual orientation, wants honesty, kindness, stability, low levels of conflict, sexual satisfaction, affection, and equality. Gay men also share with their heterosexual counterparts a strong desire for youth and physical attractiveness in potential partners. The evolutionary anthropologist William Jankowiak and his colleagues asked gay men and lesbians to rank sets of photographs of men and women who differed in age and physical attractiveness. Gay and straight men alike rank the younger partners as more attractive. Neither lesbian nor straight women, in contrast, place much importance on youth in their rankings of attractiveness. In these respects, gay and heterosexual men are alike and lesbian and heterosexual women are alike.

Gay men differ from heterosexual men, however, in the frequency of sexual encounters outside of their primary relationship. One study found that gay men were seven times as likely to have outside encounters, and other studies confirm this general finding. If gay men are more sexually permissive, it raises an interesting question about the role of jealousy in gay relationships. In principle, it could go either way. One possibility is that because gay men tend to have more outside involvements, their jealousy might become hyperactivated since they are confronted with rivals and threats of defection more often. On the other hand, perhaps gay couples quell their jealousy because of mutual agreements to permit outside sexual encounters.

Data on this question are sparse, but research is starting to reveal the outlines of homosexual jealousy. One study compared 113 homosexual men with 81 heterosexual men on a measure of sexual jealousy. Sample items from this measure are: "If _____ [romantic partner] were to admire someone of the same sex [opposite sex], I would feel irritated." "The thought of _____ kissing someone else drives me up the wall." Scores for this sexual jealousy scale ranged from 28 to 252. Heterosexual men scored 131 on average, whereas homosexual men scored only 106, which was significantly lower.

Robert Bringle of Purdue University in Indianapolis conducted a larger study of jealousy among gay men to see whether gay men really are less sexually jealous. He too found that gay men reported less jealousy than did heterosexual men in response to events such as witnessing a partner kissing someone else at a party or discovering that a partner is having an affair. Gay men, however, were also less likely to disclose jealous feelings to their partner when they had them, despite the tendency of gay men to be more emotionally expressive in general. This result raises the possibility that gay men actually experience similar levels of jealousy as heterosexual men but are simply more reluctant to report it. Gay men in committed relationships may face the same problem as heterosexuals in open marriages—how to grapple with the conflict between a desire for a more sexually liberal lifestyle and the jealousy that follows when a partner also tries to fulfill that desire. Whether gay men are truly less jealous than heterosexual men, or are merely more reluctant to express it, remains to be discovered.

What about sex differences among homosexuals in reactions to the "Sophie's Choice" of the jealousy dilemma? A team of Dutch psychologists led by Pieternel Dijkstra of the University of Groningen secured the cooperation of 99 lesbians and 138 gay men by recruiting them in gay bars in several Dutch towns. The dilemmas consisted of two infidelity scenarios, and the participants were asked which would upset them more. For example: (*a*) imagining your partner enjoying passionate sexual intercourse with that other man/woman, or (*b*) imagining your partner forming a deep emotional attachment to that other man/woman.

Another scenario asked participants to imagine that both forms of infidelity had occurred: "Imagine that your partner formed an emotional attachment to another man/woman and had sexual intercourse with that other person. Which aspect of your partner's involvement would upset you more: (*a*) the sexual intercourse with that other person, or (*b*) the emotional attachment to that other person?"

The results were different from the results of the parallel studies using heterosexuals. In response to the first dilemma, 51 percent of the lesbians found the sexual infidelity more distressing, but only 32 percent of the gay men found the sexual infidelity more distressing—a reversal of the usual sex difference. The investigators found similar results for the second dilemma, which asked "which aspect" would be most upsetting. Lesbians, in short, seem more distressed than heterosexual women about the sexual infidelity of a partner, whereas gay men show more distress than heterosexual men about emotional betrayal.

Michael Bailey of Northwestern University found similar results in

American samples. When forced to choose which form of infidelity was more distressing, gay men in his sample were more likely than heterosexual men to become upset at a partner's emotional betrayal; lesbians were slightly more likely than heterosexual women to be distressed by a partner's sexual unfaithfulness.

Based on these studies, we can offer tentative conclusions about jealousy in homosexuals. First, homosexual men appear to express less sexual jealousy than heterosexual men. This may reflect the fact that, in many homosexual relationships, it is understood that the partners will have casual sexual encounters with others, as long as they do not affect the primary relationship. Or, it's entirely possible that gay men experience the same levels of jealousy, but keep it under wraps. Lesbians appear to be more sexually jealous than their heterosexual counterparts, who overwhelmingly express more distress at emotional infidelity. The often-replicated sex differences in jealousy found among heterosexuals—with men more upset by a partner's sexual infidelity and women more upset by a partner's emotional infidelity—appear to be reversed among homosexuals. Gay men appear to be more like heterosexual women than heterosexual men in their reactions to the jealousy dilemmas. Clearly, we need additional research on this topic before reaching any firm conclusions.

The Eternal Triangle

On July 30, 1771, a man named Werther wrote a letter of distress to his brother Wilhelm. Werther had been caught by the love for a young woman named Charlotte. He had confessed to Charlotte his deep love, telling her that she was sacred to him and that he worshipped the ground she walked on. In his letter to his brother, he said that he almost fainted in her presence, so great was his love for her. The letter, however, betrayed the deep psychological agony when he compared himself to his rival, Albert, who was engaged to Charlotte:

> Albert has arrived, and I shall go. Even if he were the best, the noblest man, whom I could respect as my superior in every respect, it would be intolerable to see him before me in possession

of so many perfections. Possession! Enough, Wilhelm, the fiancé is here. A nice, dear man, whom one cannot help liking . . . His calm exterior contrasts sharply with the restlessness of my character, which I cannot conceal. He is a man of deep feeling and knows what a treasure he has in Lotte. He seems to have little ill-humor, and you know that is the sin I hate in people more than any other.

Despite his admiration for his rival, whom he describes as "the best person in the world," he deliberates on whether he should kill him, not because Albert deserved to die, but simply because his comparative superiority was intolerable to Werther. Eventually, Werther decides to kill himself instead in order to end his psychological pain.

The presence of rivals who may attempt to lure a mate away from an existing long-term mateship, by itself, may not constitute an adaptive threat. A street bum or a bag lady leering at your partner, for example, may not tempt your partner in the slightest, and so poses no threat. Rivals become relevant only when they display an equivalent or higher level of desirability.

Men's value as a mate, more than women's, is closely linked with the ability to secure resources as well as the qualities that tend to lead to resources such as status, ambition, industriousness, and maturity. Women universally desire men with good financial prospects. This preference does not diminish when women gain personal access to financial resources, nor when women achieve high socioeconomic status, nor even when women reside in cultures of relatively high economic equality between the sexes. Furthermore, since violence has been a recurrent problem women face at the hands of men, women place a greater premium on qualities that signal a man's ability to protect her, such as physical strength and athletic prowess. The ability to secure economic resources and possess athletic prowess, in short, are more central to men's than to women's overall value on the mating market. Physical attractiveness in contrast is more central to women's overall desirability on the mating market.

These fundamental sex-linked desires have enormous consequences for the triggers of jealousy in men and women, following the principle of co-evolution. Jealousy in each sex has evolved to mirror the mate preferences of the other sex. Since women desire professionally successful men, for example, men's jealousy should have evolved in tandem to be activated by a rival who excels professionally. And since men place a premium on youth and physical appearance, women's jealousy should have evolved to be especially sensitive to rivals who are younger or more physically alluring. The design of the jealousy defense, in short, should have been sculpted by generations of mate preferences imposed by the opposite sex.

Jealousy About Rivals in the Netherlands

The co-evolutionary theory of jealousy provides some powerful insights into the psychological design of jealousy, but are these insights borne out by the empirical studies? Pieternel Dijkstra and Bram Buunk conducted a study in the Netherlands to find out. They presented men and women with scenarios of rivals flirting with their partners. The following is an example of a scenario presented to the men in the study:

"You are at a party with your girlfriend and you are talking with some of your friends. You notice your girlfriend across the room talking to a man you do not know. You can see from his face that he is very interested in your girlfriend. He is listening closely to what she is saying and you notice that he casually touches her hand. You notice that he is flirting with her. After a minute, your girlfriend also begins to act flirtatiously. You can tell from the way she is looking at him that she likes him a great deal. They seem completely absorbed in each other."

After reading this scenario, participants turned the page and saw a photograph of the rival along with a personality description. In one version, the rival was exceptionally good looking, whereas in the other he was unattractive. Then the rival was described as either a dominant leader or a more passive follower. Here's how the dominant rival was described: "You find out that your girlfriend is flirting with Hans, the man in the photo. Hans is a student in Groningen [a city in the Netherlands in which the study took place] and is about the same age as you.

67

Hans is a teaching assistant and teaches courses to undergraduates. He is also president of DLP, an activities club that numbers about 600 members. Hans knows what he wants and is a good judge of character. Hans also often takes the initiative to do something new and he has a lot of influence on other people. At parties he always livens things up."

The nondominant follower was described this way: "You find out that your girlfriend is flirting with Hans, the man in the photo. Hans is a student in Groningen and is about the same age as you. Hans attends classes regularly and is one of the 600 members of activities club DLP. Hans does not always know what he wants and he often fails to understand what is going on in other people's minds. Hans often waits for others to take the initiative and is rather compliant. At parties he usually stays in the background."

After viewing the photos and reading the personality descriptions, participants rated how jealous they felt on a 5-point scale ranging from 1 (*not at all jealous*) to 5 (*very jealous*). They also rated how suspicious, betrayed, worried, distrustful, rejected, hurt, anxious, angry, threatened, sad, and upset they felt after they had perused the scenario and photograph of the rival.

The physical attractiveness of the rival did not affect men's feelings of jealousy. The dominance of the rival, however, had a strong impact. Dominant rivals evoked more jealousy among men than nondominant rivals. This effect proved especially strong in the low attractiveness version, where the dominant rival evoked jealousy scores averaging 3.5, whereas the nondominant rival evoked jealousy scores of only 2.3.

For women, the results were reversed. The dominance of the rival had absolutely no effect on women's jealousy, but the physical attractiveness of the rival had a huge impact. The attractive female rival evoked jealousy ratings of 3.5, regardless of the rival's dominance. In contrast, the unattractive female rival evoked jealousy ratings of only 2.6, again regardless of the rival's dominance.

This study provided evidence that jealousy is especially keyed to the desires of the opposite sex. Women are primarily threatened by rivals who embody what men want. Men are primarily threatened by rivals who have what women want.

Rival Jealousy in Korea, the Netherlands, and America

The Dutch study represents the first to document that the psychological design of jealousy about rivals depends on specific characteristics. How general are these results across cultures? To answer this question, my colleagues Jae Choe, Pieternel Dijkstra, Bram Buunk, and Todd Shackelford explored jealousy within the context of a larger set of rival characteristics. The American participants were 208 individuals, 106 women and 102 men, drawn from a large midwestern university. The Korean participants were 174 individuals, 83 women and 91 men, drawn from a large university located in Seoul. The Dutch participants were 182 women and 162 men from Groningen.

Each person completed a questionnaire containing background information. Then they were instructed: Please think of a serious or committed romantic relationship that you have had in the past, that you currently have, or that you would like to have. Imagine that you discover that the person with whom you've been seriously involved became seriously interested in a long-term relationship with someone else. What would upset or distress you more? Please rank order the following items on the degree to which they would upset you. Give a 1 to *the most upsetting,* a 2 to the *second most upsetting,* a 3 to *the third most upsetting* . . . all the way down to 11 for *the least upsetting.*

You found out that the person that your partner became interested in:

_____ 1. was more kind and understanding than you
_____ 2. had a more attractive face than you
_____ 3. was a more skilled sexual partner than you
_____ 4. was higher in status and prestige than you
_____ 5. was more willing to commit to a long-term relationship than you
_____ 6. had better financial prospects than you
_____ 7. had a more attractive body than you
_____ 8. was a virgin (had no previous sexual experience)
_____ 9. was physically stronger than you
_____ 10. had better future job prospects than you
_____ 11. had a better sense of humor than you

The Korean, American, and Dutch studies supported our theory of jealousy about rivals. Men in all three cultures showed greater distress than women over rivals who had better financial prospects, better future job prospects, and greater physical strength.

I witnessed this finding firsthand when I interviewed a married couple on camera for a TV documentary based on my research on jealousy. They had no previous knowledge about my research, but illustrated the theory beautifully. The couple, in their late 20s, described their marriage as solid and happy. They had just had their first child. Their colleagues and friends alike described them as exceptionally "nice people." They were as well matched on personality, temperament, and looks as any couple I'd ever interviewed. When I asked the husband whether he ever felt that his wife might be lured away by other man, he replied: "Well, we have a great relationship, and I feel like I can give her nearly everything she needs and wants. I make her laugh, I'm sweet to her, and I carry at least half of the child-care duties. There is only one thing that I feel threatened by—another man who can provide for her better than I can. I don't have a high salary. I can give her everything else she needs except that. I don't think it will ever happen, but it's the one area where I feel vulnerable."

Women in all three cultures showed greater distress than did men over rivals who had more attractive faces and more attractive bodies. One American woman, age 24, described her experience with jealousy: "I've been with my boyfriend for four years, but when we had been seeing each other for only six months, some girl came onto him at a party, and she was *very pretty*. They became friends. I became jealous of their friendship, but only after he said that he found her very physically attractive, and he told me that she was very interested in him as well—she wanted him for herself."

Another American woman, age 23, described her feelings of jealousy: "My boyfriend had been unfaithful in the past and I really felt as if he couldn't be trusted around anyone of the opposite sex. I became extremely jealous when my boyfriend was talking to another woman. She was pretty, and she made me feel like I was the ugliest girl in the world! I went up to them and stood right between them and asked 'who is this?' and he politely introduced us. I was so rude to her that she left."

The rival's sexiness also provokes a woman's jealousy. A woman in her mid-30s described this episode: "Several years ago, my best friend, who is very sexy, sat on my husband's lap just for fun, and I felt jealous and threatened for the first time in our relationship. It was her playful attitude, laughter, and her innate sex appeal that set me off—the fact that she waggled her fanny in his face. My husband and I had a huge fight later that night."

Jealousy About Rivals in Kingston, Jamaica

One of the most vivid demonstrations of the destruction caused by jealous rivals comes not from a formal scientific study, but rather from a journalist's shocking exposé of jealousy in Jamaica. In the city of Kingston, the nightlife swirls and DJs boom out songs about heart-wrenching suffering in triangular relationships. The triangles typically center on a man, his girlfriend ("matey") and the woman who's the mother of his children ("babymother"). The songs pulse and grind, the torrid beat lightened by playful lyrics that convey stories of rivalry and betrayal.

Money is scarce, but what money is available often gets funneled into sharp clothes in a plumage-like competition for desirable mates. The successfully partnered cannot rest easy. Both sexes fear being usurped by rivals. The qualities of dangerous rivals are predictably different for men and women: "the men fear being left for a better economic prospect and the women expect to be usurped by the young, up-and-coming mateys." The women look for men of means, a man with "sweets," to escape the struggle for survival and to secure a steady stream of income for their children. Men use their resources to lure young women. Cars and cellular phones signal status, so a man might say, "Come baby love. You want to come in my car? You want to talk on my cellular phone?"

Since most men lack resources, women compete fiercely for those who have them. Sandy, age 19, was among the most successful competitors when she entered the nightlife scene. She used to be a "hot girl." She dressed in the most fashionable style, name-brand clothes mailed to her from sisters in New York. And she had her own money. The most wealthy don of the area, a flashy dresser named Lucky, noticed her. He already had five babymothers, but Sandy was so young and hot that Lucky could not resist. He bought Sandy fine gifts and he swept her away. She fell in love and became pregnant. But the relationship carried a danger Sandy did not anticipate.

While shopping on a busy street one afternoon, someone tapped Sandy on the shoulder. When she turned, she was confronted with one of Lucky's babymothers, holding in her hand a bucket of liquid. Within seconds, Sandy's face and body were splashed with a volatile mixture of acid and gunpowder. Sandy screamed. The flesh on her face melted beneath the burning acid, her face permanently disfigured by her jealous rival.

Sandy spent a year in the hospital getting skin grafts, and the next two years recovering. Today she's stoic about the events: "Lucky's baby-mother had a grudge feeling. I was the hottest girl around here. I had money, I was studying, I had body suits, shorts, Fila boots, Guess shoes . . . pure name-brand. And I was pregnant—maybe that's why she did it. If a woman hears a man checking another girl, she comes to burn you up with acid. Acid you, to spoil your beauty."

Kingston, Jamaica, is not alone in the destruction caused by jealous rivalry. In Samoa, a culture that Margaret Mead once claimed was free of jealousy, wives sometimes seek out women who had sex with their husbands and bite them on the nose to reduce their attractiveness. World-wide, the co-evolutionary spiral continues. Women and men compete to embody what the other sex desires. The jealousy of each sex, in turn, is keyed to those desires. Although the acid splashing in Kingston and the nose biting in Samoa are extreme, the jealous passions they reflect burn brightly within all of us.

CHAPTER 4

The Othello Syndrome

O! beware, my lord, of jealousy.
It is the green-ey'd monster which doth mock
The meat it feeds on. That cuckold lives in bliss
Who, certain of his fate, loves not his wronger;
But O! what damned minutes tells he o'er
Who dotes, yet doubts; suspects, yet strongly loves!

                    —*Shakespeare,* Othello

LARRY AND HIS WIFE, SUSAN, had been happily married for three years. He always wore striped ties to work. For some inexplicable reason, she fell into the routine of noticing the direction of the stripe before he left for work. One day, when Larry returned from work, she realized that his tie had been retied at some point during the day.

A man named Paul purchased a trendy new overcoat with a hood. His wife had a sudden vision, which she described as an "immediate instinct," that "he got it bad for a very young girl."

Mark and his wife enjoyed reading astrology charts together. One day, she saw him read a new sign, at which point he smiled, but said nothing. She suspected that he had taken on a lover.

Victor suddenly became a Beethoven fanatic, and his wife immediately suspected that he was having an affair with a music lover.

One Christmas Eve, a man looked across the street and thought that he observed the neighbor's window lights flashing in synchrony with the lights of the Christmas tree in his own house. He concluded with utter certainty that his wife was having an affair with the neighbor. When brought to counseling by his wife, the man was declared to be "delusional" and to suffer from pathological jealousy.

As different as these cases are from each other, they all share three things. First, in each case, the people who suspected their spouse of infidelity had been referred to a psychiatrist for help. Second, in each case, the patient had been diagnosed as being pathologically jealous, with labels attached such as the Othello syndrome or conjugal paranoia. Third, in each case, the jealous person turned out to be correct! The wife of the man who noticed the Christmas tree lights, for example, turned out to be having a torrid affair with the neighbor. In each case, the persons plagued by the Othello syndrome had picked up on clues, many of which they could not even articulate, processed those clues in some way, and arrived at a correct conclusion. How can we understand the paradox of individuals being diagnosed as pathologically gripped by the Othello syndrome, yet being perfectly accurate in their inferences about their partner's infidelity? This chapter explores the Othello syndrome and examines whether it represents a true psychological disturbance or ancient wisdom we all possess.

Not all people diagnosed with delusional jealousy accurately appraise reality. Clearly some people are truly delusional, like the 35-year-old wife who was diagnosed as having pathological jealousy. Her case was sufficiently interesting to make it into a clinical textbook: "after 13 years of marriage her relationship with her husband had cooled and the couple slept in separate rooms. Following the discovery of a letter that in a circumstantial way suggested that her husband might be having an affair, she became convinced that another woman was entering the house and having sex with her husband while she was asleep. In order to check on him she insisted on tying a piece of cotton around his penis before going to bed. Her bizarre behavior persisted and was tolerated by her husband for nearly a year. He only sought medical help [for her] when her delusional beliefs extended and she claimed that her husband could not only put thoughts into her head but also exercise remote control over the movements of her body by using electromagnetic waves."

Reality or illusion? To understand this puzzle, we must return to the problem of signal detection and probe the psychology of managing errors of inference.

Error Management Theory

Humans live in an uncertain world. We rely on our senses to pick up information from that world, and then use our information processing capacities to make inferences about the true state of the world. Real threats to our survival and relationships are not always readily apparent, given the ambiguity and uncertainty of the information.

Consider a relatively simple problem of walking through the woods and fleetingly sensing a slithering object scurry underneath some leaves in the path directly in front of you. There are two possible states of reality: either there is a dangerous snake in your path or there is not a dangerous snake in your path. Given the incomplete and uncertain information that you have perceived, there are also two inferences you could make. There is indeed a dangerous snake, and you act to avoid it. Or you could conclude that there is no snake and continue walking down the path. Two states of possible reality, two possible inferences.

There are also two different ways you could be wrong. You could believe that there is a snake when in fact no snake exists. Or you could believe that no snake exists when in fact a venomous rattler is lurking right in your path. The costs of these two types of errors, however, are vastly different. In the first case, your belief causes you to incur the trivial metabolic cost of taking an unnecessary evasive action. By giving a wide berth to the area that you believe harbors a snake, you have merely gone out of your way a little, incurring a minor delay in your walk. In the second case, however, failing to detect a snake that is in fact lurking in your path can cost you your life. The two ways of being wrong carry substantially different costs.

Now imagine that this scenario not only repeats itself thousands and thousands of times in your lifetime, but billions and billions of times over human evolutionary history. Those who made the first kind of mistake tended to survive, whereas those who made the second kind of mistake tended to die. As a result, modern humans have descended from a line of ancestors whose inferences about the uncertain world erred in the direction of believing that snakes existed more than they do. These can be called "adaptive errors."

Martie Haselton of the University of Texas at Austin, Todd DeKay of Franklin and Marshall College, and I have proposed a new theory of error management (EMT) to explain errors of this sort. According to EMT, evolution by selection will favor the inference that leads to the less costly error in order to avoid the more costly error.

Consider uncertainty about whether your romantic partner is having an affair or is likely to have an affair. Affairs, of course, are almost always veiled and clandestine. Your partner's intentions are also hidden from your inquiring eyes. Who can tell what really lurks in another's mind? In many ways, the shroud of uncertainty about a partner's infidelity is even larger than the uncertainty about whether danger lurks beneath some rustling leaves. When signals coming from the world are degraded, muffled, or impoverished, accurate inferences about reality become horrendously difficult.

To explore just how uncertain people really are about a partner's infidelity, Luci Paul and her colleagues at Temple University surveyed a large sample of young men and women who were involved in long-term romantic relationships. They asked each person privately whether they were certain or uncertain that their partner had always been faithful to them. Of the women polled, 45 percent reported that they were certain their partner had been totally faithful; 41 percent reported that they were certain their partner had been unfaithful; and 14 percent reported that they were uncertain about their partner's fidelity. Now consider the men's responses: 36 percent reported that they were certain their partner had been faithful; 28 percent reported that they were certain their partner had been unfaithful; and a sizable 36 percent reported uncertainty about whether or not their partner had remained faithful.

We don't know precisely why more men than women report uncertainty. Perhaps women are better than men at detecting a partner's infidelity. Perhaps men are less skilled at concealing their own infidelities, leading to easier detection by women. Perhaps women intentionally keep their partners in a greater state of uncertainty. Still another possibility is that women are too confident when they shouldn't be. All these explanations may account for a portion of the sex difference. Regardless of the origin of this sex difference, the key point is this: a substantial fraction of both sexes report living in a state of uncertainty about their partner's fidelity.

Now consider the two possible types of errors. You can infer an infidelity by your partner when none has occurred. Or you can err in believing that a partner is eternally devoted to you, when in fact your partner passionately embraces someone else whenever your back is turned. Which error is more costly? The answer seems clear in light of human evolution. A man who mistakenly accused his wife of infidelity might trigger a fight with her, which can be costly, but it might also cause her to increase her displays of loyalty. A flare-up of jealousy can deter a partner who might otherwise stray. The costs of making this type of error are relatively low and the benefits are potentially great.

What about failing to detect an infidelity that has occurred or might occur? A man who erred by failing to detect a real infidelity may jeopardize his entire reproductive career. He would incur the many costs of infidelity, possibly directing his parenting toward another man's children and losing all of his wife's resources. If these events occurred repeatedly over evolutionary time, according to Error Management Theory, natural selection would create adaptations designed to err in one direction. The adaptive solution would be to set a low threshold for inferring a partner's infidelity, like a hair trigger on an alarm. In this way, one avoids costs of failing to detect actual infidelities, even if it means sometimes falsely accusing a partner of betrayal.

The same logic applies to women. An ancestral woman who erred in thinking that her husband violated their marriage vows when he did not would have incurred minor costs. Her neighbor who erred in failing to detect the fact that her best friend was fornicating with her husband on the side would have risked the diversion of her husband's resources and commitments to her "friend." The conclusion is clear. According to EMT, selection will favor women who err on the cautious side, setting a low threshold for inferring a husband's infidelity, even at the risk of being wrong some of the time.

Error Management Theory provides a powerful explanation for some important aspects of the Othello syndrome. It explains why men and women sometimes have "delusions" that a partner is unfaithful when he or she has remained loyal. It accounts for why men and women are highly sensitive to signals of betrayal. It explains why men and women train their eyes laserlike on rivals who flirt with their partners at parties. But EMT, by itself, does not explain the particular circumstances in relationships that might cause a sudden increase in sensitivity to a partner's possible betrayal. To explain these psychological shifts, we must turn to the conditions that actually predict when a partner might stray, starting with sexual problems in the relationship.

Erectile Dysfunction and Male Menopause

In the animal world, monogamy—mating with a single partner—is statistically rare. It occurs in only 3 percent of the roughly 4,000 species of mammals. Biologists long believed that birds differed, and they assumed that most avian species practice monogamy. DNA fingerprinting technology, however, has revealed that many bird species previously believed to be monogamous in fact engage in considerable infidelity. In some species of birds, as many as 40 percent of the chicks turn out to have been sired not by the male at the nest but by a neighbor a few territories away with whom the female has copulated clandestinely.

Among the avian species, however, some are more monogamous than others. Ring doves tend to be one of the most loyal, with quite low cuckoldry rates. Even so, ring doves experience a "divorce rate" of roughly 25 percent per season. Why? The major cause of breaking a bonded dove pair is infertility, the failure to produce offspring. Pairs that produce chicks in one breeding season remain coupled for the next one; those that fail to reproduce in one season say good-bye to their partner and seek out a replacement mate. Difficulty in producing offspring has many causes among both birds and humans, including occasional sterility of one member or genetic incompatibility of the couple. But one cause among humans is failure in sexual relations, an event that can shatter an otherwise harmonious relationship.

When the drug Viagra was introduced, it quickly became the best-selling prescription drug on the market. Millions of men flooded doctors' offices demanding it. This outpouring pointed to a problem that plagues millions of men—the problem of impotence, or erectile dysfunction as it is now called in the clinical literature. Although large-scale studies are scarce, available evidence suggests that impotence is not a rare problem. In one study of British men, for example, 120 out of 284 men, or 42 percent, reported that they sometimes, often, or always suffered from impotence.

The causes of impotence, of course, are many, ranging from organic problems such as diabetes and the ravages of age to psychological sources such as insecurity or performance anxiety. The evolutionary anthropologist Pierre Van den Berghe of the University of Washington provides a poignant illustration of the prevalence of men's anxiety about impotence in the context of intrasexual competition:

"A boy, a man, on a date, is in competition against an unknown number of invisible competitors, and in an unpredictable number of different arenas. He can be deflated and cut down when he makes the date ("I really don't anticipate a free evening for several weeks . . ."); when he comes to fetch her ("I thought you had a convertible . . ."); at the restaurant ("Oh dear, my dress is too formal for this place; if you had told me . . ."); during dinner ("You *really* don't know how to eat an artichoke?"); in conversation ("Everybody today reads Kierkegaard, of course . . .); when paying ("My father always tips at least 15 percent . . ."); after dinner ("Is there nothing more exciting you can suggest? I hate those stuffy little movie houses . . ."); on the way home ("You surely don't expect me to get that familiar on a first date?"); etc. Whatever he does, and which way he does it, he risks the possibility that his penis may be just a little smaller, just a little less adept, than someone else's."

There is no reason to believe that impotence is a new problem or merely one that plagues only modern societies. Although rarely studied in a systematic fashion, many anthropologists who have lived with traditional peoples from around the globe report cases of impotence. In a survey of the so-called Standard Sample, a data bank containing information about a wide variety of cultures, fear of impotence is explicitly reported in 80 percent of the 40 cultures for which the relevant information is available. The Mehinaku, an Amazonian tribe of Indians in central Brazil, provides a perfect illustration. Among the Mehinaku, a man's sexual failures become matters of common knowledge, since gossip travels quickly throughout this closed community. Stories of impotence are reflected in Mehinaku folklore, as illustrated by the following tale, called "The Armadillo and the Footprint":

> Armadillo left his house to wander about through the woods, leaving his penis in a basket suspended from the rafters. As he walked along the path, he saw a beautiful woman: "Hey! Come here, woman. Let's have sex."
>
> "Are you good to have sex with, Armadillo?" she asked.
>
> "I make it really delicious," he replied. Armadillo sat down on the ground in preparation for sex, looked down between his legs, and discovered that his penis wasn't there. "Oh, I forgot my penis," he said. "I'll get it."
>
> Returning to the house, Armadillo was greeted by his wife: "What's up?" she inquired.
>
> "Oh, nothing. I was just getting my bow to shoot a bird."
>
> Retrieving his penis, Armadillo left the house and returned to look for his girlfriend. "Hey, here I am!" he called. "I brought my penis with me this time. Wow, now I have an erection! Won't we have sex, woman?"
>
> Armadillo looked all over for the woman, but she had left. All he could find was her footprint, and he had sex with that. His penis "ate" the earth."

We are amused at the image of the Armadillo leaving his penis behind, a clear reference to impotence. But impotence is no laughing matter to the Mehinaku men. Impotent Mehinaku men sometimes lose their mates, who go off in search of more potent partners. One indication of the seriousness of impotence among the Mehinaku is the number of names they have for the problem. These include *maiyala euti*, which means "the penis is tired"; *iaipiripyai euti*, which means "the penis is ashamed"; and *akama euti*, which means "the penis dies."

Another indication of its significance is the extraordinary effort the men go to in order to find cures for it. These are described with the term *japujate euti*, which describes procedures designed to "make the penis angry." Among the seven cures for impotence are rubbing an entire needle fish against the penis; rubbing the head and neck of a turtle against the penis; rubbing bamboo on the penis while chanting "*Yanapi* [penis], *yanapi*, go into the vagina, *yanapi*"; rubbing sap from a latex-producing plant onto the penis; scarring the penis with the teeth from a dogfish; and *ejekeki*, which means "breath magic," consisting of an individual who blows onto the penis while chanting magical incantations.

Historically, a man's ability to reproduce was directly linked with his ability to inseminate a fertile woman regularly, which of course required recurrent erections. Ancestral men who consistently experienced impotence with one woman may have been motivated to leave her for another woman with whom he was more virile. A woman whose mate consistently failed to become erect may have been motivated to have affairs on the side or to leave him entirely, or else risk failure at reproduction herself. If impotence by a man motivated his partner to stray then we expect men to become jealous after a bout of impotence. This is precisely what we find in clinical cases of the Othello syndrome.

In one study of 36 clinical cases of the Othello syndrome, sexual problems were reported in 19. One was due to the loss of sexual desire entirely, six were due to erectile dysfunction, and 12 were due to premature ejaculation, a condition that is closely linked with impotence. One man reported: "Because of my impotence, my wife must be losing interest in me . . . She must therefore be transferring her affection to other men."

Another case involved a 68-year-old man whose long-term marriage was harmonious until he had a stroke, causing him to become impotent. He began "putting together" the pieces of evidence from a variety of sources that "proved" his wife was unfaithful. He noticed an open window, and concluded that his wife had intentionally opened it to let her lover creep into the house while he was asleep. He noticed tracks in the snow under the window. He heard voices in the kitchen, but when he checked, the voices vanished, and he concluded that her lover had fled just before he arrived. He accused his wife of infidelity and tried to restrict her activities, insisting that she not go out of the house. He became sexually aggressive with her, despite his impotence, making sexual advances so persistently throughout the night that she was forced to move into a separate bedroom. He noticed his neighbor performing routine chores, such as mowing the lawn, that he could no longer perform himself. He concluded that his wife was sleeping with the neighbor, despite the fact that the neighbor was 25 years younger than he and his wife and was a newlywed. The wife finally convinced him to see a psychiatrist when he tried to strike her with his cane and threatened to assault her, all because of his intense jealousy over her suspected infidelities.

As far as the psychiatrist could determine, the wife had remained sexually faithful throughout their marriage. But the husband's impotence triggered in him sexual jealousy, set off by what would have been a reliable signal of partner defection in ancestral environments.

As Jed Diamond, author of the book *Male Menopause,* noted: "A lot of midlife breakups are due to the projection of the men's changes onto their wives. They blame the wives for what's happening to them . . . One man, a taxi-cab driver, told me, 'I'm losing my sexual desire, my erections, and my mind. I'm afraid my wife will lose interest in me.'"

It is unlikely that one episode of impotence will impel a woman to leave her husband. But multiple episodes raise the odds. Men in our ancestral past who erred by assuming that their impotence might lead to a wife's infidelity would get jealous, prompting action designed to prevent her defection. A man who erred in the other direction, by assuming that his wife would remain faithful when she was leaning toward leaving, would have suffered more costs in the currency of reproductive success. Modern men are descendants of those who erred in the jealous direction, even when this error produced some marital friction.

Alcohol Intoxication

The sexologist Krafft-Ebing was the first to report in 1905 on the link between alcohol and jealousy. He reported that 80 percent of the male alcoholics in his study were consumed by delusions of jealousy. Krafft-Ebing argued that jealousy arose in the later phase of alcoholism and was marked by a highly organized pattern of suspicions of infidelity, believed to be delusional in nature. Once the jealousy delusion had developed,

Krafft-Ebing observed that it became "extremely fixed" and highly resistant to change.

More recent studies reveal a more modest role of alcohol in triggering jealousy. A study in 1968 revealed that 18 percent of a sample of 55 alcoholics displayed pathological jealousy. Paul Mullen found in 1985 that only 11 percent of his sample of 138 alcoholics exhibited the Othello syndrome. A 1991 study in Germany of 93 cases of "delusional jealousy" found that 12 percent were alcoholics.

By far the most systematic study, however, was an interview study in 1985 of 100 alcoholics, in which 35 percent of the men in the sample were diagnosed as extremely jealous. In 8 percent of the men, however, the man's jealousy was regarded as "justified" when it was revealed that the spouse was indeed having an affair. When this figure is subtracted from the 35 percent judged to be extremely jealous, the researchers concluded that 27 percent of the male alcoholics were "morbidly jealous." We must regard this figure with some skepticism, however, because an unknown percentage of these men might have been picking up on authentic cues to an infidelity that had been more or less successfully concealed by their wives.

A number of possible explanations exist for the modest link between alcohol consumption and jealousy. First, alcohol may lower a man's inhibitions, causing him to vent suspicions that he already has. Second, men who are concerned about their troubled marriages may be more prone to drink heavily, thus creating a link between alcohol and jealousy. Third, alcohol may directly affect jealousy, creating suspicions that were not previously present by distorting perceptions, producing errors in logic, or twisting the interpretation of facts.

Although all of these explanations may have some partial truth, there may be another explanation: the link between alcohol and impotence. To paraphrase Shakespeare, alcohol may enflame desire, but it weakens the flesh. Alcohol is clearly linked with potency problems. Since we know that impotence triggers jealousy, anything that produces impotence should be linked with elevated jealousy. And since impotence may incline a partner to leave, the fear of a partner's defection may fuel a man's jealous rage.

The wives of alcoholic men may, over time, come to find sex unpleasant. Women may develop an "aversion to the rough, brutal husband, often drunk at the time of intercourse, . . . whose pathologically tardy ejaculation causes pain through persistent and frequent attempts . . . The brutal, irritable, mentally enfeebled husband, who otherwise lives in a state of quarrel with his wife seeks and finds the cause of his sexual dissatisfaction in the infidelity of the wife." A vicious cycle is created. The husband's alcohol abuse leads to unpleasant sex, causing the wife to decline his sexual advances, which then triggers jealousy and suspicions of infidelity.

Women's Sexual Dissatisfaction

Another circumstance that might evoke a man's jealousy is his inability to sexually satisfy his partner. Over evolutionary time, women mated to men they found sexually wanting sometimes sought satisfaction in another man's arms, either temporarily through an affair or permanently through divorce and remarriage. This ancestral condition may have sculpted a psychological sensitivity in men to their ability to sexually satisfy their wives. A man's concern over his wife's sexual orgasm is sometimes attributed to "masculine insecurity." But it may instead reflect an accurate perception that her lack of satisfaction may lead her to leave. The phenomenon of women "faking orgasm" may symbolically assure the husband of sexual fidelity. The psychiatric record is filled with cases depicting men's insecurity about their ability to satisfy their wives.

In one case, an aging man started to become concerned about the quantity of his semen, which apparently had been considerable in his youth. He became increasingly jealous over time. He insisted on having sex with his wife every night, tried to prevent her from going out, and even tried to stop her from attending her weekly women's group. He insisted on reading every letter and card she received, and in one case, took a letter to a handwriting expert to analyze hidden messages. Daily he checked his wife's underpants for "evidence" of infidelity. He restricted his wife's activities. He increasingly complained that his erections were smaller than they had been and that sex with his wife was too infrequent. He asserted that his wife's vagina had changed, and believed that he could detect the "mark" of another man's penis in her vagina! He admitted all of this to the psychiatrist, but denied vehemently that he was jealous.

Similar examples abound in the psychiatric records. In one case, a man became jealous when he concluded that his penis was too short to satisfy his wife, since he assumed that she was used to a larger size from her previous partners. Another man believed that his wife had committed adultery with at least three different men. He believed that he was incapable of satisfying her sexually because one of these men, he thought, had such a large penis that it had widened his wife's vagina. His jealousy got so bad that he concluded that he must not be the father of any of his children. The jealousy tore apart the marriage. His psychiatrist was unable to contain the man's jealousy, and eventually the couple divorced.

Another case involved a 45-year-old man who was described by his wife as hardworking, sensitive, and reserved. The couple had five children, but despite this, the husband began to accuse his wife of being a "whore." He believed that she betrayed him with a bus driver, who could perform "sexual tricks" for his wife that he insisted he lacked the knowledge to do. He discovered these "tricks" by reading a book on sex. He noticed the bus driver giving his wife "fixed looks," and noticed his wife swaying her buttocks when she boarded the bus. He began to wonder whether his children were his own. He thought that only one looked like him. He wanted his wife to take blood tests, but she refused and would not allow any paternity testing, which fueled his jealousy further. She gave the impression of being trustworthy and honest, and denied having intercourse with other men. But she declared that she had not experienced orgasm in the marriage. She also stated that her husband did not understand her, which the husband interpreted as meaning that "he doesn't know how to satisfy me sexually." Treatment was unsuccessful, and the man subsequently abandoned his wife and children.

A man's inability to satisfy his partner sexually, real or imagined, appears to be a powerful trigger of sexual jealousy. The therapist of one couple entering treatment for the husband's pathological jealousy noted that the wife talked about her former lovers "all of the time and speaks disdainfully about the sexual performance of her husband."

Sexual dissatisfaction is linked with marital unhappiness, which is a good predictor of divorce. In my study of 107 married couples, we found that some women and men expressed a variety of complaints about their partner's sexual behavior. Some complained that their partner refused to have sex with them, declared a lack of interest in having sexual relations, and rebuffed their sexual advances. All these sexual complaints were linked with marital unhappiness.

Since an inability to satisfy a partner sexually causes marital unhappiness, and marital unhappiness causes divorce, it is reasonable to conclude that sexual dissatisfaction raises the likelihood of breaking up. Sexual jealousy, triggered by a perceived inability to please a partner sexually, may be a coping device designed to fend off this impending threat—an evolved product of error management, helping to prevent a permanent defection. By getting jealous when a partner is perceived to be sexually dissatisfied, a man effectively steps up his mate guarding tactics in an attempt to ward off the threat of losing her.

Women's Decline in Sexual Desire

When a woman's desire for sex with her regular partner declines, it may signal marital problems. Women sexually bored by their husbands may seek stimulation from other men. A recurrent thought among men diagnosed with "conjugal paranoia" is: "If she is not achieving sexual satisfaction with me, she must be achieving it with someone else." A woman also may be bored with the relationship itself, an ominous indicator of impending divorce. Whether the boredom is merely sexual or extends to the entire relationship, a drop in sexual interest portends trouble in a previously harmonious relationship. As Mae West once said, "It's not the men in my life that count—it's the life in my men."

Case reports of pathological jealousy contain many examples of jealous symptoms triggered by a wife's decrease in desire. In one case, a married man 43 years old was admitted to a psychiatric hospital. His complaint was that he was "tensed up" because he believed his wife to be unfaithful. He provided no evidence to support his suspicions, but reported that the idea of his wife's infidelity had been planted by a co-worker, who casually asked him one day whether he had ever suspected his partner of fooling around on him. His suspicions escalated when his wife failed to provide a satisfactory explanation for an attractive pair of boots she was wearing. His jealousy became so extreme that once he attempted to strangle his wife, which failed when neighbors intervened. Another time, dressed only in underwear, he ran out into the street in a vain attempt to catch his wife with her suspected lover. Upon further probing, the psychiatrist discovered that the husband's jealous symptoms started shortly after his wife had a hysterectomy operation, which resulted in a sharp decrease in her sexual desire. The decline in her desire whispered into the man's Stone Age brain that she might leave the relationship, triggering a massive jealousy reaction.

Differences in Desirability

Measures of desirability on the mating market are sometimes crudely translated into numbers, as when actress Bo Derek was referred to as a "10" in the movie *10*. An "8" might turn down a "6," but in turn might be rebuffed by a "10." Individuals who differ in desirability, however, do sometimes become coupled. And when they do, problems can ensue. Moreover, nothing remains static over time. An initially equitable relationship may turn into one marked by gaping differences in desirability.

Several factors cause gaps in mate value to widen over time. Consider an initially well-matched couple in their mid-20s. The woman is intelligent, young, and attractive; the man intelligent, young, and at the entry stage of a successful career. Over time, the man's career soars. Although they both age chronologically at the same rate, aging sometimes takes a greater toll on the woman's attractiveness in a man's eyes. Simultaneously, the man's elevated status opens up sexual opportunities previously absent. The adulation he experiences by attractive young women starts to contrast sharply with that of his aging wife. The reverse can happen as well. When a woman's career takes off, she may grow disgruntled with a less successful husband, since she'll be able to command a higher-status man on the mating market. As Donald Symons notes, "a woman is most likely to experience desire for extramarital sex when she perceives another man as somehow superior to her husband . . . her sexual desire may function primarily as part of the process by which women trade up in the husband market."

Although menopause has not been examined systematically as a trigger of jealousy in women, the clinical literature contains a number of cases that point to its importance. In one case, a woman was referred to a psychiatrist for her "delusions" that her husband had been carrying on numerous affairs: "Several years before her delusions, she had been mortified to hear her husband (who was her own age) express the opinion that men do well to marry women much younger than themselves. With the approach of the menopause, she became obsessed with the notion that her husband was bent on the seduction of every young woman with whom she came into contact."

Another woman, age 44, suddenly began to accuse her husband of infidelity after many happy years of marriage. She started chain-smoking cigarettes and became temperamental and easily irritated. Intercourse with her husband was too infrequent, she complained, and she believed this to be caused by his affairs with other women. She became convinced that her husband "made signs" to other women on the street, using a handkerchief waved from their bedroom window.

The husband admitted to the psychiatrist that sexual intercourse with his wife had become less frequent, sometimes with many weeks in between sexual episodes. The wife found this decrease strange and suspicious. Prior to approaching menopause, the wife had never been jealous at all! As sex grew less frequent, however, she developed "feelings of inferiority," believing that she had grown old and ugly. She became convinced that her husband would run off with a "pretty young girl." The woman's jealous feelings reached a crescendo when the couple rented a room in their house to a young woman. The wife had to be hospitalized. During her stay at the psychiatric clinic, she improved substantially, but could never expunge her jealous thoughts, especially about the young renter.

In these cases, we cannot be sure whether the menopausal woman's suspicions of infidelity were delusional or accurate. As Claire Warga, author of *Menopause and the Mind*, notes, menopause is sometimes accompanied by changes in attention, memory, and a "fluctuating agility in prioritizing" thoughts. Nonetheless, it is reasonable to suggest that women respond to modern manifestations of ancestral cues that predicted a husband's wandering eye.

A woman's loss of physical attractiveness associated with aging is a related precipitator of extreme jealousy. Consider the following case of a woman diagnosed as having "excessive and irrational jealousy" that "defied . . . therapeutic efforts" to resolve it. Betty had reached the age of 50 when the jealous episodes began. She had been married for 30 years to her husband, George. They lived in harmony for many years, sharing a home with her husband's sister, and the three shared nearly all of their leisure time together. As she approached 50, however, she developed stomach problems, and became obsessed with her health and aging. Over time, she "began to resent her graying hair, her failing eyesight, her wrinkles, her age spots." Seemingly "out of the blue" she developed a "towering jealousy" of her sister-in-law, and started to accuse George of having an affair with his sister. She started to eavesdrop on their phone conversations, snooped through letters, rifled through the husband's pockets, studied credit card receipts, suspiciously viewed any time they spent together, and vigilantly monitored all of their activities.

Oscar Wilde asserted: "Curious thing, plain women are always jealous of their husbands, beautiful women never are!" He was probably wrong. It is not the level of physical attractiveness per se, but rather a divergence between spouses in desirability that triggers jealousy. A woman who is a "6" married to a man who is a "6" should be no more jealous than an "8" married to an "8." In fact, the theory predicts a counterintuitive result that goes against Oscar Wilde's proclamation; a woman who is an "8" married to a man who is a "10" will become more jealous than her less attractive counterpart who is a "6" but who is equitably married to a man who is a "6."

In the metric of perceived attractiveness, aging often takes a greater toll on women than on men. This is especially true when the husband experiences professional success, which elevates his attractiveness. As therapist Mary Seeman noted in a report on five women diagnosed with pathological jealousy: "Because of the general respect which the husbands elicited, they were in reality constantly exposed to many young, available females. The wives' realistic opportunities for attracting men other than their husbands were far fewer."

In these cases, when questioned about the sexual fantasies they had as adolescents, all five women reported what the author describes as "a variant of the raped virgin fantasy as their most common masturbation accompaniment. Whereas they themselves had played "the heroine" in the fantasy during adolescence, they were now putting the suspected rival into that role. She [the rival] was seen as the young, resisting virgin, with the husband who cajoles her into submission."

Although each of the five women in this study was diagnosed as "pathologically jealous," each of the husbands had reported to the therapist that he felt "sexual guilt," even if he had not been unfaithful. The husbands reported in private that they frequently had sexual fantasies about precisely the acts their wives accused them of committing. The wives often guessed correctly about the women to whom their husbands were attracted. Women, like men, seem sensitive to signals of real threats of defection, even in cases that may not have culminated in sexual intercourse, a hypersensitivity explained by Error Management Theory. Women's ancestral wisdom has decreed that it is more costly to fail to perceive an impending infidelity than to suspect infidelities that won't happen. These cases also call into question the label Othello syndrome, which some psychiatrists attach to jealous individuals. Many women diagnosed with "delusional jealousy" are in fact picking up on authentic cues, if only in their husband's real attraction to other women. As someone once said in a different context, "you're not paranoid if they're really after you."

Although the idea of desirability differences widening to the disadvantage of women is part of folk wisdom, the reverse can also occur. Consider a professional couple, both ambitious and devoted to their careers. The woman's career takes off, and her income starts to exceed her husband's. As she gets promotions, bonuses, and status from work, her husband's career starts to languish. He becomes depressed; she becomes dissatisfied. Over time, his attractiveness to other women languishes along with his career failures. Simultaneously, she develops self-confidence and verve, and starts to radiate a new-found attractiveness. Men begin to notice her, and although some become intimidated by her success, high-status confident men are turned on and find her radiant.

When she comes home after a day of flourishing successes, she encounters a dour husband who has started to drink to drown his anguish. A chasm in desirability has opened that shows no signs of closing and she begins to notice other men.

Another change in desirability favoring women centers on health. Women live longer than men. At an earlier age men contract a wide variety of illness, from cancer to heart disease. A married couple initially well matched can suddenly experience a gap when the man falls ills since health is an important component of mate value. When the illness causes the man to be house-bound, with his wife free to venture into the world, jealousy and fears of defection can follow.

Although systematic large-scale studies of illness and jealousy have not yet been conducted, one study examined seven cases of "delusional jealousy" linked with failing health. In one case, a 77-year-old man had developed a severe case of osteoarthritis, which left him house-bound. His wife was eight years his junior, in robust good health, and they had been married for 51 years. Although their marriage had been generally harmonious, it took a severe turn when he developed his disease. He began to look much older and considerably more frail than his wife, creating a difference in desirability where none previously existed. He started questioning her intensely whenever she left the house. He accused her of having an affair with a taxi driver, and these accusations were increasingly accompanied by threats of violence. The psychiatrist determined that the man was "cognitively intact" in every way, other than his delusions about his wife's infidelity.

Another case involves a man, age 73, whose delusions about his wife's infidelity started when he developed Parkinson's disease, which left him cooped up at home. His delusions were so extreme they resulted in visual hallucinations in which he literally imagined that he was witnessing his wife having sexual intercourse with other men. He questioned her whenever she was about to leave the house, and accused her of being a prostitute. Prior to Parkinson's disease, he was a successful butcher, and was described by others as a "well-mannered, courteous, charming man." After his Parkinson's, he aged in appearance noticeably, looking a full generation older than his wife. Although his basic cognitive functions were largely intact, with only minor short-term memory problems, his hallucinations and delusions grew worse over time. An initially well-matched couple, the husband's failing health had created a contrast in desirability.

A final case illustrates the modern manifestations of this ancient jealousy trigger. The man was an 83-year-old, who had been married for 43 years to a woman who was eight years younger. Their marriage had been harmonious until he had a cardiac pacemaker inserted, which caused his activities to be restricted mostly to his house. He began to look much older than his wife, who brimmed with robust health. He began to harass his wife with accusations of infidelity and asserted that her "shopping trips" were really secret liaisons with her lover. He hallucinated seeing her in bed with other men and believed that she denied her infidelities in order to make him appear to be mentally incompetent. Other than the "pathological jealousy" and its associated symptoms, however, the psychiatrist could find no mental deterioration other than minor problems with short-term memory.

The fact that men's health fails, on average, substantially sooner than women's creates desirability differences where none previously existed. In ancestral times, a man's aging and ill health would in fact lower his value to his wife, since health is a key component of mate value, ranking fifth in my cross-cultures studies. As his death begins to loom, it would make adaptive sense for a women to begin seeking an alternative mate, or at least begin to lay the groundwork for it.

Marriage vows frequently dictate remaining with a partner "in sickness and in health" and "for richer or for poorer." Sickness and poverty are singled out for special precaution in marriage vows because they are key conditions that cause a person's desirability as a mate to plummet, triggering infidelity or divorce. Jealousy has evolved to defend against such defections, even though, like all defenses, it only works some of the time.

Those who are lower in desirability are more vulnerable to getting unceremoniously dumped. The person higher in mate value comes to feel "under-benefited" in the relationship, sensing that there exist better possibilities elsewhere. People act on these feelings. In a study of 2,000 people, those who evaluated their partnerships as "balanced," in the sense of roughly equal in investments and rewards, had significantly fewer extramarital affairs than those who saw their relationship as "unbalanced." The people who believed that they were superior in some way to their partner felt that they were "unlucky in marriage," and consequently felt justified in having affairs sooner and more frequently than those who felt "lucky" in marriage.

These circumstances trigger jealousy in the less desirable partner. Simultaneously, the more attractive partner becomes less jealous, knowing that better opportunities are right around the corner. The less attractive partner, in contrast, feels lucky to hold on to the current one.

How would you respond to the following question: "Who spends more time and energy maintaining your relationship?" This is one item on the Relative Effort Scale, which measures who is more committed to the relationship. The more committed partner is generally less desirable. Studies show that the less desirable partner becomes more jealous.

In one study of 220 married couples, Gary Hansen of the University of Southern Mississippi measured perceived marital alternatives. Participants were asked to imagine that their spouse would leave them over the course of the next year. Then they were asked to estimate the likelihood that they would be able to replace their partner with someone who was as desirable. The response of *impossible* (indicating the fewest marital alternatives) was scored a 1, whereas the response of *certain* (indicating the greatest marital alternatives) was scored a 4.

Hansen then measured jealousy through responses to a series of hypothetical scenarios of potential partner defection. Here are two scenarios used, the first purely sexual and the second both sexual and emotional:

Scenario 1: "Your mate returns from a business trip to a different city and informs you that he/she met a member of the opposite sex that he/she found very physically attractive. They ended up engaging in sexual relations. Your mate informs you that their relationship was purely physical (not emotional) and that they will never be seeing each other again."

Scenario 2: "Your mate has developed an ongoing emotional and sexual relationship with a member of the opposite sex. Your mate receives a high degree of satisfaction from this relationship and plans to continue it. Both you and your mate have been happy and pleased with your own relationship. Your mate views his/her outside relationship as a supplement to, not a substitute for, the relationship between the two of you."

Participants recorded how they would feel on a scale ranging from *extremely pleased* to *extremely disturbed or bothered*. Hansen then analyzed what predicted these jealous reactions, scrutinizing personality variables such as self-esteem, trust, marital adjustment, and perceived options for replacement mates. Those who perceived fewer marital alternatives and more difficulty in replacing their partner with someone as desirable as their current partner were substantially more disturbed by imagining each of the infidelity scenarios. Partners lower in desirability, in short, are more easily threatened and more jealous.

Shocking Discoveries

Adolescence is often overlooked as a critical time in human psychological development. It's the time when hormones rage, competition for mates commences, and the first halting steps toward romantic relationships begin. So it's not surprising that events in adolescence loom disproportionately large in people's memories. Avril Thorne of the University of California at Santa Cruz asked a sample of adults to describe the most vivid memory from their past and to record how old they were when the events occurred. The overwhelming majority of vivid memories occurred between ages 10 and 20. People never seem to forget their high school athletic success when the crowd roared, their teenage back-seat fumblings, or their first love. Adolescence is the time when we crystallize images of ourselves and form impressions of the opposite sex.

Several reports suggest that shocking discoveries of a parental infidelity during adolescence can heighten jealousy in adulthood. In the most detailed study, psychiatrists John Docherty and Jean Ellis described three couples who came to therapy complaining about the husband's "pathological jealousy." In each of these cases, the husband had accidentally witnessed during adolescence his mother having sex with a man other than her husband.

In the first case, the husband was 47 and the wife 41 when they came for therapy. The couple had been married for more than two decades and had three beautiful children. Although the wife had an active and rewarding social life outside the home, she found that life with her husband had turned into a nightmare. Her husband's jealousy started shortly after they were married and intensified during her first pregnancy. For this and each of the two subsequent pregnancies, the husband became convinced that the conceived child was not his own. He started monitoring his wife's phone calls, rifled through her purse, and berated her with accusations until she knelt at his feet and pleaded with him to believe her innocence. Afterward he would apologize and beg her not to be angry with him. But just as suddenly, the jealousy would return with a vengeance at some perceived flirtation, something as seemingly trivial as a friendly smile to a neighbor. The back story to this case is that when the man was 12, he had returned home from school unexpectedly and found his mother in bed with a strange man. Although he never revealed to his father what he had witnessed, he raged inside about his mother's betrayal, especially when his parents fought violently about the mother's suspected infidelities. By the time he reached adulthood, he had concluded that women could not be trusted—a sentiment that ripped apart his marriage.

The second case involved a 36-year-old man and a 31-year-old woman, married for two years when they arrived for therapy. Although there was no hint of jealousy during their courtship, the demons emerged full-blown after the marriage. The wife learned to avoid interacting with other men in order to prevent her husband's rages. He demanded that she remain glued to his side during parties. He forbade her to socialize with men, insisted on knowing her whereabouts at all times, and interrogated her daily. Any unexpected change in her routine triggered a jealous rage and a heavy bout of drinking. This husband's secret was that in his teen years, his mother frequented a local tavern, and he once came home unexpectedly and found her naked in bed with one of the men from the tavern. He did not disclose this information to his father, but the image had haunted him since.

As in many other cases reported in this chapter, not all people labeled as "pathologically jealous" are truly delusional. Consider the case of a man who reported that his mother had had many affairs, one of which he discovered firsthand. When he returned home from running a shopping errand for his mother, he found her having sex with his father's best friend. He hadn't revealed this traumatic event to anyone until he mentioned it to his therapist. The couple had come to therapy, as the other two couples had, to deal with the husband's pathological jealousy. His jealousy began when his wife started working out, joined a weight-reduction program, began to dress more glamorously, and stared looking more attractive. Strangely, he let her go on a vacation to Florida with his best friend. When they returned, his friend informed him that they had had sex. Although the husband said nothing to his "best friend," he began to berate his wife, disconnected her telephone, took away her car, and accused her of having had many affairs. His jealousy destroyed their marriage.

Although the sample of this study is small and conclusions must be tentative, it is reasonable to propose that the early adolescent trauma of witnessing a parent's infidelity evoked a hyperactivation of sexual jealousy. Each man had developed a heightened sensitivity to suspecting infidelity, just as people with early traumas involving snakes or open places develop specific phobias.

Sometimes these shocking discoveries happen in adulthood. In one case, a man showed absolutely no indications of jealousy in his first marriage. His first wife, however, divorced him for another man, and her departure came as a total shock to him. He became morose and severely depressed for six months. Eventually he returned to normal and six years later remarried. His second wife happened to be the younger sister of his ex-wife. During this second marriage he became increasingly suspicious. His second marriage ended in tragedy. While at a party, his wife began dancing with another man. When he asked her to stop, she refused, and he stabbed her to death.

Adult sensitivities develop in women as well. One 49-year-old woman came to a psychiatrist complaining of her husband's alleged infidelities. She had left him two years earlier because he was unfaithful, but returned home "for the sake of my boy." Soon after her return, she became crazed with thoughts that her husband was having sex with a number of other women. She searched the fireplace for burned letters, followed her husband surreptitiously when he went out, and spied on him from a distance. She inspected his underpants for evidence, but failed to find any. The husband admitted to the therapist that he indeed had had an affair that originally led to his wife's departure, but he vehemently insisted on his fidelity ever since. Although the wife's jealousy was destroying their reunion, she admitted that she had not yet found a single scrap of evidence that her suspicions were valid.

If these cases are any indication, the shocking discovery of infidelity can sensitize a person to subtle signs of infidelity. It is not too great a leap to suggest that prior experience with infidelity—either by a parent or spouse—leads to a hyperactivation of this ancient coping mechanism.

Symbiotic Pathology

One final complexity must be added to conclude the discussion of the seemingly pathological aspects of jealousy—a complexity that cannot be understood without viewing jealousy as a fundamentally adaptive mechanism. Some couples develop symbiotic pathologies that are precariously poised in a delicate balance. The intensity of a man's jealousy, among other things, conveys information to the woman about the strength of his commitment and the depth of his love (topics we explore in the final chapters). At the same time, the jealous man attempts to sequester his mate and cut off her opportunities to meet other men. An intensely guarded woman may feel loved, but nonetheless claustrophobically hemmed in by her husband's possessiveness. A woman whose husband fails to display any jealousy may feel free to do as she pleases, but may simultaneously feel unloved. This delicate balance sometimes leads to what experts call symbiotic pathology.

Agoraphobia is an anxiety disorder resulting in a fear of places where escape might be difficult or help not available. It is more prevalent in women than in men. A common manifestation is a fear of open spaces or public places. Agoraphobics often avoid being outside the home alone, panic when in a crowd or standing in line, shun bridges and open fields, and fear traveling on buses or trains. In extreme forms, agoraphobia becomes so debilitating that the afflicted person refuses to leave home at all.

One counterintuitive idea is that women's agoraphobia and men's sexual jealousy sometimes coexist in a delicate balance. When a woman fears going out, she stays at home, causing the husband's jealousy to subside. If her agoraphobia gets cured and she starts going out alone, her husband's jealousy may mushroom, responding to the realistic threat that she will have increased opportunities to meet other men. One study of 36 agoraphobic women explored this symbiosis. Seven of these women had husbands who displayed "abnormal jealousy." In each case, as the women improved with treatment, getting relief from agoraphobic symptoms, the husband's jealousy increased. Predictably, when a woman showed a relapse, returning to her former agoraphobic state, the husband's jealousy subsided.

Jane, a 38-year-old woman, first experienced agoraphobia shortly after meeting her husband. Her panic and fear of going out of the house became so debilitating that she was forced to quit her job. After treatment for agoraphobia, she became almost totally cured and felt the freedom of venturing outside of her home. Four months after her relief from symptoms, Jane came to the therapist distraught and declared that her husband had attempted to kill himself. His jealousy had become a monster. He interrogated her like a prisoner of war and accused her of infidelity whenever she went out alone. Arguments and accusations continued until she became agoraphobic again. She reverted from her "cured" state— being able to travel alone for the first time in years—to her early self-sequestration. Only after her agoraphobia returned and she again became terrified of leaving her house did the husband's accusations subside.

The husband denied being abnormally jealous. Instead, he attributed his "distress" to the fact that his wife no longer needed him after her recovery. She was no longer dependent on him, making him feel useless, inferior, and inadequate. When the therapist recontacted the couple a year later for follow-up, the marriage remained unchanged and Jane continued to suffer from agoraphobia. Their symbiotic pathology remained a cycle they could not break.

Another case of symbiotic pathology involved a woman who interpreted her husband's jealousy as a sign of his love, manliness, and sexual attraction to her. The trouble started when he entered therapy to reduce his feelings of jealousy. He told the therapist that when he became jealous, he became hypersexual with his wife to ensure that she remained sexually satisfied. Only by keeping her sexually sated, he felt, could he prevent her from seeking gratification elsewhere. The wife denied any infidelity, despite her husband's suspicions. The therapist administered medication, which lessened the man's jealousy. As his jealousy receded, however, his wife developed florid agitation, loose associations, cognitive incoherence, and started to complain that her husband was "not a proper man" and was "just like a little boy." As he got better, she got worse declaring that her husband did not find her sexually interesting any more.

At this point in the therapy, the wife started to accuse him of having an affair with his brother's wife. She swore that she could detect erotic messages pass between them through eye contact and body signals. One morning, she felt "moisture on his penis," and accused him of a clandestine encounter with his lover in the middle of the night while she slept. Eventually, she convinced him to stop taking his medication. Shortly thereafter, his jealousy began to flare again and he resumed his accusations of infidelity. Apart from his jealousy, however, the therapist noticed no other symptoms or psychiatric problems. On follow-up, the marriage had returned to its original symbiotic state, with the husband extremely jealous and the wife happy.

The husband's jealousy, although it troubled him enough to seek therapy, helped the marriage by making his wife feel loved and sexually satisfied. When the jealousy subsided, she developed problems, and when it returned, her problems disappeared. Like the agoraphobic women and their jealous husbands, this couple lived in a delicate symbiotic balance that more or less worked for them.

The Pathology of Jealousy

Couples seek therapy when their marriages become conflict-ridden or intolerable. According to Shirley Glass, one of the world's leading experts on infidelity, jealousy and infidelity are among the most common core problems of couples seeking treatment. Therapists who lack an understanding of adaptive functions of jealousy run the risk of treating the defense while ignoring the problems the defense is designed to combat. As noted earlier, many men and women diagnosed as "pathologically jealous" turn out to have partners who are having affairs, have had them in the past, or are thinking about having them.

In this chapter, I have proposed that over evolutionary time it was more costly to *fail* to detect an infidelity that did occur than to err in the other direction of being overly suspicious—an application of Error Management Theory. This argument does not deny that jealousy can be pathological. Sometimes it is, as when a husband has visual hallucinations that his wife is having sex with another man right in front of him. Even in these "pathological" cases, however, we often find that jealousy is responding to real signs of potential infidelity—cues such as erectile dysfunction, inability to sexually satisfy, or a widening difference between the partners in desirability.

This analysis, of course, does not deny that jealousy can be destructive. To the contrary, there may be no passion in humans that rivals jealousy in the outpouring of violence it creates, a topic to which we now turn.

CHAPTER 5

If I Can't Have Her, Nobody Can

Has anyone counted the victims of jealousy? Daily a revolver cracks somewhere or other because of jealousy; daily a knife finds entrance into a warm body; daily some unhappy ones, racked by jealousy and life weary, sink into fathomless depths. What are all the hideous battles, narrated by history, when compared to this frightful passion jealousy?

        —*Wilhelm Stekel, 1921,* The Depths of the Soul

I N *THE BEAST IN MAN* by Emile Zola, the main character, named Rouband, questions his wife about his suspicions: "'Confess,' he repeated, 'you did sleep with him' . . . he knocked her down, grabbed her hair and by it held her to the floor.

"'Confess. You slept with him. Confess you slept with him God damn you,' he cried, 'or I'll knife you!' She could see murder plain on his face . . . Fear overcame her; she capitulated just to end it all. 'All right then, yes, it's true. Now let me go.' After that it was frightful. The admission which he had so savagely extracted was a direct body blow . . . He seized her head and banged it against the table."

This episode is pure fiction. Events like it, however, occur daily by the thousands worldwide. Here are a few real-life examples of violence triggered by sexual jealousy.

The first case is told by a woman, age 19, whose husband started beating her shortly after they got married: "Tim [her husband] is really jealous. I remember once when we were at my girlfriend's house. I had to use the bathroom. The bathroom is upstairs. Well, my girlfriend's brother's room is next to the bathroom. I stood in front of his door and talked to him for a

minute on my way back downstairs. When I got to the stairs Tim was waiting for me. He called me a whore and a tease and slugged me on the side of
my head. I fell down the stairs. I can't blame Tim, though. I guess I shouldn't
have talked to my girlfriend's brother. I mean, I know Tim's real jealous."

In a second case, "the wife, confronted with yet another round of accusations and cross-questioning about a boyfriend she had before marriage
and with whom she had a child, responded that at least her previous lover
had been man enough to get her pregnant. This touched on the husband's
fears about his potency and fertility, and triggered a furious assault."

We typically think of jealous violence as being mainly perpetrated by
men, but jealousy provokes violence in women as well, as the following
case illustrates: "A lady saw a woman in the street whom she believed
(probably correctly) was having an affair with her husband. She attempted
to walk on by, ignoring the other woman; however, as she passed her, she
noticed what she took to be a look of self-satisfaction on her face. This
provoked a sudden surge of anger, and she turned and grabbed the
woman's coat. Holding her firmly by the collar, she warned the woman to
keep away from her husband. In gripping hold of the woman's clothing,
she somehow caused a degree of constriction around the woman's throat,
who began to make choking noises, presumably in an attempt to breathe
against the constriction. The sound of the other woman's attempt to
breathe triggered in the jealous assailant an association with the heavy
breathing and cries of orgasm. For her, the gasping for breath became the
sounds of this woman's orgasm with her husband. At this point, she lost
control and in truth throttled her unfortunate rival."

What are the links between sexual jealousy and intimate violence?
Why does jealousy erupt with such unbridled fury? And does this seemingly destructive behavior have a hidden function behind it, a purpose
that accomplishes some goal for the perpetrator?

Jealousy and Battering

Evidence has been cumulating for decades suggesting that sexual jealousy
lies at the root of spousal battering and may exceed all other causes combined. In one interview study of 44 battered wives seeking refuge in a

women's hostel, 55 percent reported that jealousy was one of the main reasons their husbands assaulted them. In another study of 150 cases of women who were battered by their husbands, jealousy was listed as the key problem by the vast majority. In a third study of 31 battered women in hostels and hospitals, 52 percent listed jealousy as the main cause of their husband's violence, and a whopping 94 percent cited is as it a frequent cause. A fourth study focused on 60 battered women who sought help at a rural clinic in North Carolina. In 57 out of the 60 cases, the women reported that their husbands were extremely jealous, and that "leaving the home for any reason invariably resulted in accusations of infidelity which culminated in assault." A fifth study found that 87 out of 101 battered women rated their husbands as very or extremely jealous. Although the validity of any one study can be questioned, together they strongly point to sexual jealousy as a major cause, and likely the leading cause, of spousal violence.

Violence is not limited to marital mateships. It's also prevalent during dating. More than a dozen studies have examined date violence, and the numbers are disturbing. Across these studies, the percentage who report expressing any sort of violence, including threats of violence, toward a dating partner range from 19 percent to 64 percent for men and from 22 percent to 69 percent for women, with the averages for both hovering around 40 percent. When verbal threats are excluded and only actual acts of physical violence are included, the self-reported rates of perpetrating date violence range from 14 percent to 45 percent for men and from 10 percent to 59 percent for women. Even higher percentages are reported by people when asked whether they have ever been the victims of date violence.

When dating individuals are quizzed about what causes the violence, the results are remarkably consistent. As summarized by Sugarman and Hotaling, "In every study in which a respondent had a chance to check or list jealousy as a cause, it is the most frequently mentioned reason."

Violence against partners triggered by sexual jealousy is not limited to the United States, or to Western cultures, or even to particular political systems. The cross-cultural evidence, although less systematically collected than the North American evidence, reveals a strikingly similar pattern. The anthropologist Napoleon Chagnon of the University of California at Santa Barbara has studied the Yanomamö of Venezuela for more than 25 years. His report:

"A particularly nasty husband might hit his wife with the sharp edge of a machete or ax or shoot a barbed arrow into some nonvital area, such as the buttocks or the leg. Another brutal punishment is to hold the glowing end of a piece of firewood against the wife's body, producing painful and serious burns. Normally, however, the husband's reprimands are consistent with the perceived seriousness of the wife's shortcomings, *his more drastic measures being reserved for infidelity or suspicion of infidelity.* It is not uncommon for a man to seriously injure a sexually errant wife, and some husbands have shot and killed unfaithful wives . . . during one of my stays in the villages a man shot his wife in the stomach with a barbed arrow . . . Another man chopped his wife on the arm with a machete; some tendons were severed . . . A club fight involving a case of infidelity took place in one of the villages just before the end of my first field trip. The male paramour was killed, and the enraged husband cut off both of his wife's ears."

Halfway around the globe, the !Kung San of Botswana, often described by anthropologists as a "peaceful people," show a similar pattern of male violence motivated by male sexual jealousy:

"N/ahka, a middle-aged woman, was attacked by her husband. His assault resulted in injuries to her face, head and lips. Her husband accused her of sleeping with another man . . . N/ahka and her husband had been married for many years but had no children together. Her only child was a girl of about fourteen years whose father was a Herero [a neighboring tribe] and to whom N/ahka had not been married. The father never contributed to his daughter's support, and for many years the child had been reared by N/ahka's parents who lived in a different village. When N/ahka's parents heard about the beating, they made plans to lodge a formal complaint . . . against their son-in-law. Other people, not close relatives of N/ahka or her husband, claimed that the couple had a long history of discord, allegedly because the wife liked to sleep with Bantu men."

In cultures the world over, men find the thought of their partner having sexual intercourse with other men intolerable. Suspicion or detection of infidelity causes many men to lash out in furious anger rarely seen in other contexts.

A Range of Injuries

Paul Mullen of the University of Otago documented a range of violent behavior in a sample of 138 patients who were referred to therapy because of jealousy. Some acts of jealous violence were commonplace, such as pushing, shoving, kicking, throwing objects, and destroying property. In addition, however, six men and two women wielded a knife while issuing verbal threats, and nine waved blunt instruments such as large clubs or pokers. One man pressed a gun to his wife's head while threatening her life. A full 57 percent of the sample of jealous patients had a history of committing acts of spousal violence, again varying widely in form. Ten reported throttling their wives with intent to kill, one attempted poisoning with gas, 11 beat the spouse with blunt instruments, fracturing bones in four cases. Most perpetrators seemed intent on delivering bodily damage.

The psychologists John Gottman and Neil Jacobson of the University of Washington designed a study to explore the prevalence of battering. They advertised for couples in local newspapers. Out of the 140 couples studied, 63 fell into the group labeled as "battered." Couples were classified as such only if the wife reported *six or more* episodes within the past year of pushing or shoving (low-level violence), *at least two* episodes of high-level violence such as kicking or punching, or *at least one* instance of violence deemed potentially lethal, such as being severely beaten, threatened with a weapon such a gun or knife, or sustaining injuries from a gun or knife. The only criterion for participation in the study was that the couples had to be experiencing "conflict" within their marriage. No mention of battering or abuse was contained in the ads.

I recall one case of an unusual injury with particular sadness. Several years ago, I traveled to Europe to establish cross-cultural research collaborators to conduct research on jealousy. At one university, I met a graduate student, 24 years old and intelligent, perceptive, alert, and sweet in disposition. She was a strikingly attractive woman, but she bore a strange facial feature. On both sides of her cheeks were two white scars, thin but clearly visible, each about three inches in length running vertically. The scars, she told me over coffee, were the result of her boyfriend's attack when she told him with finality that she was breaking off the relationship. He assaulted her with a straight razor, slashing her face on both sides, while screaming that he would ruin her for all other men. Fortunately, the story has a happy ending. She recovered, and the last I heard she was succeeding in graduate school and had become engaged to another man. But her face would forever bear the scars of jealous rage.

Are You at Risk for Violence from Your Partner?

In a large study of more than 8,000 participants, Margo Wilson and Martin Daly of McMaster University identified a clear association between responses to five questions and a woman's susceptibility to various forms of violence from her husband. They were asked if any of the following items applied to their partner and to answer with a yes or a no.

_____ 1. He is jealous and doesn't want you to talk to other men.
_____ 2. He tries to limit your contact with family or friends.
_____ 3. He insists on knowing whom you are with and where you are at all times.
_____ 4. He calls you names to put you down or make you feel bad.
_____ 5. He prevents you from knowing about or having access to the family income, even if you ask.

The more items you affirm as applicable to your partner, the higher the likelihood that you will be a victim of violence. Here is a sample of the statistical evidence. For item 1, 39 percent of women who said yes had experienced serious violence: in contrast only 4 percent of the women who said no experienced such violence. Forty percent of the women who said that their husband insisted on knowing their whereabouts were victims of serious violence, compared with only 7 percent of women whose husbands did not demand knowing their whereabouts. Forty-eight percent of the women who affirmed that their husband had called them names to put them down or to make them feel bad had been beaten by their husbands, compared with only 3 percent of the women who said that this did not describe their husband. It should be noted that 72 percent of the incidents meeting the "serious violence" criterion required medical attention, attesting to the severity of the violence.

It is possible, of course, to have a partner who exhibits all of these possessive behaviors but nonetheless does not use violence. Having a partner who is extremely possessive, derogating, and autonomy limiting does not invariably signal violence. But these actions are danger signs that indicate that anywhere from a third to half of such women may be in jeopardy.

Are Women as Violent as Men?

On New Year's Eve in 1989, the football legend O. J. Simpson was accused of assaulting his wife, Nicole Brown Simpson. His response was astonishment, for he declared that it was *he* who had been battered, and he was merely defending himself against Nicole's attack. He claimed, in fact, that he was a battered husband! Is this mere self-justification? Or is there any truth to the idea that women batter men as much as men batter women in close relationships? This controversy has been raging for more than two decades among researchers who study spousal violence.

The controversy was initiated in 1978, when Suzanne Steinmetz published an article entitled "The Battered Husband Syndrome." The article reviewed most of the evidence then available, and concluded that there was a large and mostly hidden side of intimate violence, with women as perpetrators and men as victims. The article provoked outrage from sociologists, psychologists, feminists, and some journalists. The controversy was fueled in part by worries that the conclusion would be used to reduce attention to battered women, perhaps curtailing funding for shelters. The controversy ignited as media sources touted headlines such as "Study Backs Up Suspicions That Husband Is More Battered Spouse" and exaggerated the actual statistics. Whereas the actual figures for battered husbands were estimated at 4.6 percent (46 men out of every thousand), or roughly two million men in America, one media source, the *New York Daily News,* mistakenly quoted a figure of twelve million battered men!

There are many statistics on the issue, but they must be examined carefully. In the most extensive American survey of domestic violence, the sociologists Murray Strauss and Richard Gelles found this extraordinary result: The frequency of acts of violence in mating relationships is indeed approximately equal for the two sexes, with half perpetrated by men and half by women. Some research on date violence suggests that women actually exceed men in some particular acts of violence. Women more than men report pushing or shoving their partner (38 percent for women and 15 percent for men), slapping their partner (22 percent versus 6 percent), kicking or biting their partner (20 percent versus 1 percent), and hitting their partner with an object (16 percent versus 1 percent). In this study, men exceeded women in only two acts of violence, both severe. Men more than women threw or smashed more objects (47 percent for men versus 40 percent for women) and forced sex on their partners (6 percent versus 1 percent). From these studies and others, it is reasonable to conclude that women are as capable of acts of violence as men are, and perform some of them with at least the frequency shown by men.

Some of these acts are clearly cases of women acting in self-defense, however, either against a specific attack or to combat a repeated history of abuse, as the following cases illustrate. The first involves a woman named Sally, age 44 and married for 25 years: "When he hits me, I retaliate. Maybe I don't have the same strength as he does, but I know how to hold my own. I could get hurt, but I am going to go down trying. You know, it's not like there is anyone else here who is going to help me. So . . . I hit him back . . . I pick up something and I hit him."

In another case, a woman used violence as an anticipatory defense strategy developed after a long history of experiencing her husband's wrath: "I know that look he gets when he gets ready to hit me. We've been married for ten years, and I've seen that look of his. So he gets that look, and I get something to hit him with. Once I hit him with a lamp. Another time I stabbed him. Usually I don't get so bad, but I was real fearful that time."

A third case involved Francine Hughes from Dansville, Michigan, who suffered years of beatings by her alcoholic and jealous husband, James Hughes. One evening, she poured a can of gasoline on Hughes while he slept after a night of drinking. She backed out of the room, lit a match, and fled with her children as her husband was engulfed in flames. She drove straight to the Ingham County sheriff's office, where she confessed to the crime. The jury eventually acquitted her, declaring that she had been temporarily insane while in the act of incinerating her husband.

Although studies show that women assault their spouses as much as men, there are two critical differences. First, women's violence is typically prompted by self-defense against a husband who is about to beat them, who is in the process of beating them, or who has had a long history of beating them. Women rarely initiate the battering, but do defend themselves when attacked. Most women are not passive victims of violence. They fight back when they can. Second, the cases above notwithstanding, women *on average* do far less damage than men when they enter the fray. There are no shelters for battered husbands, nor do hospitals house many men whose bones have been broken by an assaultive wife. True, men may be embarrassed by being beaten by a woman and show reluctance to bring such cases to light. Documented cases may underestimate the actual damage that women do. Even allowing for some underreporting, however, it's clear that men do more bodily damage than women.

Much intimate violence by both sexes ultimately can be traced back to sexual jealousy. Men assault their partners out of jealousy, and although women sometimes attack out of jealousy, more often it is in defense against a husband who is attacking them out of jealousy. In both cases, jealousy lies at the core of the conflict.

Explanations of Jealous Violence

How can we understand the brutality unleashed by the emotion of jealousy? What sort of explanation could account for the paradox that we hurt most the ones we love? According to sociologist R. N. Whitehurst, who studied 100 court cases involving husbands and wives in litigation over physical cruelty within their marriages, "At the core of nearly all the cases involving physical violence, the husband responded out of frustration at being unable to control the wife, often accusing her of being a whore or of having an affair with another man." Whitehurst explains the violence by attributing it to two factors. The first is "socialization," whereby men beat their wives because parents, teachers, and television teach them to do so. A second explanation invokes "male norms of aggressiveness," whereby men explode on their wives because American society views it as the normal and manly thing to do.

A third popular explanation for intimate violence proposes that patriarchy in Western culture is primarily responsible. As Neil Jacobson and John Gottman argue, "Our culture has been patriarchal as far back as we can trace it . . . patriarchy has sanctioned battering historically and continues to operate to perpetuate battering today; the continued oppression of women provides a context that makes efforts to end violence against women difficult if not impossible . . . In short, battering occurs within a patriarchal culture, and is made possible because such a culture dominates American society." As a result of patriarchy, they continue, "Many men still see it as their right to batter women who oppose their authority . . . marriage as an institution is still structured in such a way as to institutionalize male dominance, and such dominance makes high rates of battering inevitable . . . battering is simply an exaggerated version of the power and control that remain the norm in American marriages."

These explanations, although no doubt partially correct, run into trouble as complete explanations when we consider several facts about intimate violence. First, jealous violence is not merely an American phenomenon, nor can it be attributed to Western culture, media images, or capitalism. Spousal battering occurs in every culture for which we have relevant data. In the Ache tribe, a group residing in Paraguay, violence against mates is relatively common. Here is one report of an Ache child, translated into English:

"Dad could get really mad. He hit Mom in the forest when she had sex with another. Mom used to have sex with another (or several others). He hit Mom. They would have a fight. They would scratch faces. He would really scratch Mom's face. Dad was really strong. Mom was weak. Mom used to hit Dad in the face. Then he would scratch up her face in revenge (to defend himself). Then Mom would cry."

Napoleon Chagnon reports similar instances of violence among the Yanomamö. According to Chagnon, Yanomamö men beat their wives with sticks for a variety of reasons, ranging from consorting with another man to a violation as trivial as serving tea too slowly! Among the Yanomamö, as in the United States, jealous violence is also directed toward same-sex rivals: "Most duels start between two men, usually after one of them has been accused or caught *en flagrante* trysting with the other's wife. The enraged husband challenges his opponent to strike him on the head with a club. He holds his own club vertically, leans against it, and exposes his head for his opponent to strike. After he has sustained a blow on the head, he can then deliver one on the culprit's skull. But as soon as blood starts to flow, almost everybody rips a pole out of the house frame and joins in the fighting, supporting one or the other of the contestants."

Not surprisingly, as the men age, the tops of their heads become covered with scars, which the men proudly display. Some shave the tops of their heads and rub red pigment on the skin to draw attention to them and to demonstrate their toughness. All this florid violence—against a partner, against a rival, and sometimes involving the whole group—is triggered by jealousy over a real or suspected sexual infidelity.

Thousands of miles away from the Yanomamö resides the Tiwi tribe, located on Melville and Bathhurst Islands off the northern coast of Australia. Because of their relative isolation, the Tiwi tribe retained many of their customs at the time they were studied by anthropologists. They are described as a gerontocracy, which means that the older men tend to hold most of the power, while the young must wait their turn, sometimes for decades. The Tiwi are polygynous, with the powerful men taking as many as 29 wives, many of whom are younger by decades. Young men remain mateless. According to Tiwi law and custom, all women must be married, but the same obviously does not apply to men.

Given this mating system, it is not surprising that young wives sometimes have sexual affairs with the young men. When discovered, the husband usually beats his wife and then publicly accuses the young man of violation. Ritual requires that the accused young man stand in the village center, surrounded by all the other men in the village, while the offended husband throws spears at him. Being more athletic and agile, the young man can sometimes dodge the spears to avoid injury. But if he does, the other old men, allies of the offended husband, pick up spears and hurl them at the interloper. The most effective strategy is to attempt to receive a nonlethal spear, say in the upper thigh, which will draw a lot of blood, thereby assuaging the honor of the offended older man and preventing the young man from being killed.

As we've seen, jealous violence resides not only in North America, or in Western culture, or in cultures bombarded with media images. Neither the Tiwi nor the Yanomamö have electricity, much less television. Explanations limited to American culture, local socialization practices, or Western patriarchy fail to explain the universality of jealous violence. A deeper explanation is needed, one that traces violence back over human evolutionary history.

Is Domestic Violence Adaptive?

Let's put aside, for a few moments, our revulsion to partner battering, to consider the troubling possibility that violence may have served useful purposes for perpetrators. Does aggression sometimes pay?

Margo Wilson and Martin Daly speculate that the most plausible adaptive functions of violence against partners are *deterrence* and *control*. Men's use of violence, or threats of violence, convey an important signal to the spouse: acts of infidelity come at a steep price. By making the price of unfaithfulness sufficiently high, men hope to deter their spouses from sleeping with other men. One clue to the adaptive function of violence is the type of men most likely to use it. Wilson and Daly argue that the men most likely to resort to violence are those who lack more positive means of voluntary compliance at their disposal, such as providing resources. Violence, in this view, may represent men's last-ditch effort to hold on to partners who are on the verge of defecting. Violence, therefore, should be more prevalent when men lack the economic resources that might fulfill a core desire of women's initial mate choice.

Is there any evidence that men's use of violence actually deters women from infidelity or defection? Some battered women do remain in violent relationships, and return to them even after they have sought help at a shelter or hostel. In a study of 100 women at a shelter for battered women, a substantial number returned to their husband. Twenty-seven returned after their husband promised that he would change and refrain from violence, and 17 returned as a direct result of threats of further violence if she did not return. Another 14 returned home because they had no alternative place to go, and 13 returned because of their children. Eight women returned to their husband because they were still in love with him or felt sorry for him. A majority of the women who had been battered, many severely, returned to their partners after a stay in the shelter.

Some women respond to a man's violence by cutting off their contacts with male friends, wearing less revealing clothing, becoming more solicitous of their partner's needs and wants, and generally reducing signs of straying. Aggression, unfortunately, sometimes works if a wife is frightened enough to choose compliance over death. Recently I received a letter from a colleague who had been lecturing in an undergraduate class about the possible functions of violence. He related this story: "I had been discussing the roots of wife battering in mate guarding (sexual jealousy and proprietariness, etc.), and a student put up her hand, obviously anxious to make a point. She said that this could not be true. She had been working for some time at a shelter in Northhampton for abused and battered women, and had become familiar with many of them. When the subject of the reasons why they were abused came up, they said that getting involved with another man was the 'furthest thing from their minds.' In response, another student put his hand up and said, 'Well, I guess the abuse works.'"

Men are most likely to use violence when they discover an infidelity or suspect an infidelity. One study interviewed a sample of battered women and divided them into two groups: one group had been both raped and beaten by their husbands and one group had been beaten but not raped. These two groups were then compared with a control group of non-victimized women. The women were asked whether they had "ever had sex" with a man other than their husband while living with their husband. Ten percent of the non-victimized women reported having had an affair; 23 percent of the battered women reported having had an affair;

and 47 percent of those who were battered and raped confessed to committing adultery. These statistics reveal that infidelity by a woman predicts battering behavior in men.

In short, we can draw two tentative conclusions from the available evidence. First, men's violence against their partners does seem to serve the function of deterrence and control. By using violence, men maintain a credible threat, lowering the odds that their partner will commit infidelity or defect from the relationship. Men's violence seems most likely to rear its monstrous head when there is an increased likelihood that women will consort with another man. Second, although men's violence may sometimes represent a last ditch effort to keep a mate, and may sometimes backfire and cause a woman to leave, violence may actually deter defections. Even women who have been battered severely enough to go to a shelter sometimes return to their partners because of the threat of further violence.

The idea that spousal violence serves a deterrence function is undoubtedly disturbing. But it should not be construed as condoning or justifying these detestable and repugnant acts. Nor should this explanation be used to excuse or exonerate the cowardly men who commit them. Spousal violence is wrong according to most moral and legal systems. Only by understanding the causes of violence, however, can we hope to reduce its occurrence.

I Know You Really Love Me

In the movie *Fatal Attraction*, a married man played by Michael Douglas has a brief sexual fling with a professional colleague played by Glenn Glose. Although Douglas finds the sexual encounter exciting and intensely erotic, he breaks it off, not wanting to endanger his marriage. Glenn Close refuses to accept rejection. She begins stalking him, appearing suddenly after work at his parking garage, leaving tape recorded messages in his car, and spying on him as he enjoys a quiet evening with his family. She insists that he really loves her and refuses to be denied. All his attempts to convince her otherwise fail. Things come to a head after she boils his family's pet rabbit in a soup pot, kidnaps his daughter, and finally breaks into his house one evening brandishing a large kitchen knife. It was said that after *Fatal Attraction* came out, there was a temporary drop in the rates of male infidelity.

Stalking is a frightening behavior that has received national attention, and now all 50 U.S. states have passed anti-stalking legislation. Victims of stalking suffer greatly. A third of stalking victims seek some form of psychological treatment and a fifth lose time from their work. Stalking imprisons the victim both physically and psychologically. Victims report restricting their activities, become fearful of venturing out of familiar territory, and feel frightened even in well-frequented environments. They become anxious about answering the door, opening the mailbox, or picking up the phone. The fear stems from the barrage of harassment stalkers inflict, including repeatedly phoning the victims at home and work, ringing the doorbell, inundating the victims with letters and flowers, jumping out of the bushes unexpectedly, bombarding them with verbal insults or entreaties, and generally following them everywhere. Many stalkers spy on their victims (75 percent), make explicit threats (45 percent), vandalize property (30 percent), and sometimes threaten to kill them or their pets (10 percent). In some cases, stalkers assault their victims, and become especially violent when she or he becomes involved with a new romantic relationship.

I've interviewed many women who have suffered at the hands of a stalker, and the patterns are frighteningly similar. In one case, an attractive, well-educated, professional woman named Deirdre, age 28, became romantically involved with a man for about three months. She broke it off after he started to become unusually jealous and possessive. Over a period of six months he barraged Deirdre with hundreds of letters and thousands of phone calls. He repeatedly broke into her apartment when she was not there, leaving messages scrawled on her desk and bathroom mirror entreating her to take him back. Even a police restraining order failed to stop this stalker (80 percent of all restraining orders are violated by stalkers). Eventually, he was convicted of assaulting her and sentenced to three years in jail. In order to protect herself when her former lover was freed, she was forced to quit her job, change her name, and move to a different city. Fortunately, the story has a happy ending—Deirdre is now happily married to a man her professional and intellectual equal, and although the former stalking caused psychological scars and several years of misery, she has finally managed to put the horror behind her.

Stalking is best viewed as a continuum of activities. When the definition is broadened to include "the persistent use of psychological or physical abuse in an attempt to begin or continue dating someone else after they have clearly indicated a desire to terminate a relationship," a full 56 percent of college women report that they have been romantically harassed in this way.

How can we explain these bizarre, repugnant, criminal, and violent acts? Although some are clearly pathological, their frequency and patterning reveal that they are often extreme manifestations of men's psychology of jealousy and possessiveness—desperate measures designed to get someone back into the relationship or restore a love that was lost.

The first clue comes from the relationship between stalkers and their victims. Stalkers, of course, come in several types. Some stalk celebrities, as in the case of John Hinckley stalking the actress Jodie Foster or the bizarre case of the woman who kept breaking into talk show host David Letterman's house, insisting that she was really his wife. Some stalk total strangers or casual acquaintances. But by far the majority of stalkers have been romantically involved with their victims—as a current spouse, a former spouse, a previous lover, or a past dating partner. In roughly 60 percent of the cases, stalking by an intimate partner started before the relationship officially ended. This suggests that stalking is a violent manifestation of mating psychology, representing a frantic tactic designed to keep a partner or to coerce a partner back.

The second clue to the psychology of stalking comes from the sex of the victim. Although men and women both can be victims of stalking, studies reveal that women are four times more likely than men to be stalked. According to a research review by the National Institute of Justice, 8 percent of women and 2 percent of men say that they have been stalked. Across America, this yields the estimate that 8.2 million women will be victimized by a stalker at some point in their lives. Another survey estimates that more than a million American women have been stalked in the past year.

A third clue comes from the ages of the victims. In a study of 628 women victims of stalkers, 87 percent were under the age of 40. The overwhelming majority of these women were between 18 and 29, with the average around 28, suggesting that women of high fertility are most at risk of being stalked—a pattern strikingly similar to that found with victims of spousal battering.

Many male stalkers have a history of physically abusing their partners while in the relationship, and stalking, like domestic violence, represents a desperate attempt to regain control over a woman and coerce her back into the relationship. Most women stalking victims report that their assailants stalked them in order to keep them in the relationship, force a reconciliation, or seek vengeance against them for leaving.

Stalking, like domestic violence, is cowardly, morally repugnant, and illegal. The suggestion that it reflects an evolved male psychology of jealousy and possessiveness designed to keep or control a woman should in no way be used as an excuse for forgiving it or failing to punish its perpetrators. To the contrary, we may need stricter laws and more severe punishments to counteract these base manifestations of male nature.

If violence and stalking, abhorrent as they are, are motivated by men desperate to keep their partners, the same cannot be said for outright killing. The killing of a partner, in sharp contrast to nonlethal beating or stalking, seems genuinely puzzling, since killers lose their mates forever. Can we shed any light on the seemingly bizarre and apparently maladaptive phenomenon of wife killing?

Lethal Violence

In approaching the unsettling topic of mate murder, let's first examine some actual findings. The most extensive study of mate homicides consisted of 1,333 women and 416 men murdered by their intimate partners in Canada between 1974 and 1990. These included both officially married couples as well as common-law marriages in which partners lived together without an official marriage license. Women were more than three times as likely to be killed by an intimate partner as they were to be killed by a stranger. When this comparison is restricted to women legally married, women were more than nine times more likely to be killed by an intimate partner than by a stranger.

In a study of 25 spousal homicides, sociologist Peter Chimbos found sexual jealousy to be a prominent motive. Consider the following five accounts by husbands who were trying to explain why they killed their wives.

"She often called me a 'damned mute,' just running me down like that. Many times she would call my mother and tell her about me being 'mute' and no good. She also had refused sexual relationships with me and went out with other men."

"Her infidelity really bothered me. She had gone out with other men. It was about two weeks before the incident [killing] when she said to me: 'I want you to leave.' Then I said to her: 'What do you mean?' She replied: 'Don't you know that you are not wanted?' Then I bought a rifle to commit suicide but I never did."

"She would humiliate me in front of others on purpose. She knew I wouldn't argue in front of others and she said nasty things to me. At times she tried to belittle me about my sexual performance. She did not enjoy sex with me, but I never had any complaints from other women. I started to believe that I was impotent. I tried to talk with her about our problem but she would ignore me."

"You see, we were always arguing about her extramarital affairs. That day was something more than that. I came home from work and as soon as I entered the house I picked up my little daughter and held her in my arms. Then my wife turned around and said to me: 'You are so damned stupid that you don't even know she is someone else's child and not yours.' I was shocked! I became so mad, I took the rifle and shot her."

"We got married on a Saturday. She took the whole reception as a joke. She was really vulgar and nasty all day and she wanted to take her clothes off in front of everybody. I think she was hurt because her parents did not come to the wedding. Later that day I saw her being friendly with an ex-boyfriend of hers whom she had invited to the wedding. I started having doubts about her. I know she was a prostitute before. Anyway, that night when we went to bed I asked her why she acted that way during the reception. Then she replied to me: 'You are a bloody $20 trick just like the others.' At that moment I was so ashamed of her and felt so humiliated that I couldn't take it anymore. Then I put my hands around her neck and choked her to death."

In this study, 76 percent of the killers issued threats to the victims on the day of the killing, and 47 percent stated that their quarrels at the time of the homicide centered on sexual refusals or extramarital affairs. Infidelity and sexual rejection figure prominently in many spouse killings. Not all lethal violence is directed at the mate, however, nor is all lethal violence committed by men. Consider the following case.

In the small North Texas town of Mansfield near Fort Worth, Diane Zamora and David Graham lured Adrianne Jones to a remote lake road where they beat her with a dumbbell and shot her in the head. Diane Zamora had apparently convinced her boyfriend, David, to collaborate on this lethal act. The catalyst was sexual jealousy. Adrianne Jones had had sex with David, fomenting a ferocious rage in Diane. In order to continue the relationship, Diane insisted that David help kill her sexual rival. They were both convicted of premeditated murder and sentenced to life in prison.

These are individual cases, of course, but a wide variety of studies point to jealousy as the primary motive for killing partners and rivals. The discovery of infidelity and the finality of ending the relationship are the most common catalysts.

Martin Daly and Margo Wilson compiled evidence from a variety of sources to support this conclusion. In a study of 58 marital conflicts leading to murder in Detroit, they discovered that two-thirds were committed by men. Of these, 16 men killed their wife for infidelity or suspected infidelity. Seventeen men killed their rival or suspected rival. Two men killed their wives, allegedly in self-defense. And two gay men in the sample killed their male lover because of his infidelity.

Women kill because of jealousy, but at a far lower rate. Only six women in the sample killed their husband because of his infidelity. Three killed a rival woman. Nine women killed their husbands in self-defense, after the men became violent after accusing them of sexual infidelity. And the family members of women killed two men while defending the women against their violent partners.

Other studies report similar results. Peter Chimbos conducted intensive interviews with 34 perpetrators of spouse killings in Canada. The primary source of conflict, according to his summary, was "sexual matters (affairs and refusals)," which occurred in 29 of these cases, or 85 percent. The majority of these couples (22) had been separated as a result of infidelity and had either reconciled or had talked about reconciling. Combined, these two studies point to sexual jealousy as a key cause of partner killing in North America.

Do these findings generalize to other cultures and countries? In one study of court records in the Sudan, 74 out of 300 cases of male-perpetrated spousal homicide were explicitly attributed to jealousy. In a study of Ugandan homicides that included, but were not restricted to, spousal homicide, sexual jealousy and adultery ranked as the third leading motive, just short of robbery and property disputes.

The most extensive cross-cultural study examined the court trial transcripts of 533 homicides among a variety of African cultures, including the Tiv, Soga, Gisu, Nyoro, Luyia, and Luo. Ninety-one of these cases explicitly reported extreme sexual jealousy, infidelity of the spouse, or the wife leaving the husband as the primary motive for the homicide. This is surely an underestimate of jealous homicides, however, since in many cases a large percentage of the killings are attributed merely to "drunken arguments," with the real issue of contention left unspecified.

The second most extensive non-Western study examined the court records of 275 homicides occurring in the Belgian Congo. In many cases, no motive was explicitly recorded, but for those that did specify a motive, male sexual jealousy dominated the accounts. Of these, 59 were due to the man's jealousy, and only one to the woman's jealousy. These 60 cases were broken down into subtypes: 16 husbands killed their wives, her affair partner, or both as a result of sexual infidelity; 10 killed partners who had either deserted them, or were threatening to leave the relationship; 3 killed former wives after those wives had succeeded in obtaining a divorce; and 3 killed the new husbands when their ex-wives remarried.

Mistresses and engaged partners do not escape the wrath of male sexual jealousy, as the deaths of 13 such women attest. The one woman who killed as a result of jealousy murdered her husband's mistress. Male sexual jealousy was *not* implicated in only 20 cases in the entire sample of spousal homicides. In all these instances the motives were left unspecified, leading one to suspect that some were probably provoked by sexual jealousy as well.

Jealousy, the dangerous passion spurred by infidelity or desertion, unleashes a fury against the partner or interloper unrivaled by any other emotion. Sometimes it results in dead bodies.

An Evolutionary Explanation for Mate Killing

How can we comprehend the repulsive act of killing a mate? Martin Daly and Margo Wilson offer an explanation that may be labeled the "slip-up hypothesis." According to this explanation, spousal homicide is not adaptive, nor has it ever been adaptive for the perpetrators. Instead, dead bodies result from slips in a dangerous game of brinkmanship. Men use violence to control women and to prevent them from leaving, according to this argument. In order to make threats credible, actual violence has to be used. Sometimes the violence gets out of hand and results in a dead spouse. To quote Daly and Wilson directly: "Men . . . strive to control women . . . women struggle to resist coercion and to maintain their choices. There is brinkmanship and risk of disaster in any such contest, and *homicides by spouses of either sex may be considered slips in this dangerous game*." They elaborate in a later publication: "the fatal outcome in these homicides [spousal killings] is hypothesized to be *an epiphenomenal product of psychological processes that were selected for their nonlethal outcomes*." Men use violence to control women, and the psychology behind violent control has served a useful purpose for our male ancestors. But sometimes the violence gets out of hand, and results in "dysfunctionally extreme manifestations" that are "clearly counterproductive." Does this explanation square with the facts, or is a more disturbing conclusion warranted?

Joshua Duntley and I have proposed an alternative to the Wilson-Daly 'slip-up' hypothesis. We started by examining the known facts

121

about spousal homicide and asking whether the slip-up hypothesis explains them. Many homicides are premeditated, for example, and do not seem like mere accidents or slips.

A common refrain of killers to their victims while they are still alive is, "If I can't have you, nobody can." One Australian man, who killed his wife a month after she left him, said: "I was in love with Margaret, and she would not live with me anymore. I knew it was all finished so I bought the rifle to shoot her and then kill myself. If I can't have her, nobody can." In another case, an Illinois man issued the following threat to his wife after she had filed for divorce but before the divorce became official: "I swear if you ever leave me, I'll follow you to the ends of the earth and kill you." Unfortunately, this man made good on his promise and killed his wife in her home.

If spousal murders are really just slip-ups in a dangerous game of coercive threats and control, why do many spousal homicides seem planned and premeditated? Duntley and I argue that men have evolved a mate-killing module, a psychological mechanism whose function is not threat or deterrence, but rather the literal death of a mate. How could killing one's mate ever have been advantageous to our ancestral forefathers? We suggest several possible benefits that would have flowed to killers under some circumstances. First, in a polygynous mating context, where a man might have several wives, killing one wife as a result of an infidelity or defection could prevent other wives from cheating or leaving.

Second, in some cultures, a man's reputation would have suffered so extensively as a result of a wife's infidelity that killing her would be the only means of salvaging lost honor. Killing an unfaithful wife sometimes restores a man's honor. As Daly and Wilson note, "Not infrequently, men salvage some of their lost honor by killing an unchaste wife . . . and the male seducer. Shrinking from such vengeance may even add to their dishonor."

Third, a sexual infidelity may have inflicted such a severe cost on a man in the currency of paternity uncertainty and the associated misdirection of his investments, that killing the woman may have been a viable means of stanching the costs. If she is pregnant with another man's child, he also hurts his rival's reproductive success.

Our fourth argument hinges on the fact that one of the major triggers of mate killing is an irrevocable loss of the relationship. When a woman finally convinces her partner that she's leaving for good, the loss may be so substantial that it pushes the man over the edge into entertaining homicidal thoughts.

The final end of the relationship, in sum, historically may have put the man in triple jeopardy in the currency of reproduction. He lost entirely his access to her reproductive capabilities. He suffered severe and possibly irreparable reputational damage as a result of the loss. And if the woman was at all desirable, it was likely that she would remarry, so that a man's loss would have been his rival's gain. His same-sex rival benefited in direct proportion to the original man's loss.

According to this theory, over the long course of human evolutionary history, it has been reproductively advantageous for men *in some circumstances* to kill an errant partner, especially when the finality of her departure sinks in. A key prediction follows: Women should be most at risk of being killed when they have actually defected from the relationship, or when they have stated unequivocally that they are leaving for good.

Ironically, Wilson and Daly, the proponents of the opposing slip-up theory, provide the most compelling data in support of our Evolved Homicide Module Theory. In their analysis of the 1,333 mate homicides in Canada, estranged or separated wives are from five to seven times more likely to get killed by partners than women who are still living with their husbands. The separation time appears to be crucial. Women are at greatest risk in the first two months after separation, with 47 percent of the women homicide victims being killed during this interval, and fully 91 percent within the first year after separation.

Research conducted in three separate countries—New South Wales, Australia (1968–1986), Chicago (1965–1990), and Canada (1974–1990)—confirms these patterns.

In Chicago, for example, 44 percent of the women homicide victims who had separated were killed within the first two months of departure, and 78 percent were killed within the first year. Similar percentages were found for Canada and Australia. These results convey a warning that should be heeded by all women on the verge of separation: the first few months after estrangement are especially dangerous, and precautions should be taken for at least a year. Men do not always act on threats to kill estranged wives, of course, but such threats should always be taken seriously.

Wilson and Daly interpret these results to mean that men threaten their wives in order to control them and prevent their departure. In order to make such a threat credible, actual violence has to be carried out. They are undoubtedly correct that men sometimes use threats and violence to achieve control and deter defection. Here is what one Chicago woman declared, when asked by a friend why she did not leave her husband after he had battered her many times: "I can't, because he'll kill us all, and he's going to kill me." Men undoubtedly use violent threats to prevent women from leaving.

Nonetheless, there must be more to the story of lethal violence, something beyond the desire to exert control. This evidence supports the theory that estrangement, especially when the husband's loss is compounded by a rival's gain, may have been one of the most severe costs that a husband could incur. Homicide may have been an adaptive method of reducing this cost. As disturbing as this idea is, we must confront the demons of human nature if we are ever to understand and prevent the abhorrent act of wife-killing.

Laws About Spousal Homicide

In trying to come to a conceptual grip on the problem of mate murder, another source of evidence comes from laws throughout the land that have codified lethal violence against partners. It is clear that the laws on the books throughout the world implicitly acknowledge that the discovery of a partner's infidelity is sometimes viewed as a "justifiable cause" of mate killing, and hence deserving of less severe forms of punishment than other murders. As Daly and Wilson state, "adultery is widely construed to justify his resorting to violence that would in other circumstances be deemed criminal." Among the Yapese, for example, a husband who caught his wife in bed with another man "had the right to kill her and the adulterer or to burn them in the house." Similar provisions historically have been made in China, Japan, and other Asian countries.

In the state of Texas until 1974, the laws were lenient for killing a wife who strayed. According to the Texas penal code, such murders went unpunished "when committed by the husband upon the person of anyone taken in the act of adultery with the wife, provided the killing takes place before the parties to the act of adultery have separated." Simply put, it was not a crime to kill the lovers if you did so before they got out of bed. In New Mexico and Utah until the 1970s, a husband who found his wife naked in bed with another man and killed them was acquitted, since in the eyes of the court, no crime had been committed.

Historical English law reveals similar provisions. The killing of an adulterous wife used to be exempt from the usual charge of murder, and instead the charge was reduced to the lowest form of manslaughter on the grounds that "there could not be a greater provocation." This is apparently still the law throughout much of the English-speaking world, which relies on the "reasonable man" standard. As one legal scholar described this notion: "the judges have gone a considerable way towards establishing—so far as the law of provocation is concerned—a standard portrayal of the make-up and reactions of the reasonable man. They say he is not impotent and he is not normally drunk. He does not lose his self-control on hearing a mere confession of adultery, but he becomes unbalanced at the sight of adultery provided, of course, that he is married to the adulteress."

In the United States today, killing a wife or her lover is considered a criminal act, but the actual penalties levied against such killers tend to be more lenient than for other types of killings. Juries usually display sympathy for husbands who have killed when discovering their wife in a naked embrace with another man. Some prosecutors decide not to pursue such cases in light of the likely sentiments of the juries.

Lawmakers and everyday jurors apparently believe that stumbling upon carnal evidence of adultery is a provocation so severe that many "rational" men would resort to extreme violence. The legal system seems implicitly to acknowledge the deep roots of men's homicidal nature.

Women Who Are Most Vulnerable to Homicide

Not all women are equally vulnerable to getting killed. Women who are young, who have substantially older husbands, or who have children from former mateships are especially at risk.

Youth and Fertility of the Woman

When mate killing occurs in specific circumstances, it provides clues to the design of murderers' minds. One circumstance is the age of the partner. Young women tend to be more fertile than older women, and we know that youth figures prominently in men's mating desires. Young women are more attractive to a man's rivals, who are therefore more likely to flirt, charm, or try to lure them away from their existing partners. Men mated to young women are more often surrounded by encroaching competitors, which trips the jealousy switch.

Young women, because they tend to be desirable, are in the best positions in their lives to secure a desirable mate. At no other time in a woman's life does she have more options. Attempts to switch mates—to find a better mate to replace her current mate—may be most effective during this stage. Their husbands seem to be aware that they may be expendable.

In Daly and Wilson's study of spousal homicides in Canada from 1974 to 1983, women under the age of 20 were two and a half times more likely to be killed than women between the ages of 20 and 49. After the age of 50, when most women are postmenopausal, the spousal homicide rate drops again in half. These findings do not indicate that men view young women as lacking in worth—quite the opposite. It's precisely because a man values his young bride so much that he becomes fanatical in attempting to control and keep her.

May-December Marriages

When a man is substantially older than his partner, he may be especially vulnerable to being cuckolded and abandoned for two reasons. First, women usually want men who are only a few years older than they are, not men substantially older. Women married to much older men may therefore have a desire that remains unfulfilled. Second, a young wife is likely to elicit more interest from other men, opening up more frequent opportunities to switch mates. If men married to women considerably younger have a more tenuous hold, and their mates are in fact more prone to defection, then spousal homicide should show a frequency spike in May-December marriages.

Among the spousal homicides in Miami in 1980, 29 percent of the killings occurred in marriages where the age discrepancy was 10 years or more. Similar statistics were reported of spousal homicides in Houston (25 percent), Chicago (23 percent), Detroit (23 percent), Britain (18 percent), Scotland (15 percent), and New South Wales, Australia (19 percent). The largest sample of spousal homicides, a total of 1,749, revealed that 20 percent occurred in marriages with an age discrepancy of 10 years or more.

Not all of the May-December homicides can be explained by the theory that men might have an evolved mate-killing module. Some spouse killings are motivated by greed, some catalyzed by pathology. Some may even be accidental, as Daly and Wilson claim. But the fact remains that most young women married to older men have lots of mating options, are likely to be sexually attracted to the man's rivals, and may be tempted to leave the relationship—circumstances that our Evolved Homicide Module Theory predicts will render women more vulnerable to lethal violence.

Women with Children from a Previous Partner

From a man's perspective, women with children from a previous partner have a portion of their resources tied up. In reproductive currencies, this creates conflict between the woman and her new partner. It detracts from the resources that she has to invest in him and his children. A disturbing statistic attests to this conflict: young stepchildren are 40 to 100 times more likely to be killed than children residing with two biological parents. Does this conflict also spill over into the marital relationship itself, making the woman with children from a previous partner more at risk?

Daly and his colleagues explored this issue in Hamilton, Ontario. Mothers with children fathered by a former partner were 12.7 times more likely to be killed by their new partner than women with children fathered only by their current partner. Many of these murders occurred when the woman had left the relationship, or was in the process of leaving. Here are a few of these cases: "One woman was slain 4 days after moving out, and another was killed while walking to work from a shelter to which she had moved 5 days previously. Another couple shared the marital home while divorcing; the homicide occurred 11 days after the divorce was finalized while the victim was packing her belongings. Three more women were killed while retrieving belongings from the marital home after having moved out within the previous month . . . two were in possession of restraining orders against their husbands because of prior threats and assaults, and [another] was killed by a husband already await-ing trial for a prior assault against her . . . One wife was shot while sleeping a week after demanding a divorce. A second was allegedly planning to leave, or so her killer believed, when he drowned [the stepson] in the bath while she was at work and stabbed her to death on her return home . . . another was killed after making an appointment with a lawyer to discuss the logistics of marital separation." The presence of stepchildren from previous partners puts women at special risk, especially when they are defecting from the relationship.

Homicidal Fantasies

A final source of evidence on this disturbing theory of spousal homicide comes from research Joshua Duntley and I have been conducting on homicidal thoughts. We find that most people have had the thought of killing someone else at one point or another in their lives. Fortunately, most people do not act on these thoughts. Homicidal thoughts are thou-sands of times more common than actual killings. Nonetheless, homicidal thoughts almost invariably precede actual homicides. Potential killers work out the fantasy in their minds, envision the weapons of destruction, the step-by-step scenario of carrying it out, and often establish an alibi. If O. J. Simpson killed his estranged wife, Nicole Brown Simpson, he may have rehearsed it in his mind dozens of times, as revealed by circumstantial evidence. Prior to the killing, he had arranged a plane flight to Chicago, which he boarded shortly after the killing. By the time the body was discovered, he could declare that he had been hundreds of miles away and so could not possibly have killed her. If humans have evolved a psychology of killing, then premeditations are surely part of that psychology.

If Duntley and I are correct, then thoughts of murdering a partner should be triggered by two critical events: the discovery of sexual infidelity by a mate and the actual permanent departure of a mate. Our research reveals that men's mate-killing fantasies are triggered precisely by these two events, which vastly overshadow all other mate-killing catalysts. Here are a few samples of what men in our study reported:

Man: Age 24. Victim: Girlfriend. Reason: "Well, we got into a fight about her cheating on me. This made me think that if I can't have her all to myself, then no one will. I thought about taking a gun and shooting her in the face. I didn't just want to kill her; I wanted to destroy her beauty."

Man: Age 33. Victim: Girlfriend. Reason: "She admitted to cheating on me. We didn't talk for a week. Then we went to a bar, had a few drinks, and made up. We started sleeping together again. The next month, she came home at three in the morning smelling like sex. I thought that a good way for her to die would be in a fiery car crash, so I would cut her brake line. I also thought that it would be nice to get a syringe filled with the HIV virus and inject it into her."

Neither of these men, as far as we know, acted on their homicidal thoughts. But our studies of homicidal thoughts among thousands of men show conclusively that a lot of men start thinking of killing when they catch their partner cheating or when they get unceremoniously dumped.

What can we conclude from this evidence? It would certainly be premature to conclude that we know with certainty that men have evolved a situationally triggered mate-killing psychology. Perhaps Daly and Wilson are correct in their slip-up theory. But we know that men's homicidal thoughts occur in specific predictable circumstances. We know that the fantasies involve killing, not merely hurting or deterring. We know that the thoughts occur with some frequency and take up a significant amount of men's attention that could be devoted to other problems. If men do have an evolved mate-killing mind, then we must face this disturbing evil of human nature unflinchingly. We need to know the minds of the killers among us in order to prevent them from acting on their fantasies. Only by understanding the hidden roots of mate murders can we hope to reduce their occurrence.

We must now move to another spiral in the co-evolution of men and women and explore the events that lead to jealousy, the passions that lead a partner to stray.

CHAPTER 6

Secrets and Lies

I think a man can have two, maybe three affairs while he is married. But three is the absolute maximum. After that, you are cheating.

—*Yves Montand*

I N THE PREVIOUS CHAPTERS, we explored the psychology of jealousy and its more destructive manifestations, including the treacherous abuse of spouses and the horrifying killing of partners. But our jealous nature cannot be fully appreciated without a deep understanding of why jealousy evolved to begin with—the nature of the threats it evolved to defend against. This chapter explores the nature of infidelity.

On February 28, 1997, Monica Lewinsky entered the Oval Office for her final sexual encounter with the President, Bill Clinton. The President gave her a few gifts, and then . . . according to Lewinsky's testimony:

"We went back over by the bathroom in the hallway, and we kissed. We were kissing and he unbuttoned my dress and fondled my breasts with my bra on, and then he took them out of my bra and was kissing them and touching them with his hands and with his mouth. And then I think I was touching him in his genital area through his pants, and I think I unbuttoned his shirt and was kissing his chest. And then . . . I wanted to perform oral sex on him . . . so I did . . . And . . . then he pushed me away, kind of as he always did before he came, and then I stood up and I said . . . I care about you so much; . . . I don't understand why you won't let me . . . make you come; it's important to me; I mean, it just doesn't feel complete, it doesn't seem right."

They hugged and looked at each other, and the President said, "I don't want to disappoint you." Then, Monica Lewinsky continued to perform oral sex on the president to completion. Subsequent laboratory tests revealed that the semen stain on the dress Lewinsky wore that day contained DNA that matched the President's, providing incontrovertible evidence of a secret affair that the two had been carrying on from November 15, 1995, through their final encounter on February 28, 1997.

What was striking about the Lewinsky-Clinton affair was neither the salaciousness of the sexual acts, nor the fact that Bill Clinton was married. Affairs are commonplace and most sex partners engage in oral sex. What was arresting was the sheer volume of public attention—a feeding frenzy of unseemly obsession—in what in nearly any other context would be a rather banal sequence of events. Viewed from an evolutionary perspective, however, few domains have greater reproductive consequences than the sex lives of others. As a result, we attend to, and remember most vividly, events with reproductive repercussions. Americans' apparent obsession with every lurid detail of the sexual encounters of President Clinton and Monica Lewinsky, and not with every detail of, say, Clinton's golf game, reveals this ancient human interest.

Why would a man or woman risk so much—status, reputation, honor, marriage, children, and even personal safety—for a few minutes of sexual gratification? How can we explain the puzzling pervasiveness of infidelity that violates the marital vows?

The Prevalence of Infidelity

The prevalence of infidelity has been extensively researched, but different studies produce widely varying estimates. Shere Hite put the rates as high as 70 percent, while others such as Andrew Greeley asserted that only 5 to 10 percent of married people cheated. There are several problems with determining precise rates. First, infidelity is typically concealed and people are reluctant to talk about it. In the classic Kinsey study on sexuality, the interview questions about infidelity caused many participants to withdraw from the study, and of those who remained, questions about infidelity were often left unanswered.

Second, the methods used by studies of infidelity vary considerably. Some studies evaluate infidelity rates across the entire span of the marriage, whereas others restrict the time interval to the previous year of marriage. Some use an interview format; others use anonymous questionnaires. One study was particularly revealing about the reluctance of people to admit to affairs. The authors examined 750 individuals who entered therapy and found that 30 percent initially admitted to sexual infidelities. During intensive therapy with the same people, however, an additional 30 percent revealed clandestine liaisons, bringing the total figure for this sample up to 60 percent. Clearly, the methods used, time frame selected, and level of trust in the researcher all affect estimates of infidelity.

My own estimate, averaged across studies, is that approximately 20 to 40 percent of American women and 30 to 50 percent of American men have at least one affair over the course of the marriage. Even these figures, however, underestimate the likelihood that *at least one partner in the marriage* will be unfaithful. Anthony Thompson of Western Australian Institute of Technology argues that the probability that either the husband *or* wife will have an affair (the affair rate for the couple) may be as high as 76 percent.

Although the figures for men and women cheating at least once are fairly close, men break their marital vows of fidelity more frequently. Graham Spanier, of the State University of New York at Stony Brook, and Randie Margolis, of Harvard Medical School, found that 26 percent of the men, but only 5 percent of the women, had affairs with three or more partners. A full 64 percent of women who have affairs have them with only one partner, whereas only 43 percent of the men who have affairs restrict themselves to a single partner.

Clearly, both men and women have affairs, but the sex difference should not be hastily dismissed. I keep a file of news articles about sex scandals. Most involve married men, often in positions of power, who use their status to attract sex partners other than their wives. A recent example: "Fourth Woman Accuses 'Guru' of Sex." A Hindu guru in Houston is accused of convincing each of four women that "she must have sex with him to cleanse her womb of evil spirits." He apparently told each not to mention these episodes to his wife, since she apparently got angry at the cleansing rituals. Four women so far have come forward to complain that he abused his position as a religious adviser to manipulate them into having sex.

In my files, collected over a span of years, I found not a single case of a married woman abusing her position of power to secure sex with multiple men. Perhaps we don't hear about them. Perhaps they will emerge as women assume more positions of power. Given what we know about the gulf between the sexes in unfaithful desires, however, I wouldn't bet on it.

Lust in the Heart

Affair rates underestimate the rates of cheating hearts. Imagine an attractive person of the opposite sex walking up to you and saying, "Hi, I've been noticing you around town lately, and I find you very attractive," and then asking one of three questions: "Would you go out on a date with me tonight?" "Would you go back to my apartment with me?" "Would you have sex with me?" Of the women approached in a study that actually posed these questions, 50 percent agreed to go out on a date with the man; 6 percent agreed to go back to his apartment; and 0 percent agreed to have sex with him. Most women thought it bizarre for a man to approach them out of the blue and ask for sex. Men differed. Of the men approached by the attractive female, 50 percent agreed to go out on a date with her; 69 percent agreed to go back to her apartment; and 75 percent agreed to have sex with her! The men who refused were typically apologetic, citing a previous engagement with parents or a fiancée. Some asked for a rain check. This is one of many studies that reveal fundamental differences between the sexes in the desire for a variety of different sex partners.

The journalist Natalie Angier questions these results, arguing that women would hop into bed as easily as men in these situations, but are deterred by a concern for their personal safety. Russell Clark of the University of North Texas explored this possibility. First, he replicated the study on a different sample in a different part of the country, and the results were almost identical; more men than women were willing to have sex with a virtual stranger. Second, Clark notes that roughly half the women in each study were quite willing to go out on a date with the strangers, which seems puzzling if they were concerned about their safety. Third, when Clark's experimenters asked the participants to describe the reason for their refusal (if they refused), women's and men's answers were nearly identical; both mentioned that they had a boyfriend or girlfriend, or that they did not know the person well enough.

Perhaps a date seems safer than sex and women really do want sex with strangers, if only they could be assured of their safety. To explore this possibility, Clark conducted yet another experiment. Men and women participants were contacted by a close personal friend who testified about the integrity and character of the stranger. The participants were assured by their friends that the other person was warm, sincere, trustworthy, and attractive. The participants were then asked one of two questions: "Would you be willing to go on a date?" or "Would you be willing to go to bed?" After being debriefed, participants were asked for their reasons for their decision.

The overwhelming majority of both sexes agreed to the date: 91 percent of the women and 96 percent of the men. As for the sex, however, a big difference emerged: 50 percent of the men, but only 5 percent of the women agreed. Not a single woman indicated a concern for safety. Clearly, making conditions safer for women increases the odds that they will consent to sex with a stranger—from 0 percent to 5 percent—so safety concerns are not irrelevant. But the sex difference remains great. Most women agree to date strangers when a close friend vouches for the man's warmth and integrity, but 95 percent still refuse to consent to sex.

The difference is *not* that "women are coy," which would imply a false shyness, a pretense of lack of interest, or a childlike coquettishness. And it's not that women lack interest in sex. Once a woman makes the decision to sleep with a man, there is no reason to think that her sex drive is not as high as his. The evidence is compelling, however, that most women are careful about whom they choose to sleep with, and for the most part avoid jumping into bed with total strangers. Men are more willing. Most men responded to the sexual request by saying, "What time?" or "Why not?" and then asking for the requester's telephone number and directions to her house.

These differences hold with equal force in lust for affairs. In one study by Ralph Johnson of Sacramento State College, 48 percent of American men, but only 5 percent of American women, expressed a desire to engage in extramarital sex. In a classic older study by Lewis Terman of 769 American men and 770 American women, 72 percent of the men, but only 27 percent of the women, admitted that they sometimes desire sex with someone outside of their marriage. Germans reveal similar tendencies: 46 percent of married men but only 6 percent of married women admit that they would take advantage of a casual sexual opportunity with someone else if the chance arose. More recent studies by David Wyatt Seal and his colleagues at the University of New Mexico show similar sex differences.

Women, of course, may be more reluctant to confide their sexual desires to a surveyor, so the figures are likely to underestimate women's adulterous impulses. Nonetheless, the sex difference proves so robust across studies and methods of inquiry that there is no reason to doubt that men and women differ in desire.

The desires of men have a straightforward explanation based on evolved sexual strategies. Historically, men's reproductive success was limited primarily by the number of fertile women they could successfully inseminate. The greater the sexual access to a variety of women, the greater the reproductive success. The insatiable desire for a variety of sex partners evolved as a powerful passion in men, expressing itself in a host of behaviors ranging from patronizing prostitutes to indulging in infidelity.

Sexual Fantasies

Sexual fantasies provide another psychological window into secret desires. Fantasies are not behaviors, of course, but they reveal something about the desires that motivate behavior. As evolutionary psychologist Donald

Symons of the University of California at Santa Barbara notes in a related context: "Even if only one impulse in a thousand is consummated, the function of lust is to motivate sexual intercourse." Research conducted in Japan, Great Britain, and the United States shows that men have roughly twice as many sexual fantasies as women. When asleep, men are more likely than women to dream about sexual events. Women may be more reluctant to admit to such fantasies, even on an anonymous questionnaire, but a reporting bias is less able to explain the content of the fantasies.

Men's sexual fantasies more often include strangers, multiple partners, and anonymous partners. During a single fantasy episode, most men report that they sometimes change sexual partners, whereas most women report that they rarely change sexual partners. Forty-three percent of women but only 12 percent of men report that they never substitute or switch sexual partners during a fantasy episode. When asked, "Have you had over 1,000 sexual fantasies in your lifetime so far?" 32 percent of men but only 8 percent of women report numbers this high.

Here is one sample fantasy from a 20-year-old man who works in Connecticut sailing boats for a living: "I fantasize about having the maximum number of women at one time that I can. I know I won't be able to satisfy each of them sexually, but as it's my fantasy it really doesn't matter . . . I'm lying on my back in bed. I'm totally naked. My legs are spread wide apart and my arms are stretched out above my head. A bevy of six beautiful women walk into the room. They're all slim and naked. My cock, which has already started to stiffen, becomes totally erect as they stand around the bed . . . The first woman crawls onto the bed and straddles my stomach . . . she holds my cock and guides it into her pussy, moving her body slowly up and down so that my cock slides deep into her . . . Shortly, she moves away from me and sits on the edge of the bed. Then the next woman does exactly the same thing, but this time there is one difference. When she sucks my cock, it is covered with the love juices of the previous woman, and that excites me greatly. After each woman has done the same to me, I have already penetrated each of them with my cock." The fantasy continues in this vein, with graphic descriptions of each woman's body and the various sexual combinations and permutations he carries out with each.

Numbers, variety, and novelty dominate men's fantasies. Men focus on body parts and sexual positions stripped of emotional context. Male sexual fantasies are heavily visual, focusing on smooth skin, breasts, genitals, thighs, and buttocks. During sexual fantasy, 81 percent of men but only 43 percent of women focus on visual images rather than feelings. Men fantasize about attractive women with lots of exposed skin who show signs of easy access and no commitment. As Bruce Ellis and Donald Symons observe, "The most striking feature of [male fantasy] is that sex is sheer lust and physical gratification, devoid of encumbering relationships, emotional elaboration, complicated plot lines, flirtation, courtship, and extended foreplay." Men's fantasies reveal a mind attuned to sex with many partners.

Women's sexual fantasies, like men's, vary widely, and no two are alike, but they are more likely than men's to contain familiar partners. A few women, of course, sometimes crave what the writer Erica Jong described in *Fear of Flying* as the "zipless fuck," anonymous sex with a stranger on the train. More often, though, women's fantasies have thicker plot lines.

Consider this sexual fantasy reported by Jayne, a 29-year-old woman: "I have known my imagined partner for some time, but we have held off becoming intimate until this moment. He has spent the day showering me with attention, listening to me over lunch, looking at me with a burning desire as we have walked together, hand in hand, along crowded city sidewalks. Now, back at my apartment, he holds me close and whispers his feelings for me. He lets me know that I'm the center of his life, the only one who has ever made him feel this way. . . . Our kisses at first are tender, then we both become more passionate. We collapse on the floor, pulling at each other's clothes, then pause in our frenzy and take time to look at each other. When our bodies come together, it's not just sex but the merging of two people, hearts and souls."

Notice the emotional intimacy, private whispers, personal attention, and psychological closeness with someone Jayne already knew. None of these ingredients pervade the typical man's sexual fantasies, which more often center on raw sex with strangers. Fifty-nine percent of American women but only 28 percent of American men report that their sexual fantasies typically focus on someone with whom they are already romantically and sexually involved. Not all women's fantasies, of course, center on men they already know.

Here is one from Bobbi, a married woman in her 30s, about a man she had never met: "I'm with a man I've never met in real life. He's a cowboy and an animal lover, self-confident and strong, yet also tender. We spend the whole day together and discover that we have many common interests. He . . . [is] hanging on my every word, and looks at me with burning desire. At his home, we eat, drink, listen to music, dance close. . . . He says that I'm the only one who has ever made him feel this way. This excites me and makes me want him, too. His first kisses are gentle, and I return them that way. Then he kisses me more aggressively, and I return that energy. When we undress each other, I notice his lean, taut stomach, his contoured legs, his dark chest hair. As he caresses me, he makes me feel worshiped, adored, safe, and very sexy. He takes me to the edge with breast stimulation and oral sex, then thrusts inside me. We climax together, then cuddle in bed for the rest of the day, talking and touching."

Emotions and personality are crucial for women. Although Bobbi's fantasy centered not on her husband but on a man she had never met, they don't just jump into bed. They build up to sex by getting to know each other, sharing common interests, dancing, and eating. Bobbi becomes the center of the man's desires, arousing him like no other woman before her. He worships her, makes her feel safe and protected, all qualities that signal emotional involvement and commitment over time.

The formal studies bear out these themes: 57 percent of women but only 19 percent of men report that they focus on feelings as opposed to visual images. As one woman observed, "I usually think about the guy I am with. Sometimes I realize that the feelings will overwhelm me, envelop me, sweep me away." Women emphasize tenderness, romance, and personal involvement in their sexual fantasies, paying more attention to the way their partner responds to them.

Men's fantasies, in contrast, focus on sexual variety, since those men in the past who were inclined in this direction tended to reproduce more than men not so inclined. It's not that men lack the desire to marry, as as the journalist Natalie Angier and other critics have mischaracterized the theory. It's that men are more likely than women to be on the lookout for the occasional casual fling in addition to whatever long-term commitments they make.

It surprises me that some ideologues insist that the sexes are identical and that women lack discernment when it comes to casual sex, just like men. The data don't support these positions. Women's reproductive resources are precious and finite, and ancestral women did not squander them on just any random man. Obviously, women don't consciously think that sperm are cheap and eggs are expensive. But women in the past who failed to exercise acumen before consenting to sex were left in the evolutionary dust; our ancestral mothers used emotional wisdom to screen out losers. Lust is one thing; acting on it is another. Not all people who experience extramarital desires give in to them.

Susceptibility to Infidelity: Differences in Attractiveness

What telltale signs reveal a cheating partner? Some of these signals are obvious—an unexplained absence, a sudden decrease in sexual interest, unfamiliar sexual scents on a partner, an open flirtation with others, or catching the partner in a nude embrace with a neighbor. Many signals are more subtle, such as the personality characteristics of a partner. This section explores who is susceptible to infidelity and what clues they leave behind.

When studying the avian species of zebra finches, *Poephia guttata,* the evolutionary biologist Nancy Burley made a striking discovery. These birds were presumed to be monogamous, preferring to mate with a single partner for many breeding seasons. When she monitored the birds over the course of several months, however, she observed that some males in fact copulated with several females, others copulated with only a single female, and still others remained celibate. She also observed that the zebra finches varied in coloration, and that some colors were more attractive than others.

Burley performed an unusual experiment that probably would be unethical to perform on humans. She created bands of different colors and placed them on the legs of the birds. Some males were banded with red colors, which her observations suggested were highly attractive to females. Other males were banded with green, a color less attractive to females. For females, black bands seemed to be the most attractive to males, so some were banded with black. Others remained unbanded. In this manner, Burley varied the relative attractiveness of the zebra finches, and then observed their mating behavior over the following 22 months. Food was readily abundant in her laboratory aviary, so it did not play a role in mating.

She discovered two intriguing results when birds paired up with those who were less or more attractive than themselves. First, the birds lower in attractiveness devoted more effort than the birds higher in attractiveness to the care and parenting of their offspring chicks. It was as if the less desirable birds had "recognized" that they had to compensate for their lower attractiveness with increased parental care; the birds higher in mate value were able to trade their attractiveness for a lighter workload. Second, the male zebra finches who were more attractive than their partners more often mated with other female birds, enjoying extrapair liaisons in addition to sex with regular mates. The birds higher in mate value, in essence, traded their relatively greater attractiveness for increased opportunities for infidelity.

Do humans show a similar pattern? The first evidence for the importance of attractiveness differences for marital infidelity came from a *Psychology Today* survey. This study asked each participant: "Describe your partner's desirability: Much more desirable than I; Slightly more desirable than I; As desirable as I; Slightly less desirable than I; Much less desirable than I." Those higher in mate value were defined as those who described their partners as "slightly less" or "much less" desirable than themselves. Those lower in mate value were defined as those who described their partners as "slightly more" or "much more" desirable than themselves.

The study also asked the participants how willing they were to engage in an extramarital sexual relationship. It posed two questions: How soon after you began living with your partner did you first have sex with someone else (if you have had sex with someone else at all)? With how many people have you had extramarital affairs over the course of your relationship? Fifty-eight percent of the partners turned out to be well matched, showing comparable levels of mate value. What about those who were mismatched, where one partner was more desirable than the other? The partner higher in desirability turned out to be more likely to have more extramarital affairs with more partners than those who were lower in desirability. Furthermore, the more desirable partner in each pair was more likely to have affairs *earlier* in the marriage. They began having affairs 6 to 8 years after the wedding. In contrast, those who were equivalent or lower in desirability waited 12 to 15 years before starting an affair, if they had an affair at all. Like zebra finches, human affairs seem to be affected by the relative mate value of the partners.

In a more recent study of newlywed couples, Todd Shackelford and I explored the importance of attractiveness differences for susceptibility to infidelity in more detail. We studied 107 couples using three sources of data: self-reports, partner reports, and interviews with each couple. When the couples were physically separated to preserve privacy, we asked each spouse to estimate the likelihood that their partner would perform various acts of infidelity over the course of the next year. These included flirting with a member of the opposite sex, passionately kissing, going out on a romantic date, having a one-night stand, having a brief affair, and having a serious affair. Subsequently, they all estimated their own likelihood of engaging in each of these types of infidelity over the course of the next year. Participants were then asked two questions: If this event occurred, what is the probability that *you* would end the relationship? If this event occurred, what is the probability that *your partner* would end the relationship?

Following these private estimates, each couple was interviewed together by a pair of trained interviewers, one man and one woman, drawn from a rotating team of eight interviewers. Immediately after the interview, the staff members independently judged them on their "overall attractiveness as a potential mate," which we defined as "market value to opposite sex." The separate judgments of each interviewer were then combined to form an overall measure of everyone's mate value. To evaluate dissimilarity, we then calculated the disparity between the married partners in their overall attractiveness as a potential mate.

We discovered that the partner higher in mate value was significantly more likely to commit infidelity, confirming the results of the *Psychology Today* study. Women married to more desirable men, for example, judged it more likely that their husbands would kiss, date, have a one-night stand, and have a brief affair with someone else. Furthermore, we discovered that dissimilarity was linked with the likelihood of ending the marriage if their partner had an affair, but this was only true for the more serious types of infidelity. If the less desirable partner flirted or kissed someone else, this could be overlooked, or at least would not result in divorce. If the less desirable partner had a one-night stand, brief affair, or a serious affair, however, the more desirable partner would seek a divorce. The less desirable partners, in contrast, would tolerate infidelity by their more desirable partner and stated that they would not seek divorce.

These findings have some degree of cross-cultural generality, as illustrated by a study by Bram Buunk and his colleagues of 82 Dutch men and 132 Dutch women, all married, with an average age of 41. They examined the effects of relative mate value on a person's desire for extramarital sex and on their actual frequency of extramarital sex. Desire was assessed through this question: "How many times did you want to have sex with another (wo)man during your marriage or cohabitation?" They were also asked how many extramarital partners they had had.

The effects of relative mate value also proved especially strong for the Dutch women. Women who perceived themselves as higher in mate value than their partners were more likely to express a desire for extramarital sex and were more likely to act on those desires. Women who felt that they were well-matched with their partners, equals in what they brought to the mating table, were the least likely to desire or engage in affairs. All these studies point to a singular conclusion: those who are higher in mate value are especially prone to infidelity.

The Principle of Diminishing Returns

Time and effort in each person's life are finite. Life can be viewed as a series of decisions about how to spend one's time. Time spent at one activity necessarily precludes time for others. Some of the most important decisions men and women face are how much effort to spend pursuing various life tasks, such as finding a mate, getting ahead in the workplace, and raising a family. Effort devoted to getting ahead takes time away from the family. With each activity, however, we reach a state of diminishing returns, where additional effort yields less and less payoff.

Consider a simple example—time spent securing food, either through hunting or gathering. Clearly, the first few morsels of food are highly valuable. They may make the difference between starving and surviving. Subsequent portions of food the same day, however, are progressively less valuable. In the extreme case, the hundredth hunk of meat has almost no value; it's left to rot uneaten. This logic suggests that time spent searching for food is effort that shows diminishing returns. Natural selection should have created decision rules for spending a certain amount of effort toward getting food, but then ceasing this activity when the returns dip too low.

The same logic applies to the time and energy we allot toward attracting partners, what evolutionary biologists call "mating effort." Time and energy spent in enhancing one's appearance, trying to attract potential mates, and pursuing extramarital affairs may be profitable up to a point, reproductively speaking, but as a general rule, each individual will reach diminishing returns. Additional effort spent enhancing one's appearance may make only a trivial difference, for example, and so it's not worth the time or added expense. The same logic applies to effort devoted to attracting mates and securing affair partners.

But here is the catch: the rate of diminishing returns depends heavily on the mating success of the individual. According to the theory of diminishing returns, the mating payoff for highly attractive men should be far higher than the payoff for less attractive men. Attractive actors such as Matt Damon or Ben Affleck would achieve more sexual success per unit of mating effort than less attractive actors such as Steve Buscemi or William Macy. A man's attractiveness to women, therefore, should influence his decisions about how much effort to spend on mating.

To find out, David Waynforth at the University of New Mexico tested 56 men in western Belize, a predominantly Mayan population that has been relatively isolated. The villages studied, San Antonio and Cristo Rey, were inaccessible except by canoe, at least until recently. Their primary mode of subsistence is through slash-and-burn agriculture, a process known among the Belize population as "milpa." When Waynforth studied the Belizeans, all the marriages were assumed to be monogamous, although a few of the men had been married and divorced and remarried. Despite the norm of monogamy, some men had extramarital affairs.

Waynforth interviewed the men extensively about how they spent their time when not working. The two major categories were "time spent with family and kin" and "mating effort," which in this case was restricted to time devoted to casual pickups. The time spent with family and kin included chores done around the house, time spent with one's wife, and time spent with siblings, parents, grandparents, and children. The time spent on casual encounters included all time spent in situations where the men were likely to meet other women. Two men hanging out at a village store was counted as mating effort, since women frequent the village store, and it was clear from the men's behavior that they were there to attract women. Waynforth photographed each man, and then subsequently had him rated by a panel of judges for facial attractiveness.

The results supported the theory of diminishing returns. More attractive men spent little time at home with wives and kin, but spent a lot of time engaged in activities in which they would meet other women. In contrast, less attractive men, usually unsuccessful in charming women, allotted far more time to tending the home nest, doing household chores, teaching children, and investing in the family. A man's attractiveness, in short, affects how he allots his limited time to getting outside sex or tending the home fires.

It's a law of nature that everyone reaches diminishing returns in spending time and energy on particular adaptive problems. Some individuals, by virtue of their greater attractiveness, take longer to hit the wall of wasted effort where what is reaped is not worth the effort expended on getting it. Sooner or later we all hit that wall.

Emotional and Sexual Satisfaction

Common sense and everyone's grandmother could tell you that people who are sexually and emotionally unhappy in their marriages are more likely to have affairs. Sometimes, however, the world is not what it seems.

The earth appears flat to us, but it is in fact round. The universe appears to us to have three dimensions of space and one of time, but astrophysicists tell us that it has as many as 11 dimensions. So it is with the psychological dynamics of marriage. Our folk wisdom sometimes leads us astray, or in the case of unhappiness and infidelity, partially astray.

Shirley Glass and Thomas Wright explored the link between marital happiness and extramarital affairs. To their amazement, the level of marital happiness seemed to have no effect on men's likelihood of infidelity. In fact, 56 percent of the men who were having affairs judged their marriage to be "very happy."

Glass related the following incident to illustrate the shattering of her initial beliefs about marital harmony and affairs: "Being a woman, I believed that if a man had an affair, it meant that he had a terrible marriage, and that he probably wasn't getting it at home—the old keep-your-husband-happy-so-he-won't-stray idea . . . I found that she could be everything wonderful, and he still might stray . . . a man I knew, married for 40 years, had recently died and his wife was so bereaved because they had the most wonderful marriage. He had been her lover, her friend, and her support system. She missed him immensely. I thought that was a beautiful story. When I told my husband about it, he got a funny look that made me ask, 'What do you know?' He proceeded to tell me that one night when he took the kids out for dinner to an out-of-the-way restaurant, that very man walked in with a young blonde woman. When he saw my husband, he walked out.

"I wondered what that meant. Did he fool his wife all those years and really not love her? How is it possible to be married for over 40 years and think you have a good marriage? It occurred to me that an affair could mean something different than I believed."

The link between marital dissatisfaction and affairs differs for men and women, and also depends on when in the marriage the affair takes place. In general, the marital satisfaction of all couples tends to show a gradual decline with the length of the marriage. The sole exception occurs with men who have affairs. Unlike all other groups, these men remained unusually happy with their marriages. This link failed to occur however, when the affair erupted early in the marriage. Early affairs signal disaster, and these men were extremely unhappy. But many men appear able to have affairs even when perfectly happy with their wives, contradicting grandmother's wisdom.

Folk wisdom, however, turns out to be absolutely on target for women. Most women who had affairs stated that they were extremely unhappy with their marriages. This sex difference provides a clue to the realization that affairs serve different adaptive functions for men and women. Men's affairs are more likely to be purely sexual; women's affairs are more often emotional. In Shirley Glass's study, 44 percent of the men who were having affairs declared that they had little or no emotional involvement with their affair partner. In the words of one man, "Why can't women understand that it's no different than playing tennis with a different partner; you'd get bored if you played with the same partner every time." The same study found that only 11 percent of the women having affairs reported little or no emotional involvement, revealing a huge sex difference.

In another study, Glass and Wright asked 148 men and 155 women what would justify an affair: "Here is a list of reasons that people sometimes give to explain why they have been involved with someone of the opposite sex outside their marriage in a very close relationship. To what extent would each of the following reasons justify either an emotional or a sexual extramarital relationship for you?" Women were far more likely than men to say that emotional factors, such as love, intimacy, sharing, and companionship would justify their affair. Men, in contrast, were more likely to cite sexual justifications—sexual novelty, change, experimentation, or mere curiosity.

Although the motives for men's affairs vary, and certainly some men have affairs because they are miserable in their marriages, the majority seem to have affairs to satisfy their lust for sexual variety, a lust that historically had a clear adaptive impetus. The functions of women's affairs remain more mysterious and complicated, and so warrant an entire chapter (see chapter 7).

One final sex difference must be described: what constitutes infidelity. Women think that spending time with someone of the opposite sex and keeping nonsexual secrets from one's partner constitutes infidelity; men do not. Men, on the other hand, are more likely than women to state that any sexual interaction with someone else constitutes an infidelity. The sexes evidently differ in the very definition of infidelity. This difference in our intuitive understanding of what constitutes an infidelity likely stems from the different adaptive threats men and women have faced over the long course of human evolution. Men, as we have seen, have faced the threat of paternity uncertainty, women the threat of loss of a partner's commitment. These differences influence how we define betrayal.

The Personality of the Unfaithful: Is Character Destiny?

Although most research has focused on the aspects of relationships such as relative desirability and emotional dissatisfaction that lead to affairs, an often-overlooked predictor of infidelity is personality. Are people with certain personality characteristics more likely to leap into the arms of another? To answer this question, Todd Shackelford and I gave an extensive battery of personality tests to a group of 107 married couples in their newlywed year. Rather than settle for mere self-reports of personality, we secured three relatively independent evaluations: self-reports, reports from the spouse, and reports from two interviewers, a man and a woman. More than 100 measures of personality were examined, ranging from adventurousness to zaniness, but only three proved to be strong predictors of susceptibility to infidelity.

The first was narcissism. People high on narcissism have a grandiose sense of self-importance, often exaggerating their accomplishments or talents. They expect to be recognized by others as superior, and often get infuriated when such admiration is not forthcoming. Typically preoccupied with fantasies of unlimited success, power, status, or brilliance, they believe that they are "special" and unique, and that the usual rules and norms of social life do not apply to them. Narcissists require excessive admiration and go to great lengths to evoke it from others, often in a socially charming manner. A hallmark of narcissism is a profound sense of entitlement. Narcissistic people have unreasonable expectations of favorable treatment, expect that others will automatically comply with their expectations, and become furious when they don't. They take advantage of others, and although all people sometimes use others for their own ends, narcissists turn interpersonal exploitation into an art form. They make friends specifically for their wealth, generosity, and connections, and especially for the ease with which they can be exploited. Narcissists selectively choose those whom they can exploit, neglecting people who are more skeptical of their grandiose claims of superiority and specialness.

Perhaps most central for infidelity, narcissists typically lack empathy for the pain and suffering they cause others. The are so preoccupied with their own needs and desires, they neglect to consider how their actions might hurt even those closest to them. Finally, narcissists are frequently envious of others, resentful of those who might have more success, power, or prestige. Their envy may be linked to their fragile sense of self-esteem, since narcissists oscillate between feelings of grandiosity and feelings that they are worthless. Good behavioral markers of narcissism include showing off one's body (exhibitionistic), nominating oneself for a position of power (grandiose), taking the best piece of food for oneself (self-centered), asking for a large favor without offering repayment (sense of entitlement), laughing at a friend's problems (lack of empathy), and using friends for their wealth (interpersonally exploitative). All of these qualities seem conducive to gaining gratification outside marriage.

Narcissism proved to be highly linked with susceptibility to infidelity, even in the first year of marriage. Narcissists admitted that they are more likely to flirt with others, kiss others passionately, and go out on romantic dates with others. Their spouses concurred. They were also judged to be more susceptible to having one-night stands, brief affairs, and even serious affairs, and again their spouses concurred. These judgments of susceptibility to infidelity were borne out over the next four years. On follow-up, we found that those who scored high on narcissism during their newlywed year were indeed more likely to have sexual affairs with others. Interestingly, narcissism proved to be as strong a "risk factor" for infidelity in women as in men.

Narcissists, of course, can be very charming, entertaining, and highly engaging in social contexts. But those married to them are in for some suffering. Because of their excessive self-absorption, wild sense of entitlement, and lack of empathy for the harm they cause others, narcissists seek sexual gratification and esteem boosts from affair partners. They undoubtedly justify their actions—after all, they are special, not subject to the same petty rules that others must slavishly follow, and so deserve special sources of gratification.

Two other personality characteristics make it more likely that a spouse will stray: being low on conscientiousness and being high on a scale labeled *psychoticism*. Low conscientiousness is characterized by traits such as unreliability, negligence, carelessness, disorganization, laziness, impulsivity, and lack of self-control. Good behavioral markers of low conscientiousness include neglecting to pay one's bills on time, forgetting to pick up a friend after promising to do so, forgetting to thank others for their help, arriving late for a meeting, forgetting to turn off the lights after leaving a room, and impulsively purchasing an item without considering whether it's affordable.

The psychoticism scale is something of a misnomer, since high scorers are not really psychotic. Rather, high scorers tend to be very impulsive and lack inhibitory control, much like those low on conscientiousness. In extreme cases, high scorers closely resemble the clinical picture of *sociopathy*, a personality disorder marked by a short-term sexual strategy, social conning, manipulativeness, and interpersonal exploitation. High scorers on this scale also lack empathy, like those high on narcissism. Good behavioral markers of psychoticism include laughing when a dog is hit by a car, showing indifference when a child is injured, suddenly breaking off friendships without warning or explanation, disappearing for several days without explanation, and impulsively shouting "obscenities" at other drivers he believes cut him off. Men, as you might guess, score higher on psychoticism than do women.

Both low conscientiousness and high psychoticism proved to be solid predictors of marital infidelity. Like those high on narcissism, these people flirted, kissed, and dated others more frequently than their more conscientious and less impulsive peers. And they more often leaped into bed with others without thinking of the consequences, both for one-night stands, brief flings, and even more serious affairs. These personality predictors showed remarkable consistency for men and women. Neither sex, it seems, is exempt from the long reach of personality in luring some married people into the enticing arms of others. A selfish, manipulative, and impulsive personality does not inevitably cause infidelity. But it raises the odds.

Do Some Spouses Drive Their Partners into the Arms of Others?

A more subtle predictor of infidelity involves the qualities of the spouse of the cheater. Do spouses with certain personality characteristics make married life sufficiently miserable that their partners seek love from others? To answer this question, Shackelford and I examined each of the personality characteristics of husbands and wives, and correlated them not with their own susceptibility to infidelity, but rather with their partner's susceptibility to infidelity. Two personality characteristics emerged as significant predictors: emotional instability and quarrelsomeness.

Emotional instability is a broad personality characteristic marked by large mood swings. During the normal stresses and strains of everyday life, emotionally unstable people tend to get thrown out of whack more easily than their more stable peers. Furthermore, they have a longer latency in returning to baseline, remaining upset for a longer duration after the distressing event. Good behavioral markers of emotional instability include obsessing over something they can do nothing about, putting themselves down repeatedly and without good reason, and agreeing to things without understanding why and without taking a stand of their own. On the positive side, emotionally unstable persons are more emotionally responsive than others, and this quality is sometimes linked with creativity. On the other hand, highly unstable individuals can turn a loving marriage into a living hell, and sometimes drive a partner to seek solace in the embrace of another.

When emotional instability is linked with another personality characteristic—quarrelsomeness—marriages turn into cauldrons of conflict. Precisely how this works was revealed in our long-term study of married couples. Quarrelsome spouses are condescending toward their partners, insist that their own opinions are superior to their partner's opinions, and

151

call their partner stupid. They neglect and reject their partner, laying the groundwork for the partner's needs to go unmet. They tend to abuse their partners emotionally, call their partners nasty names, and demean them in front of others. The combination of emotional instability with quarrelsomeness proves disastrous for the quality of the marriage, increases the probability of divorce, and can drive a spouse into another's arms.

The spouses of emotionally unstable and quarrelsome individuals are more likely to flirt, passionately kiss, and romantically date others. These spouses are also more likely to cross the sexual line and have intercourse with others, either for a single night or for a more enduring extramarital affair. It is as though affair partners provide a safe haven from the nightmare of their marriage, a refuge where they are appreciated rather than abused. It is not inevitable that quarrelsome and emotionally unstable individuals drive their spouses to seek gratification elsewhere, but these qualities raise the odds.

Cues to Infidelity: Sensitivity to Subtle Signals

The unfaithful rarely broadcast their betrayals. On the contrary, they take great pains to conceal all clues, meet in out-of-the-way places, mask telltale sexual scents, create alibis for unexplained absences, get close friends to cover for them, and generally try to act as if everything is normal. Concealment creates a co-evolutionary arms race between deception and detection of deception. Because the costs of discovery can be catastrophic, the unfaithful have become more and more skilled at evading detection. Because the costs to the betrayed are so severe, however, selection favors those who penetrate the mask of deception. In short, the co-evolutionary arms race has created exquisite sensitivity to the most subtle signals of betrayal, while simultaneously creating extraordinarily skilled evaders of detection.

In 1997, Todd Shackelford and I explored an array of cues to infidelity. As a first step, we asked 204 men and women to list clues that they believed would evoke suspicions of sexual or emotional infidelity, separately. On one form, labeled "Cues to a Partner's Sexual Unfaithfulness," we asked people to think of a past, current, or future romantic relationship, and then asked them: "What cues would lead you to suspect that your partner is sexually unfaithful to you?" On a separate form, labeled "Cues to a Partner Falling in Love with Someone Else," we asked: "What cues would lead you to suspect that your partner is falling in love with someone else?" We ended up with 170 cues, which provided the raw information for the subsequent study.

Our next study determined which cues were most diagnostic of sexual and emotional infidelity, and furthermore determined which cues were *differentially diagnostic* of the two types of infidelity. That is, which cues are more likely to signal a sexual betrayal rather than an emotional betrayal and vice versa?

The most diagnostic signal of *sexual infidelity* was rather obvious: actually discovering a partner in bed with someone else. Other signals were subtle. Physical signs include detecting the odor of sex or other unfamiliar scents, such as perfume, on the spouse. Another important signal involves abrupt or unexpected changes in the sexual interest of the spouse. A partner might suddenly have difficulty becoming sexually aroused, for example, or become more mechanical and bored when having sex. Rapid increases in sexual interest can also signal sexual infidelity—acting more interested in sex than usual, talking about sex more, or suddenly trying out new sexual positions.

Changes from the normal routines of everyday life can trigger alarm bells. Suddenly buying new clothes or changing clothing styles, for example, can signal a sexual infidelity. One woman, married to a dentist she found dull, started having an affair with an exciting and successful professor. She suddenly started wearing more tight-fitting clothing, had her belly button pierced, and walked with more flair and confidence. Eventually, after her husband discovered the affair and she broke it off with the professor, she returned to her previous duller style of clothing, had her navel ring removed, and appeared more demure in demeanor.

Other changes can also set off alarm bells—changes in food preferences, musical tastes, or even choice of books. The clinical literature brims with cases of the Othello syndrome inspired by a partner coming home with a trendy new shirt, developing a sudden interest in hip-hop or jazz, or becoming an avid reader of Updike or Nabokov.

We discovered that other signals are more diagnostic of *emotional infidelity*. The most obvious involved actual discussions of dissolution. The partner might start talking about the end of the marriage, for example, declaring that the love has gone out of the marriage, or might even suggest they begin seeing other people. A more subtle cue is emotional disengagement, such as failing to respond to a spouse's declaration of love. Ceasing to say "I love you" proved to be one of the most diagnostic cues of emotional infidelity. Forgetting their wedding anniversary, the spouse's birthday, and other special dates, as well as not sharing personal feelings with the partner are all manifestations of emotional disengagement. Displays of guilt proved more diagnostic of emotional than sexual infidelity: failing to look the partner in the eyes, being unusually apologetic toward the partner, and acting guilty after having sex with the partner.

Showing either a reluctance to discuss a specific person or an increased reference to a specific other person stand out as signals of emotional infidelity. Avoiding talking about another person or acting nervous when that person's name crops up in conversation revealed the reluctance side; beginning to mention another's name more frequently reveals the increased reference side. Perhaps most devastating, accidentally calling one's spouse by another person's name proved to be an especially strong signal, not to be recommended under any circumstances, but especially not when in bed with one's spouse! One woman I interviewed said that she made a point of calling both her husband and her lover "sweetheart" to avoid the possibility of slipping up in this manner.

Another potent cue to emotional infidelity involves becoming increasingly angry, critical, or inconsiderate of one's spouse. Looking for reasons to start arguments with one's partner, failing to consider the partner's needs, acting rude and abrupt, finding fault with trivial things, and becoming less gentle during sex also signal emotional detachment. The final sign is an increased apathy toward the partner. A spouse might get less excited than usual, less often invite the partner to spend time with him or her, fail to invite the partner to attend social events, and generally act bored.

An interesting pattern of sex differences surfaced in judgments of how diagnostic each cue was of infidelity. First, women are more likely than men to judge a wide array of clues as symptomatic of emotional infidelity: sexual disinterest, a partner's guilt and apathy, displays of anger and criticality, and emotional disengagement. It's important to stress that men are not oblivious to these signals. Rather, women seem more finely attuned to the subtle emotional changes in their husbands that might betray a change in emotional commitment.

The second sex difference pertains to a sensitivity to signals coming from the opposite sex. In our study, both men and women evaluated each cue when it was discovered in either a man or a woman. Women judged exactly the same cues—for example, emotional disengagement—to be more typical of men's infidelity than women's infidelity. Similarly, men judged cues such as emotional disengagement to be more characteristic of infidelity in women than in men. Women appear to be more sensitive to men's defections, and men to women's defections, which makes good adaptive sense. After all, the most severe adaptive threat comes from the infidelity of one's partner, not from the infidelity of members of one's own sex, except when same-sex friends lure one's partner into an affair— a double deception.

Aside from death, nothing is inevitable or assured, not good health, not lifelong love, and certainly not the fidelity of one's partner. Cues to infidelity get intentionally muted and muffled. Human minds have evolved to be extraordinarily sensitive to these inconspicuous whisperings. Our psychology of infidelity detection amplifies these signals because they pose an adaptive threat. We are sometimes wrong. Emotional disengagement might indicate a stressful day at the office rather than a passionate involvement with another. But those in our evolutionary past who ignored subtle signals of betrayal suffered reproductively relative to those who detected them.

Breaking Up

Worldwide, infidelity is the leading cause of divorce. In studies of Western cultures, as many as half of all divorcees cite a spouse's sexual infidelity as one of the primary reasons for the divorce. One woman put it this way: "I tried to forgive him, but every time we made love, the image of his lover invaded my mind. I saw her in my husband's arms, him embracing her, whispering into her ear. I could not shake these images, and so I had to end it." Not all couples, however, divorce following an infidelity. Some manage to stay together, patch things up, muddle through the bad part, and emerge from the violation to a new beginning. What distinguishes couples who stay together following an infidelity from those who break up?

As part of the study of 107 married couples, Shackelford and I asked each husband and wife, in private and separated from the glare of their partner's eyes, whether they would seek a divorce if their spouse engaged in intimacies with another. Husbands and wives, on average, showed strikingly similar estimates. In response to a partner flirting with someone else, only 4 percent of the husbands and 3 percent of the wives declared that they would seek divorce. This jumped to 20 percent and 21 percent for a partner passionately kissing someone else, and 36 percent and 37 percent for a partner going out on a romantic date with someone else. Responses to the more serious forms of sexual infidelity resulted in larger percentages. For both sexes, 49 percent declared that a partner's one-night stand would trigger a divorce, and 56 percent indicated that a partner's brief affair would trigger a divorce. The greatest estimates of divorce were reserved for a partner who had a serious affair. Fully 67 percent of the husbands and 69 percent of the wives avowed that this greatest of all violations would produce an irreparable breach. The most remarkable finding from this study is not that the severity of the infidelity raises the odds of divorce; rather, it's that nearly a third of the sample professed that they would *not* seek divorce, even after their partner had a serious affair with a rival. Who are these forgiving souls?

The relative mate value of the partners proved crucial, but primarily from the woman's perspective. Recall that male and female interviewers evaluated the physical attractiveness of each person and their "overall attractiveness as a potential mate (market value to opposite sex)." Wives judged as more physically attractive than their husbands stated that they would be more likely to divorce unfaithful husbands. Similarly, wives higher in mate value than their husbands declared that they would break from unfaithful husbands. Women who were *lower* than their husbands on attractiveness and mate value, in contrast, were more forgiving. These women indicated that they would probably remain with their husbands, even if these men had a one-night stand or a brief affair. It's as though these women thought: "I'm really lucky to be with him, and would have enormous difficulty replacing him with someone as desirable, so I'll stick it out."

A long-term study of 2,033 married couples supports this interpretation. Early in the study, each person was asked about their perceived marital alternatives. "These days, there are many uncertainties, and marriages break up unexpectedly. While it may be an unlikely event, I would like to ask you a few questions about how you would get along on your own if your marriage ended in divorce or separation. How difficult do you think it would be for you to find another (husband/wife)? Would it be very difficult, somewhat difficult, not too difficult, or not difficult at all?" The researchers also gathered information about each participant's income. The results dovetailed with those of our study. Women who perceived that they would have difficulty replacing their current partner were more likely to remain married if their husband cheated, whereas women who perceived their mating alternatives as more promising were more likely to get divorced. Furthermore, women who had higher levels of income were more likely to get divorced than women with less personal income.

Divorce is not an inevitable consequence of sexual infidelity. The odds depend heavily on the relative desirability of the partners. Those who are more desirable relative to their current mate have better options elsewhere, and hence are more likely to dump a cheating partner. With this background of the secrets and lies of married life, we now turn to a more targeted question: why women stray.

CHAPTER 7

Why Women Have Affairs

*You never seem to want to do anything with me anymore . . . When I try to talk
to you you never listen, you just put it down to my hormones, or it's a woman's
thing. I felt alone, insecure, unattractive, and stupid, lately, that's how you
make me feel. Robert makes me feel alive, and sexy, and interesting.*
— *Kitzinger and Powell*, Engendering Infidelity, 1995

WOMEN BEAR THE PLEASURES AND burdens of childbearing. Nine
months of internal gestation is metabolically costly, restricts a
woman's mobility, and makes her more vulnerable. Women don't have a
choice. No woman can scale back her investment to, say, four, six, or
eight months of pregnancy. Nor can the man directly share the load. One
woman I interviewed declared that she wished men could carry half of
the pregnancy, "preferably the second half!" In exchange for nine months
of a woman's obligatory investment, the man need put in as little effort
as it takes to complete a single act of sexual intercourse—an evening, an
hour, a few minutes, or even a few seconds. There are individual differences among men, of course, but the inescapable fact is that the biology
of reproduction is more costly for women.

These fundamental physiological sex differences led to the evolution
of several psychological sex differences; men view sex one way, women
another. Men evolved a more powerful desire for sexual variety, which
increased their chances of impregnating women. Men express a desire for
more than four times as many sex partners in their lifetimes, have more
than twice as many sexual fantasies, more often engage in partner switching during the course of a single fantasy episode, lower their standards to

abysmal levels in casual sex, let less time elapse before seeking sexual intercourse with a new partner, spend more time trying to initiate sex, and are more willing to consent to sex with a total stranger.

So powerful, direct, and obvious are the reproductive benefits to men who succeed in a quest for sexual variety that scientists have largely overlooked a fundamental fact about short-term mating: the average number of sexual partners for men and women who engage in short-term mating, of which infidelity is a primary variety, must be identical. Every time a man has sex with a particular woman for the first time, the woman is simultaneously having sex with that man for the first time. In fact, men could not possibly have evolved a desire for sexual variety without women who were willing. As noted by the feminist evolutionist Sarah Hrdy, of the University of California at Davis: "females . . . potentially determine the direction in which the species will evolve. For it is the female who is the ultimate arbiter of when she mates and how often and with whom."

If men's desires require willing women, willing women require benefits. Our ancestral mothers must have reaped advantages sufficiently weighty to more than exceed all of the treacherous costs of infidelity. Natural selection could not have forged a female psychology of infidelity if it failed to carry substantial advantages.

The idea that women are not by nature monogamous makes many men nervous. Women's sexual strategies, however, have evolved not for men's benefit, not for the good of the group, not even for the good of the species. Women's sexual psychology, including their desire to stray, exists today solely because that's what benefited ancestral women.

Co-evolution guarantees that women's sexual desires for men other than their husbands sometimes will be held in check. Men's jealousy drives them to control, sequester, constrain, coerce, restrict, stifle, isolate, lock up, box out, bind, enslave, encircle, truss, and shackle women. A man's jealousy tethers a woman's sexual strategies, preventing her from pursuing what is best, evolutionarily speaking, for her.

The principle of co-evolution also dictates that women will not accept jealous control passively. Over human history, women fought back, evolving an array of strategies specifically designed to escape men's control. Women have evolved concealed or cryptic ovulation most likely to disguise their time of ovulation, making it more difficult for men to target their mate-guarding to specific times of the month. But the fact of concealed ovulation, even if it evolved to escape a husband's control, does not explain why women stray. We now have some answers to this enigma.

The Scent of Symmetry

The logic of the mating market dictates that women will generally be able to get a more attractive partner for a casual sexual encounter than for a permanent husband. Attractive men are often willing to have sex with less desirable women, as long as they do not become encumbered by entangling commitments. Rock stars and sports stars perfectly illustrate this logic. They often have groupies for casual sex with no hint of commitment. This mating market logic leads to a disturbing consequence. Women married to men matched to their level of desirability will sometimes be tempted to have affairs with men whom they find sexier than their husbands.

Why risk discovery, ruin a good reputation, and chance abandonment by having an affair with a man higher than her partner on the mate value scale? Steve Gangestad and Randy Thornhill proposed one answer: Women can acquire better genes from higher value extrapair matings than from their regular mates. Good genes may bring better resistance to disease, increasing the health and hence survival of their children. Women, of course, don't think about these things consciously. Their passions for other partners are blind to the evolutionary functions that have shaped them. Women just need to find other men sexy; knowing why is unnecessary.

One indicator of good genes has emerged over the past decade: symmetry. Humans, like many organisms, show a physical arrangement characterized by bilateral symmetry. If you draw a line straight down the middle of your body, starting with your face, the two halves are more or less mirror images of each other. The "more or less" qualifier is the key, since no one is perfectly symmetrical. Each of us carries a host of small deviations from perfect symmetry, ranging from Cindy Crawford's small mole to Lyle Lovett's lopsided grin.

Deviations from symmetry have many causes, but they have been most strongly linked with two determinants. First, symmetry signals "developmental stability," a genetic resistance to pathogens and mutations. A person who is genetically susceptible to pathogens and mutations will develop a more lopsided face and body than those who are genetically resistant to pathogens and mutations. Second, symmetry is a sign of a genetic resistance to a host of other "environmental insults," such as extreme temperatures, poor nutrition in childhood, and exposure to toxins. It is, in short, a genetic marker of health.

Symmetry can be measured in practically any organism. With humans, researchers typically take a variety of measurements, such as feet, ankles, hands, wrists, elbows, and ears. By taking multiple measurements, researchers achieve a higher level of reliability in their index of actual symmetry. To study the effects of symmetry on human mating, Gangestad and Thornhill studied 203 heterosexual couples who had been involved in a romantic relationship for at least one month. After assuring participants of confidentiality and anonymity, they questioned each person about whether they had ever had sex with someone else while in their current relationship. They also queried participants about whether they had sex with someone else whom they knew was already married to, or seriously involved with, someone else. They then applied steel calipers to assess participants' degree of symmetry, taking seven measurements from each side of the body.

Gangestad and Thornhill discovered a groundbreaking result. Women preferentially chose symmetrical men as affair partners. Assuming that symmetry is a marker for genes for health, women who have affairs appear to select men who, for genetic reasons, are unusually healthy and whose genes then make children more healthy and resistant to diseases. Men who are rather asymmetrical are especially prone to being cuckolded by their more symmetrical rivals.

How do women "detect" such symmetrical men? The most obvious answer is simply to look. In extreme cases of asymmetry like Lyle Lovett or symmetry like Denzel Washington, women merely need to gaze through their own eyes. But there is a more subtle means by which women can detect symmetry—through their sense of smell. In an innovative study, Gangestad and Thornhill asked men who varied in symmetry to wear the same T-shirts for two days straight without showering or using deodorants. They instructed these men not to eat any spicy food— no peppers, garlic, onions, and so on. After two days, they collected the T-shirts, and then brought women into the laboratory to smell them. The women rated each shirt on how good or bad it smelled. They were of course not aware of the purpose of the study in advance, nor did they know the men who had worn the T-shirts. The fascinating finding was that women judged the T-shirts that had been worn by symmetrical men as more pleasant smelling, but only if they happened to be in the ovulation phase of their menstrual cycle. So one clue to the mystery of how women detect men with good genes lies with the "scent of symmetry."

Some women pursue a "mixed" mating strategy—ensuring devotion and investment from one man while acquiring good genes from another. Women detect the scent of symmetry, prefer that scent when ovulating, and choose more symmetrical men as affair partners. This may not be good news for lopsided men. After all, the genes a man is born with are beyond his control, and it may seem a gross injustice that women are more likely to cheat on these men. But women's sexual psychology is designed neither for fairness for nor justice. It is designed to help women reproduce more effectively, regardless of the pain inflicted on their partners.

There are two potential criticisms of this reasoning, but they turn out to crumble under close examination. The first is that modern women often don't want to have babies with their lovers, and so one might argue that the quality of their lover's genes is irrelevant. Women's sexual psychology, however, was forged in an evolutionary furnace lacking birth control. Sex led to babies regardless of a woman's conscious desire to reproduce or not. Ancestral women who had affairs with healthier, more symmetrical men tended to bear healthier, more symmetrical babies. Modern women have inherited from their successful ancestors an attraction to these men. The fact that roughly 10 percent of children today have genetic fathers other than their putative fathers suggests that these internal whisperings continue to operate today in the modern world.

A second possible objection is: Why wouldn't women want symmetrical mates as husbands as well as affair partners? The answer, of course, is that they should and do. But the economics of the mating market means that most women are able to attract a more symmetrical man as an affair partner than as a husband. Some women, in short, are able to get the best of both worlds—attracting investment from one man while obtaining superior genes from another.

Sexy Sons

Men's obsession with a woman's physical appearance and sexual availability results in what many women experience as objectification, or being treated as "sex objects." But men don't hold the monopoly on sexual objectification. The modern phenomenon of female rock groupies provides a perfect example. Groupies typically get neither investment nor attention nor much time from the rock stars whom they seek for sex. As Pamela des Barres observed in her book *I'm with the Band: Confessions of a Groupie,* a half-hour "quickie" can make a groupie's day. Most of these women do not delude themselves that the male rock star will fall in love with them, have a relationship with them, or even remember their names in the morning. And they risk a lot by such brief flings—the loss of their regular boyfriends and the possibility of contracting sexually transmitted diseases. Why do they do it?

My studies with Heidi Greiling support an intriguing idea known as the theory of "sexy sons." Women who mate with sexy men tend to bear sexy sons. When these "sexy sons" grow up, they attract an above-average number of women, thereby gaining a genetic edge on the competition. Their mothers gain in ultimate reproductive success through the increased reproduction of their sexy sons.

When evaluating what qualities women want in a one-night stand outside of their regular relationship, women topped out in requiring the following attributes (using a 1–9 scale): sexy (8.7), highly desirable to the opposite sex (8.2), desires sex with you a lot (8.2), sensuous (8.2), physically attractive (8.6), good looking (8.3), sought after by members of the opposite sex (8.3), thinks you are sexy (8.3), and greatly desires you (8.3). Contrary to what women want in a regular partner, women seeking brief flings appear to go for the "studly" charmers who have what it takes to bed a variety of women. These are precisely the qualities that would give their sons a mating advantage in the next generation.

These same qualities shine through when women express the minimum percentile they require for various types of relationships. The contrast between the minimums women express for regular mates and for one-night stands is especially striking because women relax their standards for many qualities when seeking brief encounters. For degree of education, for example, women required husbands to be in the 61st percentile, but for one-night stands they required only the 47th percentile. In sharp contrast, women became more exacting in a one-night stand on precisely the qualities one would expect according to the theory of sexy sons. Whereas they wanted their husband to be in the 58th percentile on sexiness, they wanted their brief flings to be in the 76th percentile. On physical attractiveness, they required husbands to be only in the 54th percentile, but demanded the 77th percentile for one-night stands. In brief encounters, it seems, women demand sexy partners who are highly desirable to other women, perhaps because their sons stand a greater chance of being sexy themselves. Women, of course, do not think these thoughts; there is no conscious calculus of genetic effects. They just find some men sexy and that's all they need to produce sons who will be sexually successful.

Mate Insurance

Imagine that you are on a camping trip. You wake up in the morning with an empty stomach and a need to urinate. As you go about your business, the sun beats down on your head and thirst parches your throat, and you quickly come to appreciate the nearby stream with its cold, clean water. But it's time to head off for the day. You pack your gear and look around. Your growling stomach signals the need to eat. Your crying baby is hungry. You want to venture out, but there are possible dangers—wild animals, snakes, and perhaps hostile humans. Now imagine that this camping trip lasts not a few days or weeks, but your entire lifetime. This is what our ancestors faced, roaming the savannas of Africa.

In our ancestors' daily struggle to survive, they obtained food through their own labors—gathering or hunting—or else garnered it from the labors of others. Cold winters battered precarious shelters. Deep freezes rendered fruit and game scarce. Hungry children cried at night, signaling the extra mouths that needed feeding. Could a woman always have relied on only one man? What if he left her to be with another woman? What if he became sick or injured, hampering his ability to hunt? And what would she do when her husband left for three or five days on an extended hunt, leaving her vulnerable to possible exploitation at the hands of other men? One solution to all these problems is to take out mate insurance—cultivate an affair partner as a backup mate.

People normally purchase insurance as a hedge against unpredictable disasters: car insurance in case of an accident, house insurance in case of a fire or flood, and disability insurance in case of unexpected personal injury. Mate insurance works in an analogous manner. Cultivating a backup mate provides security in the event that a regular mate gets injured or killed, infected with some disease, loses status within the group, fails to provide food, becomes abusive, mistreats the children, or defects from the relationship. The monthly premiums women pay for mate insurance are not financial; they are sexual.

The backup mate can serve many functions when the regular mate is not around. He can defend against predators, fend off aggressive men who might otherwise exploit the absence of a regular mate, or provide food during a shortage. As the biologist Robert Smith notes, "Females could likewise venture sex on a good prospect against the possibility of some future return in material resources . . . a hedge against the possibility that a principle mate will be unable or unwilling to supply sufficient resources."

According to the mate insurance hypothesis, women should select affair partners in part based on their ability and willingness to provide resources and protection. To explore what women want, Heidi Greiling and I asked a large sample to rate the desirability or undesirability of 139 characteristics in a potential affair partner. The rating scale ranged from

1 (*highly undesirable in an affair partner*) to 5 (*neutral*) to 9 (*highly desirable in an affair partner*). Any characteristics rated 7 or higher are considered very desirable.

The protection factor permeated women's preferences. Women expressed a desire for affair partners who were athletic (7.7), protective of her (9.0), strong (7.8), muscular (7.8), and physically fit (8.2). All these qualities are signs of a man's ability and willingness to protect a woman and her existing children. In our in-depth interviews with women about what they wanted in an affair partner, most vehemently denied that they were looking for someone with the physique of an Arnold Schwarzenegger or a Sylvester Stallone. They found those bodies overblown and worried that muscle-bound men were overconcerned with their physical appearance. But they did want a man who could handle himself physically with other men—a man in good shape, fit, strong, athletic, well toned, and willing to step in when the situation called for it.

Although most systems of morality condemn women who have affairs, these relationships apparently served an extremely important function for our ancestral mothers, providing mate insurance in the event that they needed protection from abuse or if something unfortunate befell their regular mates.

Trading Up

The famous anthropologist Margaret Mead once was asked why she had such a long history of failed marriages. She replied: "I have been married three times, and not one of them was a failure." A woman I interviewed told me that relationships with men are like tires; some get better mileage than others, but eventually they all wear out. These two anecdotes, of course, do not add up to scientific evidence. But the fact is that a host of circumstances could cause a woman to want to "trade up" in the mating market, and affairs can be used to evaluate potential husbands.

According to Helen Fisher, several ancestral conditions set the stage for the evolution of women's psychology of trading up. First, a woman's partner may decline in mate value due to injury or disease. Second, a woman's own value may have increased over time as she became more proficient at gathering, extended her political alliances, or proved to be especially fecund. Third, in ancestral times, contact with a new tribe may have increased exposure to more desirable potential partners.

There are several other circumstances that might have caused a woman to trade up. Her regular mate might have become emotionally or physically abusive, inflicting costs that were not apparent when she selected him. One modern woman described her affair in these terms, implicitly implicating her abusive husband as a reason: "Yes, I'm not as afraid to say what I want to say. I don't think I kowtow to my husband as much as I used to, I don't let him hurt my feelings as easily as I used to 'cause I silently think that someone else loves me. And if this man, my husband, is getting mad and raging at me, ridiculing me, then I don't bow and paw as much as I used to."

Some husbands become "slackers" over time, failing to provide resources that they formerly provided. A man could start affairs with other women, diverting a portion of his resources to his affair partners and their children. He could prove infertile, rendering the relationship reproductively barren. For all these reasons, selection may have fashioned a female sexual psychology of mate switching.

To test the trading-up hypothesis, Heidi Greiling and I examined the desires women express for affair partners, and contrasted them with desires women express for one-night-stand partners and long-term mates. If an important function of affairs is to evaluate the affair partner as a potential long-term mate, then a woman's desires for an affair partner should be similar to what she wants in a spouse, but different from those expressed for a one-night-stand partner. Women in our study supported this idea. In both an affair partner and a husband, women wanted men who were above the 70th percentile on the following qualities: dependable, affectionate, successful, emotionally stable, easygoing, intelligent, mature, faithful, honest, open-minded, and unselfish. In sharp contrast, women's minimum thresholds for nearly all of these qualities in a one-night-stand partner dipped below the 50th percentile.

Our studies of women's perceptions of the benefits of affairs and the circumstances that impel them also supported the trading up function. One woman told us that her affair made it easier to break up with her husband. Another revealed that her affair made her realize that she could find someone more compatible with her than her husband. A third said that she had married young, and the affair made her realize that she did not have to settle for a man who failed to meet her standards.

Mate switching is the result of two related conditions: being stuck with a regular mate who fails to bring in economic resources, thus violating her desire for provisioning; and meeting someone who can better provide those resources. Each woman in our study evaluated three crucial circumstances as predisposing her to have an affair: When her current partner can't hold down a job, when she meets someone who has better financial prospects than her current partner and who seems interested in her, and when she meets someone who is more successful than her current partner.

This does not necessarily imply that a woman always marries her affair partner. Sometimes she does, sometimes she doesn't. But even when she doesn't, the affair typically gives her enough confidence in her own desirability to catalyze a break. The affair, by boosting a woman's self-esteem, makes her more certain that she can trade up to someone better. Here is what one woman reported:

"Yes, it built up my confidence and ego seeing that other men were attracted to me, things that I really didn't know before. It's given me a whole new way of looking at myself. It changed my whole way of dress, just my whole appearance. I felt attractive again. I hadn't felt that way in years, really. It made me very, very confident."

The most common domain of self-esteem enhancement pertains to the woman's body and sexuality—qualities critical to her value on the mating market for trading up. One woman reported these effects of her affair: "I think I'm more sure of myself and I don't think I have to prove any kind of sexiness like I used to." After interviewing 50 women who were having affairs, Lynn Atwater concluded that "most of the change in self-confidence was rooted in a sense of being more physically appealing because they knew other men were interested in them." Since physical attractiveness is critical to a woman's mate value, an affair can elevate a woman's self-appraisal of her physical desirability, giving her the confidence to leave her current partner in the quest for trading up to someone better.

Not all boosts in self-confidence as a result of affairs were linked with sexuality and appearance. One woman reported: "I have more self-confidence, a feeling of independence and self-reliance that I didn't have before . . . an understanding that I have resources and abilities too to meet those needs if I have to, and that I could call on them again if I need to."

Our more systematic studies of women's perceptions of the benefits of affairs supported the case-report evidence. Greiling and I found that women who had affairs judged the effects on self-esteem to be among the most beneficial consequences of affairs. On a 5-point scale, women judged the following consequences of affairs to be among the most beneficial: "Affair partner made me feel better about myself than any man had done" (3.87); "I felt good about myself because my affair partner respected me" (3.68); "Because my affair partner was interested in the details of my life, I felt good about myself when I was with him" (3.55); and "Because my affair partner was emotionally sensitive to me, my self-esteem increased" (3.43). The mate-switching benefit of affairs is supported even more directly in the following item, which also ranked among the most beneficial consequences of women's affairs: "I was able to make better decisions about long-term partners because I felt good about myself" (3.23).

Women see "being made to feel beautiful" as an extremely important benefit of affairs, especially after a husband's long-term boredom has set in. Finding a fresh partner who appreciates one's assets can give new meaning to life. And let's face it—the hundredth time a husband tells you that you are beautiful, usually out of habit, does not have the same toniclike effect as the first few times from a fresh lover. The boost in self-esteem is undoubtedly enhanced when the affair partner profoundly values the woman in ways that are not just sexual. Women judged the items "My sexual partner made me feel important" and "My sexual partner made me feel intelligent," for example, to be among the most beneficial aspects of affairs.

Girls Just Want to Have Fun

"Oh, Christ, I could write a book! Ah, comparatively, he is a fantastic lover . . . The physical thing, you know, between Jim and I is absolutely incredible. It's probably—it's the major thing even with all this intellectual closeness, it's primarily, you know, a good fuck . . . He has really opened me up as a lover even more than my first. I do things with him that I can't do at home."

"Sexually it was really great for me. He was more sexually satisfying, more physical. I was more physically attracted to him, I was just absolutely in love with his body."

"Our sexual relationship is totally different. I guess that's where the crux of it is. It's certainly where it initially was and although all other things with Peter are wonderful, it's still the main drawing card to stay involved in the relationship. I'm orgasmic with both. Sex with my husband is straight fucking and oral-genital contact which is all nice, but it's not passionate. It's pretty much all we do. My husband and I almost never, ever kiss. There is little time spent in bed before we fuck. We don't fuck very often . . . It's not really a turn-on like it is with Peter. I think Peter is the greatest lover in the world. That's obviously subjective, but I will bet that other women who've made it with him will say that, too."

When Heidi Greiling and I began to interview women about their affairs, one prominent theme emerged repeatedly: sexual gratification. In our very first study of women's perceptions of the benefits of affairs, sexual gratification was at the top of the list. Our initial sample of 90 women judged it to be "highly likely" that a woman would receive sexual gratification from an affair partner, more likely than any of the 28 potential benefits in the initial study. When we asked women to evaluate which circumstances would be most likely to open them up to an affair, sexual unhappiness with regular partners loomed large: "my current partner is unwilling to engage in sexual relations with me"; "sexual relations with my current partner have been unsatisfying for a long time"; and "sexual relations with my current partner are too infrequent for me."

Moreover, women rated experiencing sexual gratification with an affair partner to be one of the most important benefits of an extramarital affair. Orgasms in particular seem especially important, as women rate these as more beneficial than merely receiving sexual gratification.

Our exploration was motivated in part by a theory of female orgasm that may provide an explanation for the importance women place on sexual gratification with an affair partner, the "sperm retention" theory proposed by two British biologists, Robin Baker and Mark Bellis of the University of Manchester in England. To understand the sperm-retention theory, we must introduce the broader theory of sperm competition.

Sperm competition occurs when the sperm from two different men inhabit the woman's reproductive tract at the same time. Although the woman's egg, once ovulated, is only viable for 12 to 24 hours, men's sperm have a longer shelf life. Sperm can remain viable within the woman's moist tract for up to seven days. The upshot is this: if a woman has sex with two different men within the span of a work week, then she sets the stage for the men's sperm to compete with each other in the race to her valuable egg.

Is there any evidence that humans have a long evolutionary history of sperm competition? The answer now is a resounding yes, for both men's and women's physiology and passions have been adapted to the demands of sperm competition. One source of evidence comes from studies that attempt to determine the rates of "misidentification" of the father. Averaging across a handful of studies of paternal discrepancy from Europe, Africa, North America, and Oceania, Baker and Bellis estimate that roughly 9 percent of children have genetic fathers who are different from those who believe that they are the father. A medical researcher I interviewed confirmed this estimate. She conducted a large-scale study of the genetics of breast cancer that required DNA fingerprinting of children and their parents. Although it was not the goal of her study, she calculated the incidence of mistaken paternity and found a paternal discrepancy rate of 10 percent—findings she did not publish because she feared that her grant funding might be jeopardized. These surprising statistics tell us that women sometimes conceive and bear children by men who are not their husbands, and probably have done so throughout human evolutionary history.

Physiological clues also betray a long history of sperm competition. First, men's testis size and sperm volume are far larger than those of the more monogamous primates such as gorillas or gibbons. This clue suggests that men have evolved a larger ejaculate to increase the odds of successful competition by crowding out the sperm from competing men. Second, men's sperm come in several predictable shapes, not merely the government-issue conical shape sperm that are designed for swimming speed. As discussed in chapter 1, men possess "kamikaze" sperm, coil tailed and terrible at swimming, that have been observed in laboratory studies to wrap themselves around competing sperm and destroy them while simultaneously self-destructing. Furthermore, these sperm appear designed to position themselves within the female reproductive tract to interfere with the progress of their competitors in the race for the eggs.

The early work on sperm competition often emphasized the male arsenal, with women more or less passively setting the stage for the battle. Recent work, however, has focused on the active role that women play in influencing the outcomes of what has variously been described as a "lottery," a "race," and more ominously a "war."

Imagine taking a field course in biology in the exotic location of Calahonda, Spain. You are grouped with 50 undergraduate students, eight graduate students, and three senior instructors. The sex ratio is slightly biased—more men than women. You've left your regular partner behind, hundreds or thousands of miles away. You sleep under the stars on a flat roof of the villa, along with everyone else. The brilliant beaches, azure days, and starry nights provide a romantic setting, as you work side by side with others in the group exploring the mysteries of life on earth. This was precisely the setting for one of Robin Baker's studies, and human nature being what it is, romances often developed as the memory of the partner at home faded with the sunset. People shared their exotic experiences with new partners.

According to Baker, women's concealed ovulation is among the major weapons women have evolved to shop around for superior genes for their children. By concealing ovulation, women made it more difficult for a regular mate to guard them during their more fertile time of the month. Concealment set the stage for sperm competition, giving women the opportunity to be fertilized by men of their own choosing.

In the Calahonda study, 37 percent of the 57 women arrived in Spain without their regular partner. Of these women, 21 percent ended up having an affair. Given that the field course lasted only two weeks, this rate of infidelity is unusually high. Perhaps women drawn to a field course in biology in such an exotic location might differ from women more likely to stay at home. Or perhaps the romantic locale, combined with the distance from their regular partner and the low risk of discovery, led to the high rate of infidelity.

Two factors predicted whether mated women would have sex with a new partner: symmetry and length of relationship. Women who were more symmetrical tended to stray more than women who were less symmetrical, perhaps because they were judged to be more attractive, and hence had greater opportunities. And women in longer relationships tended to remain more faithful than women who had been coupled with their distant partner only briefly.

One of the most startling findings to emerge from the studies of sperm competition, including the surveys and the Calahonda study, centers on women's sexual orgasm, one of the factors most closely linked with women's sexual satisfaction. Women have more "high sperm retention" orgasms with their affair partner than with their regular partner, as indexed by the amount of sperm contained in the "flowback" collected after intercourse. Furthermore, women seem to time their orgasms with their affair partners to coincide more closely with when they ovulate. These findings, together with the theory of sperm competition, may solve the puzzle of why women place such importance on sexual gratification as a benefit from extramarital liaisons.

In the modern world, with many women taking contraceptives, the connection between sexual orgasms and actual reproduction may be severed. But women's sexual psychology, forged over millions of years in an ancestral world devoid of the pill, continues to get played out in the modern world. The importance to women of sexual gratification, and orgasms in particular, may be a key motive driving women to act on their unfaithful passions.

It's possible, of course, that this theory is wrong. Don Symons argues that female orgasm lacks an adaptive function. He draws an analogy to men's nipples, which have no function, but are merely incidental byproducts of the common design men share with women early in development. Women's nipples and men's orgasm have clear functions: to breastfeed a baby and to ejaculate sperm into the woman's reproductive tract, respectively. But women's orgasm, like men's nipples, have no evolutionary purpose, Symons suggests. He may be right. But the weight of the evidence from several labs around the world is weighing in against the interpretation that women's organism is a byproduct.

Women I've talked to tend to have strong opinions on the topic. When I recently gave a lecture on these findings at the London School of Economics, a woman afterward gave me a cartoon that beautifully illustrated this point. Two peahens are staring at a peacock, who is striving valiantly to display his plumage to them with a maximum of flourish. One of the peahens tries to stop him with this quip: "Cut the crap and show us your willy!"

Whether women's orgasm proves to have a function, as seems likely, or whether Symons turns out to be right, the competing theories have had the healthy effect of stimulating more research on this neglected side of women's sexuality.

Some Women Some of the Time

Generalizations about "women" are always problematic for one fundamental reason—not all women are alike. General trends are important, but we must also consider the variability within each sex. Some women delight in affairs, gaining self-esteem and a bounty of other benefits. Other women express horror at the mere thought of breaking marital vows. Women have a varied menu of sexual strategies at their disposal. The strategic combinations they select depend on individual circumstances.

Do women who pursue a strategy of extrapair mating have a different cost-benefit evaluation system than monogamous women? Is their behavior driven by the perception that more profound benefits will flow from casual flings? If so, precisely which benefits do these women perceive to be forthcoming?

To answer these questions, Heidi Greiling and I contrasted women who were actively pursuing a short-term sexual strategy with those who remained monogamous. They differed substantially in their perceptions of benefits. The short-term strategists perceived two key benefits as more likely to be reaped: receiving sexual gratification from an affair partner and elevating their self-esteem because more than one man found them sexually attractive.

The greatest differences between the two groups, however, centered not on how likely these benefits were to be received, but rather on how beneficial they would be when they were received. Women who are short-term sexual strategists perceive the direct sexual rewards to be far more beneficial than do women adopting a monogamous strategy—rewards such as engaging in sexual experimentation, experiencing more sexual orgasms, getting pleasurable sexual stimulation aside from orgasms, and receiving oral sex from the affair partner that her regular partner was unwilling to provide. Sexual benefits seem more important for women who persue a multiple-mate strategy.

Other rewards centered on the acquisition of resources: receiving expensive designer clothing, becoming friends with high-status others, discovering other attractive partners through the affair partner, and advancing a career. The more promiscuous women appear to capitalize on their sexuality by using multiple partners to gain status, material goods, and access to a wider pool of potential mates. These women have the sex appeal to secure such benefits.

The final cluster of rewards involves the cultivation of new skills and abilities: improving techniques of attraction, for example, and being better able to seduce a man because of experience gained through an affair partner. Some women see affairs as vehicles for honing their mating skills to become more successful at implementing a short-term mating strategy or to attract a more desirable permanent partner.

Why do some women pursue a monogamous mating strategy while others opt for a strategy of multiple partners? One possibility is that casual strategists possess more abundant sexual assets that allow them to be more successful in garnering the various benefits from a short-term strategy. A woman with less sex appeal may be more limited in her successes in this domain. According to this explanation, casual strategists should be viewed as more "sexy" than monogamous women, although not necessarily more "attractive." Although sexiness and attractiveness are correlated, some women are more sexy than attractive, whereas others are more attractive than sexy. The actress Ellen Barkin, for example, might be judged highly sexy, but not necessarily at the top in pure beauty. Meryl Streep, in contrast, might be judged to be highly attractive, but not necessarily at the top in raw sex appeal. If the "ability to successfully implement the strategy" explanation is correct, then Ellen Barkin would be more able to thrive in short-term pursuits, whereas Meryl Streep would be more successful going for monogamy.

Another possible explanation is that some women lack the ability to hold on to a highly investing man in the long term, and so opt for a strategy of multiple partners. Which strategy a woman pursues depends on a variety of circumstances: the time in her life, the assets she can parlay, and the social setting in which the sexual strategy is implemented.

Why Not to Stray

With all the potential advantages women can gain through affairs, one puzzle is why more women do not stray more of the time. To understand why many women decline to go after superior genes, additional resources, mate insurance, or trading up, we must return to the principle of co-evolution and identify the costs of infidelity.

Benefits from a woman's affairs come at a cost to her regular mate. Men don't like being cuckolded. Co-evolutionary logic tells us that men have evolved strategies to prevent reproductive losses by guarding their wives more diligently and punishing them for signs of straying through verbal abuse, emotional manipulation, jealous rages, beatings, and sometimes the threat of death. Men make it costly for women to stray—costs that deter many women at least some of the time. Women's infidelity, in turn, has become more cryptic, enigmatic, and deceptive over evolutionary time to evade these costs. Each increment in female concealment creates selection pressures on men to be even more vigilant and inflict even more deterrents. In the current never-ending co-evolutionary spiral, both sexes are armed with weapons and defenses, counter-weapons, and counter-defenses.

Each woman's decision to stay or stray hinges on cost-benefit calculations based on the quality of her regular partner, the benefits she could gain through an infidelity, the odds of discovery, and the costs she will suffer if discovered. Heidi Greiling and I explored 50 of these costs. Only one occurred regardless of whether the affair was discovered—an increased probability of contracting a sexually transmitted disease. The other 49 potential costs hinged on whether the infidelity was discovered.

The most obvious toll is the loss of the woman's regular partner. A female friend told me that she seriously contemplated an affair after the boredom from her 10-year marriage set in, but she refrained solely because she did not want to risk losing her husband, a medical doctor with a healthy income. As Laura Betzig documented in her massive cross-cultural study, infidelity more than any other cause impels men to divorce their wives.

Another obvious cost centers on violence at the hands of the husband, as documented earlier. Unfaithful women risk being beaten or killed. The actual acts of destruction are as revealing as they are abhorrent. In one study of 100 battered women, the researchers catalogued women's injuries and found that they had been attacked with fists, kicks, and belts, and had suffered from suffocation, burns, and scalds. Some women had broken noses, teeth, and ribs, and others had dislocated shoulders and jaws. Nine of the 100 women required hospitalization, and two of these were unconscious at admission. Two suffered retinal damage, resulting in permanent defective vision; one sustained an injury that penetrated her skull; and two developed epilepsy as a result of their head injuries. Our studies confirm that women are acutely aware of these costs, admitting that being physically abused by a partner when he found out about the affair was highly likely, and they evaluate it to be 4.9 in costliness on the 5-point scale.

The damage caused by abuse is also borne by the woman's children. If she is injured or dies as a result, she is unable to protect and provide for them. If her husband abandons her as a consequence of her betrayal, her children are in jeopardy of greater violence at the hands of others. Stepchildren suffer a 40 times higher rate of physical abuse compared with children living with both biological parents, most often by the step-father, who typically lacks the deep love for the child that comes naturally to the genetic parent. Children without an investing father can suffer a 10 percent lower survival rate.

Even if the man decides to stay, he may continue to punish her for straying. On top of psychological and physical abuse, some men retaliate with an affair of their own. Since men typically channel resources to sex partners, the wife and her children also risk losing those resources.

Women whose affairs are discovered sometimes risk abuse at the hands of their fathers or brothers as well. In some Mediterranean cultures, brothers kill their sisters and fathers kill their daughters in order to salvage the "family honor" when the women are caught betraying their husbands. In less extreme cases, family members may ostracize the woman, and refuse to invest in her children. In our study, women judged the item "family stopped supporting me emotionally when they found out about my affair" as one of the most costly consequences, giving it a 4.8. Women judged "family stopped supporting me financially when they found out about the affair" to be nearly as costly, giving it a 3.9 on the 5-point scale. Loss of investing kin could have been catastrophic for ancestral women and their children.

In addition to these hardships, women whose affairs are discovered jeopardize their social reputation. I recall a recent case of a woman who discovered another woman's earrings in a crease in the sofa one afternoon while cleaning. When she confronted her husband, he confessed and revealed the owner of the earrings, who happened to be the wife's "best friend," married, and a member of a garden club to which both couples belonged. At the next meeting of the garden club, the aggrieved wife stood up and denounced her friend as a "slut" and a "whore" for sleeping with her husband. Thereafter, the other members of the garden club shunned the adulteress, and she was forced to quit the club.

Our study revealed several facets of reputation damage, all hovering around 4.0 on the costliness index. Women risk social shunning by friends, family, work colleagues, church groups, social clubs, and higher-status peer groups. They also risk losing the respect of their children when they find out about the affair, which women in our study judged to be 4.9 in costliness.

The final cost centered on a loss to self-esteem, which may seem paradoxical, since women's self-esteem is often boosted as a result of an infidelity. The apparent paradox is resolved when we consider the different sources of esteem. We often base our evaluations of ourselves on the esteem in which we are held by others. Women who suffer social shunning, therefore, will lose self-esteem. The boost in a woman's self-esteem, in contrast, comes not from her peers but from the affair partner who finds her intelligent, charming, and attractive. The end result is that a woman's infidelity can have two different, and contrasting, effects on her self-esteem: the boost in self-esteem comes early in the course of the infidelity, prior to its discovery; the loss comes later, and only if the infidelity is discovered and ends in disaster. As Robert Frank of Cornell University observes, "With the illicit affair, the difficulty is that the rewards occur right away. Its costs, by contrast, are both uncertain and in the future."

Although the benefits from straying can be substantial, the potential damage often offsets these gains. There is a double standard in these costs. Women caught having an affair, in contrast to men caught having an affair, suffer a greater risk of physical abuse, more severe damage to their reputations, a higher risk of being shunned by family and friends, a greater loss in self-esteem, and a higher vulnerability to abandonment. My study concerning the psychology of reputation in Zimbabwe, Eritrea, China, Guam, Russia, Brazil, Poland, Korea, and Transylvania verifies that the double standard is widespread.

To Fling or Not to Fling

We inhabit a modern social landscape that is forever changed from the Stone Age world in which our sexual psychology evolved. The anonymity of large city living creates more opportunities to carry out affairs undiscovered, compared with the small group living arrangements of our prehistoric ancestors in which it was hard to conceal a sneeze, much less a torrid affair. By lowering the risk of discovery, modern conditions lower the odds that women will suffer the costs of infidelity.

In contrast to the ancestral pattern of small group living with only a handful of potential partners to choose from, modern urban living provides thousands. Opportunities for trading up present themselves daily.

Repeated exposure to new potential partners, whose flaws remain concealed on first encounters, can create dissatisfaction with a current partner whose charms have worn thin with time.

Modern work conditions also differ from ancestral ones. In hunter-gatherer societies, division of labor often kept the sexes segregated. Women brought in economic resources through gathered plants and tubers, cared for children, prepared meals, and kept the home fires burning. Men hunted large game, mostly in the company of other men. In the modern sexually integrated workplace, men and women who share similar interests work side by side for eight or more hours each day. Repeated workplace flirtations flower into perilous passions.

Modern women share with their ancestral mothers the strategy of infidelity within their menu of mating. Our sexual strategies have changed little, but the social world we now inhabit differs profoundly. These changes increase the benefits of infidelity and decrease the costs, tilting cost-benefit calculations toward a greater temptation to stray. In a world of fast food and fast mating, we must learn to cope.

CHAPTER 8

Coping Strategies

Once habit has dulled the edge of jealousy, a number of men may drink from a single love chalice without repugnance and without rancor while the woman knowing that she is desired and being skilled in the art of rendering happy those who seek her out, proceeds to dispense her caresses and her affections in just and sapient nature.

—*Paolo Mantegazza,* The Sexual Relations of Mankind, 1935

Big boys don't cry.

—*Guerrero and Reiter,* Sex Differences and Similarities
in Communication, 1998

JONATHAN USED FIELD GLASSES TO spy on his wife from afar. After pretending to leave the house for work, he would secretly reenter the house in an attempt to trap his wife with her lover. He searched the house repeatedly for evidence of her infidelity. He accused his children of conspiring to conceal their mother's "lechery." Several times he threatened neighbors with violence. He developed a "sinister habit" of walking around with a razor in his pocket. He frequently expressed the wish to keep his wife perpetually pregnant so that he could keep her "fully occupied." He kept her up late many nights attempting to satisfy what he thought was her "insatiable lust" in order to dissuade her from satisfying it elsewhere. His methods of coping kept his wife faithful, but at a tremendous cost to himself and his family.

In Barbados, Verity, a 43-year-old woman, worked as a nurse, pulling down a small but reliable salary. She lived with her husband for three years before they married. Although most of these early years were marked by poverty, she felt content as long as her husband loved her. But the love soon started to wane, and Verity became increasingly unhappy at her husband's failures to provide, both emotionally and materially. He frequently asked her for money, leaving her with bills unpaid and shelves unstocked. Before long, Verity learned that her husband had been having an affair with a very young girl. She discovered not only that her husband had been spending *her* money on the other girl but also that they had sometimes had sex in her own bed. The final straw was Verity's discovery of two plane tickets for a vacation for her husband and his lover, tickets purchased with Verity's hard-earned money.

To cope with this escalating sequence of betrayals, she sought the advice of a woman renowned for her wisdom and took the following steps. Verity first depleted all the money from their joint bank account and went to another bank to open an account solely in her own name. Next, she traveled to the city where her rival resided. She sat on her rival's stairs for hours until the young woman appeared, then "just grabbed her, and I just take her [inside] near the cooker and near the pot," threatening to dunk the young woman's face in boiling water if she did not keep her hands off her husband.

Verity did not divorce her husband, since she feared that he would get the house and all of their possessions, acquired through her own labors. But she did take a lover. She concealed her own infidelity from her husband, instead meeting her lover in his car, always away from areas where they might be known or discovered. Although none of this erased the pain she felt about her husband's betrayal, she finally felt a measure of control over her life, both financially and emotionally.

The strategies used to cope with jealousy and infidelity are almost as varied as the people involved and the unique circumstances they confront. So pervasive and ominous has been the threat of infidelity that it would be surprising if humans had not developed a veritable arsenal of weapons to combat its occurrence. In this chapter we witness the principle of co-evolution at work. Coping strategies came into existence to contend with real and recurrent adaptive problems. Since affairs produce a cascade of consequences for all players in the eternal triangle, no single coping strategy will suffice.

Jealousy, of course, lies at the source, leading first to rage, then to soul-searching, and finally to dramatic action. But the action it incites is so diverse that it defies singular depiction. Violence and homicide, covered in detail in chapter 5, represent only the most desperate of coping mechanisms. This chapter delves into the broader array of coping strategies, from denial to revenge.

Clinical Treatment of Jealousy

The clinical and self-help literature on coping with jealousy and infidelity reveals a bias that ignores the usefulness of jealousy. The central coping issue is typically framed as, How can jealousy be overcome? as though the problem lay solely or primarily with the jealous person. Therapists exhort the jealous person to "take responsibility" for the jealousy. In one common therapeutic technique, called *systematic desensitization*, patients first list the situations that would trigger their jealousy and then rank them according to the intensity of jealousy they evoke. Having one's partner make eye contact with a rival might evoke mild jealousy, followed by flirting or cheek-kissing. Deep "French kissing" might evoke yet more jealousy, especially if accompanied by groping and fondling. Witnessing a loved one giving oral sex to someone else, however, might push a person over the edge into an uncontrollable rage.

After this jealousy hierarchy is established, patients are taught a progressive relaxation technique, whereby different parts of the body are mellowed in succession. Finally, the therapist instructs the patient to start imagining the jealousy-evoking events, beginning with the mild ones, while maintaining bodily relaxation. If the patient tenses while going through the hierarchy, the therapist retreats to a milder level until relaxation is again established. The ultimate goal is to become so relaxed and comfortable that vivid images of the partner trying out different sexual positions with a rival are no more likely to evoke jealousy than an innocuous handshake.

Given the deep roots of the dangerous passion, eliminating jealousy is unlikely. It could only be done if there were a zero probability of infidelity or defection: if people never flirted with others, never smiled at others, and never danced with others; if rivals never showed the slightest interest in each others' mates; if people never became dissatisfied with their relationships; if all couples were perfectly matched on mate value; and if all changes in desirability occurred equally and in precisely the same way for each member of each couple. But short of locking couples alone in isolated chambers devoid of all social interaction, these conditions will never be met.

Therapists are not alone in the view that jealousy is an emotion that should be purged from our psychological repertoire. Some researchers argue that jealousy is a malady that requires intervention. Several recommend "cognitive reconstrual," whereby remaining in a relationship despite suspected affairs is viewed positively—a kind of happy-idiot solution. Some recommend thinking about positive aspects of oneself as a method for "relieving jealousy," reminiscent of the palliative "just say no" as a magic solution to making drug use disappear. And some view violent expressions of jealousy as signs that a person is merely "reaching out for help in learning how to cope with these powerful and complex emotions," as though a man who has just murdered his wife in a jealous rage just needs a bit of warm, unconditional love. All of these recommendations ignore the fact that, in most instances, it's not the experience of jealousy per se that's the problem but rather the real threat of defection by a partner interested in a real rival.

Obviously, episodes of extreme, irrational, or pathological jealousy can destroy an otherwise harmonious marriage, as we saw in the chapter on the Othello syndrome. Coping strategies that carry the sole goal of eliminating jealousy, however, would be like smashing a smoke alarm to solve the problem of a house fire. Successful coping requires dealing with the fire.

One common coping strategy is to visit a therapist. Therapy can sometimes be an enormous aid, clarifying the nature of the problem and offering a rational set of alternative solutions. We must recognize, however, that therapy may not be the perfect panacea. Therapists sometimes approach the problems with moral judgments and personal biases that do more harm than good. In a chapter in the *Clinical Handbook of Couple*

Therapy, Frank Pittman, one of the leading experts in marital infidelity, asserted: "Infidelity is not normal behavior, but a symptom of some problem." Given that as many as half of all married individuals have affairs, then according to this expert, as many as 50 percent of the population must be considered "abnormal."

Marital experts often recognize that therapy cannot always solve the problem of marital treachery. In one case, a man could not decide between his wife and his affair partner, a co-worker: "The cuckolded wife threatened divorce if he could not make up his mind. He assured her that he was not seeing the other woman anymore, and although sex resumed in the marriage, the intimacy was not renewed, as would be expected if he really were away from his affairee. The wife kept finding clues, such as lipstick-stained cigarettes in his ashtray and a woman's underpants in his glove compartment. He told her it was her imagination. She found his car in the woman's driveway, and rammed it through the woman's laundry room, playing havoc with the plumbing. She demanded that the affairee come to the therapy session with the couple. In the session, she informed the affairee that she was still sleeping with her husband, and that he was lying to both of them. The affairee felt betrayed and stalked out, saying something to the effect that all men in her experience betray their wives, but only a real asshole would betray his girlfriend." Therapy was unsuccessful in this case.

Although the therapist's office is sometimes a safe haven to work out adulterous triangles, passions can overheat to the point of destruction: "The triangle meeting had been planned, but the ever-patient betrayed wife and the long-standing affairee both failed to show up. As we discussed the matter with the infidel [husband] in the office, we heard a scuffling in the hall. The two women were fighting. The wife had been running late and the affairee had been hiding in the stairwell, waiting for her. The affairee was trying to hit the wife with a pocketbook when the husband came out and broke it up. He pushed his bruised wife away as he comforted his sobbing affairee, and thus finally made the decision that broke the impasse." At least in this case, the therapy forced a decision, although not one the wife liked.

185

As another example of therapy failing to heal a marriage, consider the following case in which the husband refused to give up his affair partner, but finally consented to go to therapy with his wife. He used the therapy to deliver a hurtful blow: He "explained to his wife that she was lucky to be married to him because she was such an ugly woman. She should feel proud to be married to a man who was able to get such a beautiful affairee, and she should appreciate the increased status that would come from accepting the new woman into a ménage à trois." Although the wife's self-confidence plummeted to an all-time low, she still had enough courage to get up and leave her husband for good.

Despite their best intentions, therapists lacking extensive knowledge of the real roots of jealousy can formulate diagnoses that may create more havoc than healing. In one case, a man diagnosed as irrationally jealous "expressed his helplessness in the face of a wife who, having returned to the workforce after child rearing, now earned more than he and also expected him to undertake tasks at home that contradicted his firmly held but unacknowledged canons of manhood. In this case, jealousy was an element in a power struggle by a man deprived of the supports for his fragile masculinity; he felt that his wife had rendered him useless and robbed him of his self-esteem. He wanted her home and dependent, but . . . it was easier to accuse her of adultery than to voice . . . blatantly sexist demands."

In attributing this man's jealousy to sexism and fragile masculinity, the therapist failed to recognize that women place a strong value on men's earning capacity. He failed to recognize that women who earn more than their partners are indeed more likely to leave them for sound adaptive reasons. And he failed to recognize that women who work are more likely to have affairs. In this particular case, we do not know whether the man's wife actually had an affair, nor do we know whether his concerns were justified. What we do know is that he was responding to a genuine threat, since over the long expanse of human evolutionary history, men in these situations were more likely to suffer from a mate's infidelity or outright defection. This is not an argument, of course, for women to stay at home or curtail their careers. Rather, it suggests that the laying of blame for

186

jealousy at the fashionable doorstep of "fragile masculinity" and "sexist demands" fails to identify the real underlying causes, and may lead to therapeutic interventions that fail.

Culturally Prescribed Coping Strategies

Since jealousy and infidelity are human universals, it should come as no surprise that every culture has prescribed methods of dealing with them. When it comes to laws and other sanctions, the Golden Rule applies with a vengeance; those who have the gold make the rule. Throughout human recorded history, most laws have been written and legislated by men, so they reflect a male rather than a female psychology. Across most cultures over human recorded history, an infidelity by the wife is considered to be analogous to a "property violation" against the husband. Laws and other cultural sanctions mete out punishment both to the rival who has trespassed and to the wife who has betrayed.

In some cultures, these sanctions have been severe. Among the Bue of Fernando Po, an island off Equatorial Guinea, unfaithful women are subjected to an escalating series of punishments: "For the first offense, the offender's hand is cut off and the stump is immersed in boiling oil; for the second offense, the operation is repeated with the right hand; for the third, the offender's head is cut off and then there is no need of oil."

Among the Baiga of Central India, one woman informant revealed an episode in which her husband caught her in an embrace with her lover. The husband attacked the rival with a blazing log, and then later inserted hot chili peppers into her vagina as punishment.

Inflicting disgrace has been a common cultural strategy for coping with infidelity. Among the Cumae in Campagna in ancient Italy, "the adulterous woman was stripped and exposed to the insults of the crowd for many hours, after which she was ridden on an ass through the city. She remained dishonored forever after, and was called 'she who has mounted the ass.'" In North American Indian tribes, adultery was commonly punished by various forms of body mutilation, such as cutting off the adulteress's hair, ears, lips, or nose.

In cultures with written laws, sexual infidelity is almost always targeted for special legislation and punishment. This point is worthy of pause. Throughout the entire world, wherever humans have written laws, who may sleep with whom has always been legislated—a telling clue about human nature.

Among the Yap in the Micronesian islands, adultery by a woman is classified as a theft, along with "the theft of personal goods, coconuts and so forth." In various groups in Africa, such as the Kipsigis of Kenya, women are purchased by payment of cattle and other livestock. When a man is caught sleeping with another man's wife, the offender must compensate the husband in kind with a payment of cattle.

Sanctioned methods of coping, codified in law, sometimes claim the Bible or other religious documents as their sources. According to one passage, for example, the Lord dictated to Moses to enjoin the people of Israel to bring women suspected of infidelity to the priest, who would then make them drink "water of bitterness." If the woman was innocent, the bitter water would have no ill effect. But if the woman was guilty of infidelity, she would absorb the water, which would make her body swell with pain.

One culturally approved method of guarding against female infidelity involves genital mutilation, which is widespread in cultures across northern and central Africa, Arabia, Indonesia, and Malaysia. Clitoridectomy, the surgical removal of the clitoris, dramatically reduces the sexual pleasure that women experience, presumably deterring them from straying. Clitoridectomy is inflicted on millions of women in modern times, although there are movements under way to eliminate the practice.

The writer Alice Walker describes a number of heart-wrenching episodes of clitoridectomy. Here is one from Mali, Africa: "Among my people, girls are not excised before they have breasts, before they develop and are mature. I left my village to go to the capital when I was twelve, and up to that time my father hadn't asked me to be excised . . . when they asked me to go through the excision with the other girls, I made an excuse that I was ill, because I'd already asked how they did the excision. I knew they cut something off, that it was very painful, and that some of the girls were badly traumatized . . . I had a friend whom I loved a lot who died as a result of the excision . . . When I told my father I didn't want to submit to the excision . . . he did not accept it, he hit me . . . So I tried to explain to my fiancé when he came at night to see me; I hoped that as my future husband he would understand. I explained to my fiancé that I was frightened; I told him how painful it would be and that my friend had died and I might die, too . . . He didn't try to understand; he said he could not accept it either . . . He said he could not be proud of a woman who would be dirty, who would be like a whore, and he would be ashamed . . . He abandoned me." This young woman managed to escape the brutality of clitoridectomy, but her story and many others like it reveal that concern with female fidelity lies at the core of genital mutilation.

Another practice common in Africa is infibulation, the sewing shut of the labia majora, sometimes done after clitoridectomy. According to one estimate, 65 million women living today in 23 African countries have suffered this form of genital mutilation. Infibulation effectively prevents sexual intercourse. It is sometimes performed at the insistence of a woman's kin as a guarantee to a future husband of the woman's fidelity. After marriage, infibulated women must be cut open to permit sexual intercourse, because otherwise the vaginal opening is too small. If the husband goes away for a while, however, his wife may be reinfibulated. The decision to reinfibulate usually rests with the husband and his appraisal of his wife's likelihood of infidelity.

Western nations have historically enacted laws that perform similar functions, although by less brutal means. Today, industrial nations have laws that approach a single standard for adultery, applicable equally to both sexes, but this trend has been extremely slow in coming. Adultery committed by a husband was nowhere considered a crime until 1810, and even then, true equality was not codified. French law made it a crime for a man to keep a mistress in the same house with his wife only if his wife objected to it. It was not until 1852 that Austria (the first country to do so) made male and female infidelity equal criminal acts. Historically, however, among the Aztecs, Incas, Mayans, the Germanic tribes of western Europe, the Chinese and Japanese, in older cities in the land now called Iraq, and in many other east Asian cultures, the familiar double standard ruled: adultery was a crime against the husband, and the laws permited recompense or revenge by the victim.

Vigilance

Our studies of dating and married couples have focused on personal, rather than legal or culturally codified, coping strategies. Maintaining vigilance is the first line of defense. When faced with an uncertain threat, men and women alike start calling their partners at unexpected times to see if they are where they said they would be. Other strategies include snooping through the partner's personal belongings, dropping by unexpectedly, and reading personal mail. Husbands and wives keep a close eye on their partners at parties, maintain close physical proximity when rivals might be around, and even ask friends to keep an eye out on their potentially errant partners.

Vigilance yields information that helps to clarify whether an adaptive threat is real or not. Once it is determined to be real, however, a new set of coping strategies kicks in.

Fulfilling a Partner's Desires

One fundamental coping strategy involves self-enhancement. The evolutionary psychology of desire actually predicts the qualities a person targets for self-enhancement. Because men place a premium on women's appearance, whereas women care more about men's resources, successful tactics of self-enhancement should be sex-linked to correspond to the desires of one's mate. Does the evidence bear out this prediction?

Imagine watching a videotape of a couple sitting on a couch engaged in conversation. They cuddle, kiss, and touch each other for a minute. Then, one of the partners gets up to refill their glasses with wine. Seconds later, an interloper enters and is introduced as the old girlfriend or boyfriend of the partner who remained on the couch. The partner stands up and briefly hugs the interloper, then the two sit down on the couch. Over the next minute, they kiss, touch, and sit close to each other. Then the absent partner returns, stops in his or her tracks, wine glasses in hand, and looks down at the partner showing affection to a rival on the couch. The tape ends. Joyce Shettel-Neuber and her colleagues at San Diego State University had both men and women watch sex-specific videotapes;

the men watched a version with an old boyfriend interloper while the women watched a version with an old girlfriend interloper. If you were the one standing there holding the wine glasses, what would you do? How would you cope with this rival, a former mate of your partner?

Women who see the tape are nearly twice as likely as men to report that they would try to make themselves more physically attractive to their partner. They would redouble their efforts at beauty treatments, hair styling, and working out. Women enhance their appearance as a coping strategy when threatened with a rival. The men reported that they would get angry or get drunk.

Our studies of 107 newlyweds confirmed that a common strategy women use to cope with threats of infidelity is to enhance their physical appearance. In a follow-up study of this newlywed sample four years later, women who felt the need to guard their partners continued to use appearance enhancement as a primary coping strategy.

Appearance enhancement emerges prominently in case studies of coping strategies, both in the clinical literature and in our studies. In one case, a woman who had been married for 14 years and given birth to three children one day discovered her husband in bed with another woman. She became hysterical when he confessed that the affair had been going on for five years. She considered a variety of options, including killing him and committing suicide. After many months, she still struggled with her husband's betrayal. Every woman she met on the street evoked images of her husband in a bed of betrayal. Every woman caused her to wonder: "Would he find her more attractive than me? Should I exercise more, attempt to become sexier, have my hair tinted or fixed more often?" She became obsessed with how she looked and took steps to improve her appearance.

Men have at their disposal a parallel strategy—capitalizing on women's desire for men who show the ability and willingness to commit attention, effort, and resources to them. Our studies of 107 married couples and 102 dating couples discovered that men are far more likely than women to increase their display of resources when feeling threatened with a mate's possible defection. Men report buying their partners gifts, flowers, and jewelry, and taking them out to expensive restaurants. These increases in resource display occur when men feel the need to step up their efforts at mate guarding to discourage their partner from seeking love in the arms of another man.

According to the biggest rock group of all time, the Beatles, "love is all you need." Although this proclamation undoubtedly overstates the case, it carries an important message for coping with a partner's threat of defection. Although both sexes prize love in the long term, women are especially sensitive to its signals. Love carries the promise of commitment over the long haul. When faced with signals of a partner's defection, we found that both sexes, but especially men, redouble their displays of love and affection. Consider these specific actions: I told her that I loved her; I went out of my way to be kind, nice, and caring; I complimented her on her appearance; I was helpful when she really needed it; I displayed greater affection for her. All of these love acts scored in the top 10 percent of effective mate retention tactics. In fact, these five acts were judged to be the most effective tactics of mate retention out of the entire set of 104 acts we examined.

Two other key findings are worthy of note. First, the love tactic showed the largest sex difference of all the tactics examined in its effectiveness at mate retention. Men who are successful at keeping their partners often step up their displays of love when threatened with a possible partner defection. Men who fail in these displays tend to be losers in love. Second, the display of love is closely linked with three key factors among the dating couples: number of months they have been involved, emotional closeness, and the probability that they will be together over the long term. Only emotionally close couples who plan to stay together express their mate retention tactics through love.

Emotional Manipulation

One strategy of coping with a partner's possible defection is to induce guilt. Why did humans evolve to experience guilt in the first place? According to evolutionary theorist Paul Gilbert, guilt evolved as an internal monitoring mechanism that allowed individuals to keep track of reciprocity in relationships. Benefits bestowed and costs inflicted cannot get too far out of balance in intimate relationships. If they do, participants run the risk of being exploited (if they give more than they receive) or being branded an exploiter (if they take more than they give). According to this theory, the greater the love, the more strongly one is motivated to reciprocate, and hence the more guilt one will experience at reciprocation failures. Guilt is evoked when you perceive that you've caused pain and suffering in loved ones, falling short of their expectations.

Once guilt has evolved, it is susceptible to co-evolutionary exploitation as a mate retention device. In our studies of mate retention tactics, participants told us that they intentionally induce guilt in their partners by crying when their partners indicate interest in others, by threatening to harm themselves if their partner leaves them, and by pretending to be mad about a partner's flirtation. A few became borderline anorexic, blaming the partner for their loss of appetite. A few even threatened suicide to induce guilt.

Contrary to common stereotypes, men and women use guilt tactics equally. We discovered that these coping tactics were equally effective in retaining a mate for both sexes, each scoring in the moderately effective range. Stereotypes of women as the more emotionally manipulative sex, at least when it comes to mate retention strategies, are false.

Inducing guilt through emotional manipulation acquires its effectiveness by exploiting people's evolved psychology of relationship balance and reciprocity. By indicating that one is psychologically injured, the strategist evokes attempts to restore balance by increasing commitment, by redoubling love, by avoiding contact with others, and ultimately by remaining with the mate. It works in part because crying and despondency convey the depth with which one partner values the other—a signal that such commitment will be difficult to replace. Becoming irreplaceable may be the key to commitment. It can only work, however, if the target of this tactic is prone to respond by restoring the balance.

Over the long run, emotional manipulation through guilt induction is a "weak tactic" because it signals dependency on the partner and a deficit in mate value. Inducing guilt may lose potency with frequent use, but its sparing application, when used in conjunction with other coping strategies, may keep a mate from straying and keep emotional commitments in balance.

Psychological Coping Strategies

That some coping strategies entail inward psychological recalibration rather than outward action should come as no surprise. Actual or suspected infidelities can shatter long-held worldviews of monogamy and marital harmony, cause a person to question her or his own worth as a mate, and more generally call for a reassessment of one's life course. Psychological methods of coping may be indispensable weapons in the arsenal required to deal with betrayal.

Denial

In the course of interviewing married couples, one woman—I'll call her Tiffany to preserve confidentiality—reported that she suspected her husband of cheating. Tiffany detected two clues. First, she discovered jewelry in their bedroom closet just before her birthday. Believing that her husband had bought the gift for her, she carefully rewrapped and replaced it. Her birthday came and went, but she received no jewelry. When she confronted her husband, he told her that she must be imagining things. So she let it drop. Second, when giving him oral sex, Tiffany noticed that he tasted and smelled like latex, even though they used pills rather than condoms as birth control. These suspicious clues coincided with days when he stayed late at the office. The signals screamed of infidelity, but her husband adamantly denied it. When I asked her whether she thought that her husband was having an affair, she told me that she didn't think so. "He's the most honest man I know," she said, "and if he says he's not having an affair, then he's not."

At first blush, this denial seemed surprising. The clues provided overwhelming evidence of betrayal. But knowing the details of her life made the denial more understandable, if not supremely sensible. Tiffany had four children and without a paying job was economically dependent on her husband. If she failed to believe her husband and forced the affair into the open, it could have resulted in a disastrous divorce. So she convinced herself that she had imagined the clues and that all was well in her marriage after all.

As it turned out, this coping strategy worked well. Over time, Tiffany's husband grew bored with his affair. He stopped staying late at the office. When they had sex, he no longer smelled of latex condoms. Today, they are happily married and enjoy raising their four beautiful children in a stable marital environment.

Although both sexes sometimes use denial as a coping strategy, a recent study revealed that men use it more frequently than women. In a study of 351 individuals in Dunedin, New Zealand, Paul Mullen and J. Martin studied strategies used to cope with jealousy. They found that 21 percent of the men, but only 13 percent of the women, used denial, ignoring threats of infidelity in the hopes that they would go away.

Although denial may seem like a strange or maladaptive coping strategy, there are clearly circumstances in which it is effective. Some problems simply go away over time without anyone doing much of anything at all.

Self-Reliance and Self-Bolstering

Imagine that you phone your romantic partner at home and an unfamiliar voice answers. Now imagine that your romantic partner has lunch with an attractive person of the opposite sex. Finally, imagine that your romantic partner visits a former lover. How would you cope with these potential threats? The psychologists Peter Salovey and Judith Rodin conducted a systematic analysis of psychological coping strategies. They asked 95 people to rate the degree to which they used 15 different coping strategies in response to a variety of possible threats to romantic relationships, ranging from a partner having lunch with someone else to a partner having a florid affair with someone else.

Through the statistical procedure of factor analysis, these researchers identified two primary psychological coping strategies. The first, labeled *self-reliance*, involved psychological attempts to refrain from thinking about, or becoming emotional about, the infidelity threat—not feeling angry or embarrassed, and not thinking about the unfairness of the situation. This mode of "becoming philosophical" about the matter, however, is tough to do since one's self-esteem can experience a tremendous blow.

The second psychological coping method is *self-bolstering*, which involves attempts to shore up self-esteem. People report consciously thinking about their good qualities, doing something nice for themselves, and bolstering how they feel about themselves. Self-bolstering obviously would not be necessary if self-esteem did not plummet in the face of an infidelity threat.

Suppressing and Evoking Jealousy

No emotion can shatter dreams and bones as much as jealousy. It's an adaptive signal of an impending threat to a primary love relationship. It's an emotion that can drive a woman to obsessive vigilance, or a man to reckless violence. It becomes all the more puzzling, therefore, that fully 50 percent of all individuals who reported on specific episodes of jealousy indicated that they intentionally tried to conceal their jealousy from their partner and kept their feelings to themselves. Why would this adaptive emotion be suppressed? Why would the alarm bell be concealed from the very person responsible for triggering it to begin with?

The answer to this mystery lies with the logic of mate value. While the experience of jealousy serves as a signal of external threat, the display of jealousy is often interpreted as a sign that the jealous person is lower than his or her partner in desirability. Those who remain indifferent to a partner's flirtations, confident in their mate's fidelity, assured in their view that their partner cannot do better on the mating market, do not display jealousy. On the other hand, those who feel that their position is indeed threatened, that their partner might leave, that they might find it difficult to replace their current partner, cannot help but experience pangs of jealousy.

So the co-evolution of signals takes over. What started out as an emotion designed to deal with a real adaptive problem has turned into a signal that can be interpreted by one's mate and all others as a sign of relatively low mate value. At this stage in the co-evolutionary arms race, most people infer that the more jealous partner is the partner lower in desirability. And it is this awful inference, which itself can lower a person's self-perceived desirability, that has led to monumental efforts to suppress the outward display of jealousy. By keeping it concealed, the jealous person avoids getting compared unfavorably with a rival, avoids reputational damage, and above all, reduces the odds that the regular mate will view him or her as a loser. By concealing jealousy, a person can conceal the display of feeling threatened and mute perceptions of a difference in desirability.

Another common strategy is to intentionally evoke jealousy in one's partner. In our studies of mate retention tactics, we found that some individuals intentionally talk to members of the opposite sex at parties to make their partner jealous, show overt interest in others to make their partner angry, and even smile and flirt with others in front of their partner to evoke jealousy. Women proved to be twice as likely as men to intentionally elicit jealousy from their partner. Given that men's jealousy is the root cause of most violence against women, why would a woman go out of her way to deliberately provoke an emotion that could unleash a torrent of abuse?

A clue to this puzzle comes from the lab of Gregory White, who identified the circumstances in which women consciously evoke their partner's jealousy. White asked men and women to indicate who was more involved in the relationships—themselves or their partners. He found that whereas 50 percent of the women who view themselves as more involved than their partner intentionally provoke jealousy, only 26 percent of the women who are equally or less involved resort to this mode of coping. Differences in involvement, of course, signal a gap in desirability; the more involved partner is generally less desirable, whereas the less involved partner is generally more desirable.

During subsequent interviews, women admitted that they are motivated to evoke jealousy in order to inspire greater commitment and possessiveness in their partner, as well as to increase psychological closeness.

They also instigate jealousy to test the strength of the relationship, a topic we will explore in the final chapter. Although motivations for arousing jealousy are varied and complex, one function seems clear—an attempt to rectify the imbalance in perceived mate value. By eliciting jealousy, women convey a vital message to their partners: "Others are interested in me; I'm highly desirable; don't take me for granted."

Derogation of Competitors

If suppressing one's own jealousy and evoking jealousy in partners are two tactics for coping with problems of relative mate value, a third coping strategy involves derogation of competitors. In one study, students who were currently involved in serious romantic relationships of at least three months' duration were asked to indicate their perceptions of their partner's preferences in an ideal mate. Then they evaluated their own standing regarding each of these traits, how they measured up to their partner's picture of an ideal mate. The qualities included honesty, sociability, warmth, sincerity, good looks, wit, popularity, reliability, charm, spontaneity, the right height, activity level, intelligence, emotional expressiveness, humor, and generosity.

After rating their partner's preferences and then their own standing, participants read the following instructions: "A jealousy situation usually involves three persons: yourself, your partner, and a third person to whom you or your partner is attracted. Please try to remember the last instance in your present relationship when you felt jealous because you thought that your partner was attracted to another person; if you are currently jealous because you think your partner is attracted to another person, you should choose this instance. Please answer the following questions about your perception of this other person."

The participants then provided background information on their rivals and the rival's relationship with their partner, and then rated their rivals on the 18 attributes. Jealousy turned out to be extremely important in the lives of most of these participants. A full 59 percent believed that their partner had had some kind of sexual contact with their rival, 45 percent reported that their rival was at the same university, and 59 percent had some kind of direct contact with their rival. So the threat of a partner's potential defection was not just hypothetical; it was a reality, or at least a perceived reality, for a majority.

The most important finding was that people denigrated their rivals on precisely the dimensions they believed that their partner valued. If their partner prized intelligence in a potential partner, then participants derogated their rivals by evaluating them as stupid. If their partner valued honesty, participants rated their rivals as deceitful. If their partner appreciated height, participants rated their rivals as Lilliputian. Whatever qualities their partner admired, participants found rivals woefully lacking in precisely those qualities.

The author of this study interprets these findings according to a standard theory of self-esteem: people's self-esteem is threatened when their partners are attracted to rivals, and so denigrating the rival is a method of restoring feelings of self-worth. This interpretation is endorsed by two leading jealousy researchers, Gregory White and Paul Mullen: "The goal of derogation of the rival is to reduce the . . . threat to self-esteem."

The importance of this coping strategy has roots deep in human history, probably traceable to the origin of language itself. But the first codified version appeared in Ecclesiasticus: "The blow of the whip raises a welt, but the blow of the tongue crushes bones." The psychologists Gordon Allport and Leo Postman put it more precisely: "Rumor is set in motion and continues to travel by its appeal to the strong personal interests of the individuals involved in the transmission." Running down a rival does more than make a person feel good; it serves a valuable purpose. Derogation is an adaptive strategy that succeeds when it effectively decreases a rival's mate value. It's an excellent method for coping with an infidelity threat, provided it succeeds in rendering the rival less desirable. Lisa Dedden, David Schmitt, and I tested this idea through a series of studies of derogation of competitors. We first wanted to find out all the ways in which men and women grapple with rivals by attempting to damage their social reputation.

We started by asking men and women to tell us what verbal barbs they have used themselves, or heard others use, to render their rivals less desirable to their romantic partners. People were loquacious on the topic, mentioning slurs ranging from men telling their partners that the rival enjoyed "using" women, to women telling their partners that the rival has a sexually transmitted disease. From these nominations we derived a list of 83 things people could do to render their rivals less desirable. Next, we wanted to discover which derogation tactics men and women used and how effective they were likely to be. We found remarkable sex differences in how often each tactic was used, precisely in line with our theory. Men tended to denigrate their rival's resources, indicating that their rival lacked money, drove a run-down old car, was viewed as a loser, and was likely to do poorly professionally. Women, in contrast, tended to deride their rival's physical appearance, making fun of the size and shape of the rival's body, laughing at the rival's hairstyle and clothes, and pointing out blemishes and asymmetries. The tactics were also sex-linked in their perceived effectiveness. It proved to be far more effective for men than for women to derogate a rival's resource potential, present or future, whereas women achieved greater success by ridiculing a rival's appearance.

These findings were disconcerting for one very obvious reason: men can clearly observe a woman's physical appearance for themselves, so how could mere words alter those observations? Would a man really be dissuaded if his romantic partner declared to him, "You shouldn't be attracted to supermodel Claudia Schiffer . . . she's really a dog!" Wouldn't direct observation give lie to these verbal efforts at psychological manipulation?

Further exploration revealed that these verbal tactics can work in two ways. First, making public one's disparaging opinion of another woman's appearance can enhance its effectiveness. The fact that others in one's social world believe a woman to be unattractive can damage a man's reputation by association. Since men's social status is affected by the physical appearance of his partner, men are highly sensitive to how others view their partner's looks.

Second, this tactic can work by steering a man's attention to flaws that are not otherwise directly observable or may not have been noticed. In one episode, a friend reported attending a party with his girlfriend, but ended up flirting with another woman, which the girlfriend observed. Driving away from the party, the girlfriend, in the most casual and offhanded manner, happened to mention that the other woman (her rival at the party) had heavy thighs, but said no more. The next time the man encountered the object of his flirtation, he found himself staring at her thighs, and concluded that, indeed, they were a tad heavy. What started out unnoticed became amplified in his attentional field. His girlfriend's coping strategy worked. Our actual perceptions of a person's beauty can be influenced in subtle ways by the views of others.

The story turns out to be a good deal more complicated, of course. Many derogation tactics attain their effectiveness because they are difficult for the target to verify directly, such as impugning a rival's intentions (he just wants to get laid) or implying a sexually transmitted disease (who really wants to verify this directly?). Still others capitalize on informational ambiguity, as in implications that the rival "might be bisexual." Others exploit the fact that a person's future is always highly uncertain, and so it is hard for the target to check out whether someone really will do poorly professionally several years down the road. Derogation tactics also take advantage of the fact that prior behavior is often difficult to substantiate (hinting that one's rival has had many past sex partners, or has slept with the entire football team, for example).

Many put-down tactics involve sweeping inferences about personality characteristics. Derogators emphasize that their rivals are weak, wimpy, cowardly, and lacking ambition; insensitive, selfish, uncaring, and inconsiderate; cheating, disloyal, exploitative, loose, and undisciplined; emotionally unstable, flighty, and prone to cry easily; and dumb, boring, stupid, and "dizzy." These tactics acquire their effectiveness from the personality traits that people in cultures around the world want in a romantic partner—someone who is active, bold, agreeable, dependable, emotionally stable, creative, and intelligent.

Derogation tactics exploit the evolved desires of partners predisposed to seek specific qualities in a mate. A man who tells his partner that his rival lacks ambition would only be effective if she were disposed to reject slackers. Similarly, a woman pointing out her rival's unattractive qualities

201

would only work if a man were disposed to reject women with these qualities.

In our initial study, we found that, contrary to our expectations, it was not particularly effective for women to derogate their rivals by labeling them as promiscuous sluts. In our follow-up study, we figured out why. We evaluated the effectiveness of this derogation in both casual and long-term mating contexts. Once we separated out these circumstances, the mystery evaporated: It proved highly effective for women to derogate their rivals by impugning their loose sexual codes of conduct *only* if the man was seeking a long-term relationship, such as a wife. For men seeking a temporary sex partner, a woman's casual sexual attitudes did not dissuade them in the slightest.

Loyalty and the Concorde Fallacy

When Hillary Clinton was interviewed about a rumor about her husband's infidelity with Gennifer Flowers, she declared that she was no "Tammy Wynette," standing by her man no matter what. But when President Bill Clinton's affair with Monica Lewinsky become public knowledge, Hillary gained near-universal respect by doing precisely that. There are two related coping strategies behind loyalty of this sort: how a woman copes with a husband's infidelity and how she wants to be perceived by others as coping.

How do people really feel about remaining in a relationship after an infidelity surfaces? Jeff Bryson of San Diego State University asked women and men to imagine how they would react to a partner's infidelity. One of Bryson's female respondents said, "I would feel that I had invested too much of myself in this relationship to break it off, and would hope that he would come back to me." Another woman thought that, "I would love my boyfriend enough that I would try to overlook what he had done. What would be important to me would be how I feel, not what others feel or say about my boyfriend, so I would stick by him. I would try to ignore what my boyfriend was doing and hope that he would see how foolish it was and come back to me."

One common refrain I've heard from women whose husbands have strayed is echoed in the loyalty-coping cluster: "I've already put so much into this marriage, I can't bail out now." This sentiment may reflect a psychological glitch known variously as the "Concorde Fallacy" or the "sunk cost fallacy." The term *Concorde Fallacy* originated when it became clear that building Concorde airplanes would not be profitable, and a rational economic analysis suggested abandoning the project. But since so much money had already been invested in its development, the decision was made to push through to completion. The project was continued after arguments were advanced that "we have already spent so much on it that we cannot back out now." More abstractly, the Concorde fallacy describes a decision to continue to invest in a project because of the resources you have already invested in it, rather than making the decision according to its yield in the future. According to economists, what should drive the decision is future yield, not prior investment. Yet psychologists have documented that humans are highly susceptible to overweighing their previous investments when making critical decisions. It turns out that even digger wasps commit this fallacy, for they fight for burrows with other wasps not in proportion to the true value of the burrow, but rather in proportion to the amount of time they have already invested in the burrow.

Although technically correct, the economists often overlook one important fact about this supposed fallacy when applied to human relationships. The amount of prior investment is often the single best guide to how much future investment will be needed to abandon the current project and acquire another relationship with sufficient depth and emotional commitment. Starting from scratch can be an enormously costly endeavor—in the search for a new mate, attracting and courting that new mate, and developing the relationship to the point where the couple becomes an intimate union.

The effectiveness of sticking it out as a strategy to cope with a partner's infidelity, of course, hinges on a variety of factors. How good is the current relationship apart from the infidelity? Will the infidelity destroy trust permanently, or can trust be regained? What are the costs to the kids? Are there good prospects for finding someone else? If the relationship is tenuous to start with, if trust is irrevocably destroyed, if the costs of leaving are minimal, and if alternative desirable mates beckon, then it's perhaps best to drop off the key and make a new plan. If not, it may pay to stay.

Revenge and Retribution

When Jeff Bryson studied a wide variety of responses to jealousy-evoking situations, he found that one revolved around revenge, retribution, and getting involved with others. The core components of this coping strategy, as articulated by the particparints, were "flirt or go out with other people," "do something to get even," "do more than my partner has done and then tell him/her about it," and "do something to make my partner jealous."

In one case, a professional couple, Amber and Marc, had been married for 16 years and had several children. The marriage suffered a fatal blow when Amber discovered that her husband had been sleeping with his young research assistant, an attractive woman 13 years his junior, the last in a long series of affairs she uncovered when he finally confessed. Marc, a successful professor of anthropology, refused to terminate the affair. He declared that Amber should understand that, given his professional success, he was "entitled" to be a polygamous man. Amber refused to tolerate the affair, and instead, immediately started an affair of her own with a man eight years younger than she, and started divorce proceedings.

Although her affair with the young man turned out to be transient, it served several important functions for her. It immediately signaled to her partner that she was sufficiently high in mate value to attract desirable alternative mates, which would help with a reconciliation, an option she wanted to keep open. It helped her self-esteem, for she realized that she was highly attractive to a wide range of men and had many other mating alternatives that might serve her better than her philandering husband. It helped to salvage her honor and social reputation with mixed success—some cheered her on and others frowned on her involvement with a younger man. After a few months, Marc grew tired of his young mistress and tried to get back together with his wife. But by this time, Amber realized that she was better off without him, got a divorce, and eventually married a man with whom she had a wonderful relationship. As of this writing, Amber is happily remarried and Marc has gone from one transient relationship to another, never having fully recovered from the loss of his wife.

Some marriages cannot be salvaged after an infidelity, and so the best strategy of coping is to move on. Extracting revenge on a mate who strayed by jumping into another's arms is not necessarily the most effective mode of coping, for it can backfire if a person is attempting to salvage the marriage. But in some circumstances, it succeeds in launching the process of remating—a coping strategy that takes emotional wisdom.

CHAPTER 9

Emotional Wisdom

Give me that man that is not passion's slave.

—*Shakespeare*, Hamlet

I N 1931, MARGARET MEAD DISPARAGED jealousy as "undesirable, a festering spot in every personality so afflicted, an ineffective negativistic attitude which is more likely to lose than to gain any goal." Her view has been shared by many, from advocates of polyamory, a modern form of open marriage, to religious advisors. Kathy Labriola, a leading advocate of polyamory, calls jealousy the "biggest obstacle to creating successful and satisfying open relationships." Social scientist Jan Wagner denounces jealousy because it supports the institution of monogamy, destroys freedom, and undermines living in the present. Even Zen Buddhists argue that "jealousy is the dragon in paradise; the hell of heaven; and the most bitter of all emotions." And so, perhaps, it is. But these views focus on only one side of the dangerous passion, ignoring its potential benefits. Consider the following case, which illustrates one of the benefits of jealousy.

The husband, a physician in his mid-forties, sought help because his marriage of twenty-one years was in trouble as a result of his wife's jealousy. His wife expressed her unfounded jealousy by raging at him and harassing him on the telephone at the hospital where he worked, which caused him a great deal of embarrassment.

The husband was instructed [by the therapist] to act the part of the jealous spouse and to keep this strategy from his wife. Having learned over many years how a jealous person behaves, he was able to perform the role of the jealous husband so skillfully and subtly that his wife didn't realize he was role-playing. While he had seldom called home in the past, he now called his wife frequently to check on her, to see whether she was home and to ask exactly what she was doing. He made suspicious and critical remarks about any new clothes she wore, and expressed displeasure when she showed the slightest interest in another man.

The result was dramatic. The wife, now feeling flattered by her husband's attentiveness and newfound interest, stopped her jealous behavior completely. She became pleasant and loving toward her husband and expressed remorse over her earlier behavior. At an eight-month follow-up, the husband reported that his wife continued to behave more lovingly toward him, but as a precaution he still played the role of the jealous husband from time to time.

The husband in this episode exercised emotional wisdom, implementing his knowledge of the dangerous passion to save his marriage. Properly used, jealousy can enrich relationships, spark passion, and amplify commitment. It is an adaptive emotion, forged over millions of years, linked inexorably with long-term love. The total absence of jealousy, rather than its presence, is a more ominous sign for romantic partners. It portends emotional bankruptcy.

This book has explored the destruction jealousy can create: the severing of social ties that make life meaningful; the psychological torture that torpedoes self-esteem; unwanted stalking; the battering that terrorizes a partner; and the paradoxical killing of a loved one. We have identified many of the key triggers of jealousy, signals that currently are, and historically have been, associated with a partner's sexual infidelity or outright defection. We have explored the hidden passions that impel people

207

to betray their partners and the strategies that men and women deploy to cope with the torments of jealousy and infidelity.

This final chapter turns to a brighter side—the positive uses of jealousy, the co-evolution of sexual harmony, and the cultivation of emotional wisdom.

The Testing of a Bond

Why do children hang on their parents to the point of annoyance? Why do lovers intentionally start fights with their partners? Why does a girlfriend lean up against her boyfriend just as he begins talking to another woman? Why do couples early in their relationship hold hands for hours and put their arms around each other until their limbs grow numb? And why do lovers kiss, placing their tongues in each other's mouths, thereby putting each other at risk of transferring diseases?

All these puzzling phenomena may have a common function—the testing of the bond. Humans (and other animals) who form relationships confront a profound problem: knowing just how committed the other is to the relationship. Mistakes inflict misery. A woman who overestimates her lover's commitment risks abandonment, damage to her reputation, and the hard work of raising a child alone. Overestimating commitment also leads to opportunity costs; the time spent with an undercommitted partner reduces the chance to attract a better-matched mate.

Underestimating the true level of a partner's commitment can also be costly, leading to a self-fulfilling prophecy. Miscalculating, for example, could cause you to reduce your own commitment, impelling your partner to do the same, thereby producing a downward spiral of mutual retreat and resentment. The bitter result could dissolve the relationship as both partners search their social world for deeper, more meaningful engagement.

Accurate evaluation of a partner's psychological involvement is also critical, because commitments can change from month to month, day to day, and even moment to moment. Many forces modulate commitment. A partner's reputation can rise or fall. Physical appearance can change over time as a function of age, health, stress, and status. Even temporary absences, something all relationships endure, can lead a partner to a "lost weekend" or the lure of a new love. For all these reasons, testing the strength of a bond is not merely a useful tool when forming a new relationship, it's an adaptive necessity over a life span. As the detective in the Coen brothers' film *Blood Simple* notes: "I don't care if you're the president of the United States, the Pope of Rome, or Man of the Year; something can always go wrong."

It's difficult to test the strength of the bond because commitment is a state of mind and therefore cannot be observed directly. It must be inferred in the face of ambiguous and uncertain signs. Amotz Zahavi, a biologist at Tel Aviv University, offers a surprising and paradoxical answer to the question of how best to gauge commitment: inflict pain intentionally. "The only way to obtain reliable information about another's commitment," he argues, "is to impose a cost on that other— to behave in ways that are detrimental to him or her. We are all willing to accept another's behavior if we benefit from it, but only one truly interested in the partnership is willing to accept an imposition . . . all mechanisms used to test the social bond involve imposing on partners." We hurt the ones we love, Zahavi proposes, to test the strength of the bond.

Zahavi may be guilty of exaggeration when he says that the only way to obtain accurate information is to inflict pain. Observing how a partner treats you over time surely provides valuable information about commitment—when a partner surprises you with flowers, for example, or carries you off for a romantic weekend at the shore. The smoke signals of betrayal can also be read without creating intentional tests. A partner who forgets your birthday or accidentally calls out someone else's name in the heat of sex surely reveals something about commitment without you having to inflict anything at all.

People also gain knowledge about commitment when they bestow benefits and then note how their partner reacts. When a woman refuses to accept a piece of jewelry from a man she's been seeing, for example, it may reveal something about her absence of deep psychological engagement. But Zahavi is correct that commitment is more difficult to discern when the waters are calm and the relationship sailing is smooth. By inflicting a hardship on your partner and then gauging the reaction, you can gain more revealing information.

Early courtship, prior to heavy investment, calls for special kinds of tests. In some species of birds, males first establish territories that are highly attractive to females. When females enter a male's territory, however, the male typically attacks her. In fact, he attacks every female who comes around, which prompts most of them to fly away. A few females, however, persist, and reenter his territory again and again. Over time, the male's attacks on the most persistent female lessen and eventually disappear altogether. The pair then proceeds to mate for the rest of their lives. Aggression is the most reliable means this male bird has for evaluating a female's commitment to their future together. Females that regard the male as a temporary convenience refuse to put up with the attacks, and quickly depart. Those that intend to commit to him as a lifelong mate endure the onslaught early in the courtship.

The theory of bond testing can explain many otherwise puzzling aspects of relationships. It explains why young children sometimes hang onto their parents to the point of annoyance. It explains why good friends who have not seen each other for a long time slap each other on the back and insult, tease, and taunt each other (only a close friend would tolerate such otherwise offensive behavior). And it explains why, after a substantial absence, lovers rush into each other's arms, embrace, and kiss passionately. Whether a bond is resolute and resistant to outside hostile forces, or fragile and vulnerable to rupture, requires tests of evaluation and appraisal. How do we go about this delicate task?

Benefits of Evoking Jealousy

Have you ever intentionally brought up an old lover's name just to see how your partner would react? Have you ever intentionally ignored your partner at a party? Have you ever been unusually friendly to someone else when your partner was present? Have you ever told your partner that someone had "hit on" you or asked you out for a date? If you have done any of these things, the chances are that you've engaged in the strategy of intentionally evoking the jealousy of your partner.

Once jealousy evolved in the human repertoire, it became fair game for partners to exploit for their own purposes. Eliciting jealousy intentionally emerged as an assessment device to gauge the strength of a mate's commitment. Both sexes do it, but not equally.

In one study, 31 percent of women, but only 17 percent of men reported that they had intentionally elicited jealousy in their current romantic partner. Women reported using several key tactics for inducing jealousy. By far the most common was discussing their attraction to other men, with 51 percent of women reporting this tactic; actually dating others came in second at 24 percent; lying about being attracted to someone else was the third favored technique at 14 percent; and talking about former partners was reported by 11 percent.

In our study of newlyweds, we found similar sex differences. Women more than men report flirting with others in front of the partner, showing interest in others, going out with others, and talking to another man at a party, all to make their partner jealous or angry.

William Tooke and his colleagues at the State University of New York at Plattsburgh have conducted the most thorough investigation of the strategic induction of jealousy. They found strong sex differences in several clusters of acts designed to induce jealousy. First, women intentionally socialize with other people. One woman said that she purposefully neglected to invite her partner along when she went out with her friends. Another said that she made a point of talking with members of the opposite sex when she and her boyfriend went out to a bar. A third indicated that she made sure to casually mention to her boyfriend how much fun she had when she was out partying without him.

The second jealousy-inducing strategy centered on intentionally ignoring a partner. One woman reported acting distant and uninterested in her partner to make him think that she didn't really care about him that much. Another woman said she deliberately failed to answer her phone when she knew her boyfriend was calling so that he would think she was out with someone else. Yet another told her boyfriend that she did not have time to see him, even though it was the weekend.

The third mode of strategic jealousy induction was especially effective at pushing men's jealousy buttons—direct flirtation with other men.

One woman reported dancing closely and seductively with someone whom her partner didn't like while he stood on the sidelines. Another woman bought a small gift for another man while out shopping with her partner. Several reported going out to bars with members of the opposite sex and coming back to the boyfriend a bit intoxicated. And others reported that they dressed in especially sexy outfits while going out without their boyfriends, a sure method of fanning a man's jealous flames.

A more subtle and ingenious tactic for evoking jealousy involves merely smiling at other men while out with a partner. Antonia Abbey of Wayne State University discovered a fascinating difference in how men and women interpret a woman's smiles. When women smile, men often erroneously read into it sexual interest, mistaking friendliness for romantic intent. Women say they are just being friendly, not sending sexual signals. Martie Haselton and I have labeled men's sexual inference an "adaptive bias" in mindreading because it's part of men's unconscious strategy of casual sex. By inferring sexual interest when a woman merely smiles, men are more likely to initiate sexual overtures in their pursuit of a short-term mating strategy.

So when a woman smiles at another man while at a party with her partner, she deftly exploits the evolved psychology of two different men. It causes the target of the smile to think she's sexually interested in him, so he makes advances. Simultaneously, it evokes her partner's jealousy, so he gets angry both about the rival and about his perception that she's encouraging the other man. The upshot might be a confrontation between the two rivals or a lover's quarrel. But who can really blame a woman just for being friendly? No other method for strategically inducing jealousy is as effective, for it makes two men dance to a woman's tune with merely a well-timed glance.

Why do women walk such a dangerous tightrope, trifling with a male mechanism known to unleash violence? Women report a variety of motives for intentionally evoking jealousy. Gregory White conducted an in-depth study of 150 heterosexual couples in California to find out. He first asked each of the 300 participants whether they had ever intentionally tried to make their partner jealous. Then he asked the participants why they did it. Only a few women reported that they induced jealousy to punish their partner. Eight percent reported doing it to bolster their self-esteem. Ten percent admitted doing it to act out feelings of revenge on a partner for a previous wrong. Increasing a partner's commitment, however, exceeded all these reasons, being cited by 38 percent of the women.

By evoking jealousy, a woman causes her partner to believe that she has attractive alternatives available, and that if he does not display greater commitment she might kiss him good-bye and depart for greener mating pastures. Women who successfully use this tactic are more likely to keep the commitment of their mates.

Forty percent of the women also reported that they evoke jealousy to test the strength of the bond. By evoking jealousy, a woman gains valuable information about the depth and consistency of her partner's commitment. Women reap this benefit most at a time in the relationship when the need to test the strength of the bond is especially strong. Women whose partners have been away for a while, women whose partners experience a sudden surge in status, and women who feel they might be perceived as being less desirable than their partner all need these vital appraisals of a man's commitment.

Gregory White confirmed this conclusion by asking all the partners in the study of 150 couples to rate themselves on whether they were more involved, equally involved, or less involved in the relationship than their partner. Relative involvement, of course, is a powerful clue to which partner is more desirable on the mating market, according to the principle of least interest—the less interested partner has the upper hand on the scale of desirability. Although 61 percent of the couples were well matched in their level of involvement, 39 percent showed a mismatch. Does this index of relative involvement predict who will deploy the jealousy-induction strategy? The effect for men was modest: 15 percent of those who were less involved intentionally induced jealousy; 17 percent of those equally involved intentionally induced jealousy; and 22 percent of the men more involved intentionally induced jealousy. So there is a slight tendency for the less desirable men to attempt to evoke more jealousy.

The results for women were more dramatic. Whereas only 28 percent of the women who were less involved reported intentionally inspiring jealousy in their partners, 50 percent of the women who were more involved than their partner reported intentionally provoking jealousy. The more involved women are thus nearly twice as likely as less involved women to report inducing jealousy. Since women who fall below their partners in overall desirability confront commitment problems more poignantly than other women, they induce jealousy in an attempt to correct the imbalance.

Strategically inducing jealousy, in short, serves several key functions for women. It can bolster self-esteem for some women because of the attention it attracts from other men. It can increase the commitment of a partner by making him realize how desirable she really is and that she would have little difficulty replacing him. And it can test the strength of the bond because she can use a man's jealousy as a barometer of the depth of his love. If he reacts to her flirtations with emotional indifference, she knows he lacks commitment; if he gets jealous, she knows he's in love. Evoking jealousy, although it inflicts a cost on the partner, provides valuable information that's difficult to secure through any other means—and it often works.

Virgil Sheets and his colleagues at Indiana State University discovered that one of the most common reactions in men whose jealousy is aroused is to increase the attention they pay to their partners. After becoming jealous, men report that they would be more likely to "try to keep track of what my partner is doing," "do something special for my partner," and "try to show my partner more attention."

Tampering with the dangerous passion requires emotional wisdom so that it doesn't backfire. Inspiring excessive jealousy, for example, can result in violence or dissolution of the relationship. Consider one man's report: "I had an old girlfriend who liked to dress provocatively. Guys— no, make that *big* guys—would hit on her constantly. At first, I found this a real ego boost—at the end of the evening, every guy saw her leave with me. But after a while, I grew weary of even going out. She was trying to prove that she was so hot, I'd be foolish to leave her behind, but in the end it backfired. She put me in too many unnecessary and potentially violent situations (shooting pool in a really short skirt, for example) and I let her go. Let some other fool be her guardian."

So although evoking jealousy can serve a useful function, it must be used with skill and intelligence to avoid unleashing unintended consequences.

Igniting Sexual Passion

Jealousy can also spark or rekindle sexual passion in a relationship, as the following illustrates.

"Let's call him Goatee Boy. He had all the late '90s options: the goatee, an earring, tattoos, baggy cords, and Keds. There on that small sofa, he was hip, cool . . . and hitting on my girlfriend. And she was playing along.

"I watched from the bar, sipping something strong and feeling something stronger. It wasn't the booze. It was something electric, a surge through my bones, tendons, and flesh that could have blown fuses at a power plant. Long story short: I walked over to my girlfriend. In a shaky but determined voice, I said, 'Let's go.' She looked at me, looked at Goatee Boy. Then she got up and we left. That night, we flew through more sexual positions than you'd find in a Kama Sutra paperback. And I had no idea I'd been had."

Or consider the case of Ben and Stacy, a couple attending an intensive five-day jealousy workshop conducted by the Israeli psychologist Ayala Pines. Ben, 15 years older than Stacy, had been married before, but had been divorced for five years when he first got involved with Stacy. Although Stacy had had a few romantic relationships, she was still a virgin when they met. Ben was flattered at the attentions of a woman as young and attractive as Stacy, but he soon became bored with their sex life, and yearned for sex with other women. This unleashed intense jealousy in Stacy, which brought them to the workshop to solve what Ben described as "her problem." He saw no rational reason why he should not sleep with other women.

During the early days of the workshop, Ben brought up Stacy's insecurity and jealousy, indicated his disapproval of her problem, and proceeded to flirt with the other women in the group. During one of these sessions,

Stacy was being berated by the group for being so jealous. Tears streamed down her cheeks and the others in the group responded with hugs and affection. The most attractive man in the group was especially supportive. He continued to comfort her, even after the session ended and Ben and the others left the room. Hugging turned to kissing, and eventually they had passionate sex right on the floor. They did not use contraceptives.

When Ben discovered the infidelity, he became furious, saying, "You hurt me more than any other woman has done, and I trusted you to protect my feelings." Over the next two days, the therapy group focused now on Ben's jealousy. But when asked by the therapist whether any good had come of the event, he replied: "When we made love afterward, it was the most passionate sex we had ever had. It was unbelievably intense and exciting. I can't figure out why." Stacy agreed. Ben's jealousy revived the sexual passion in their relationship. Why?

Astute readers already have clues to the most probable explanations. A man whose partner has just been inseminated by another man is most at risk for genetic cuckoldry. By having sex with Stacy immediately following her infidelity, he reduced the odds that she would become pregnant with another man's child, although he obviously did not think about it in those terms. The passionate nature of the sex implies that she had an orgasm, which causes the woman to retain more sperm and release less "flowback." Increased sperm retention, in ancestral times, would have meant an increased likelihood of conception. Ben was merely a modern player in an ancient ritual where men competed with each other in the battle for successful fertilization.

There is another reason for the sudden revival of passionate sex between Ben and Stacy. The other man's attentions reaffirmed Stacy's attractiveness and evoked jealousy in Ben. When it penetrates men's minds that other desirable men are interested in their partners, they perceive their partners through new eyes as more sexually radiant. As a consequence, erotic attraction ignites, sparking passionate love. I've witnessed this mechanism firsthand. For several years I played tennis with a very attractive married woman. One day after our match she announced to me: "You've been the best thing for our sex life. Dan is incredibly jealous of you. On days that you and I play tennis, Dan and I have the greatest sex!" From outward appearances, Dan was a calm and cool guy who was not easily ruffled. But once his jealousy was aroused, he perceived his wife as more sexually radiant, leading to a surge of passionate lovemaking.

Clinical cases also testify to the increased ardor following episodes of jealousy. In one study, Mary Seeman found that 17 percent of women reported enhanced sexual desire as a result of their jealousy: "Visions of what the spouses and the rivals might be doing together occupied much of their thought and, they reluctantly admitted, 'sexually excited' them." One woman in Seeman's study "seemed to be in continuous states of sexual arousal, which were both pleasurable and agonizing. This state contributed to frequent and massive pleasure in sex, which bonded the pair more closely and which accounted for much of the secondary gain derived from jealousy." In his book *The Kreutzer Sonata,* the great Russian writer Tolstoi observed: "Our arguments were terrifying . . . and so much more striking in that they were followed by equally incensed paroxysms of animal sexuality."

In one unusual case in Florida, a husband actually paid other men to come to his home and have sex with his wife. He hid in the closet and secretly watched his wife in the other man's embrace. His jealousy inflamed sexual passion, apparently the only way that he could sustain an erection. Going to such lengths to stimulate sexual interest is unusual, and using jealousy in this manner can backfire, often evoking disgust or violence. But for some couples, jealousy provides the sexual spark that can renew the passion that has dwindled over time. And sometimes it intensifies love.

The Sea of Love

One testament to the universality of love and its obstinate refusal to be extinguished can be found in societies that have attempted to banish it. In the 19th century, the Oneida Society articulated the view that romantic love was merely disguised sexual lust, and saw no reason to encourage such deceit. The Shakers, to take another example, in the 18th century declared romantic love undignified and threatening to the goals of the larger community, and so sought to banish it. The Mormons of the 19th century also viewed romantic love as disruptive, and sought to discourage it. In all three societies, however, romantic love persisted among individuals, sometimes underground, refusing banishment, hidden from the harsh eyes of the group's elders. Within cultures, as the story of Romeo and Juliet declares with universal resonance, love can be fueled by the efforts of others to suppress it. Lovers have no choice; they can quell their feelings temporarily or muffle their expression, but they cannot exorcise them entirely.

Cultures that impose arranged marriages and permit polygyny provide a test case, for what system could be better designed to undermine love? Does love have any place within a mating system where a man's first wife is chosen for him? Even when his elders choose a man's first wife for him, such as in polygynous Arabic cultures, men often marry a second wife for love. Taita women in fact prefer to be the second or third wife, believing that they will more likely be married for love and hence will receive more favorable treatment from their husband and experience more emotional closeness.

Another testament to the universality of love comes from studies that simply ask men and women whether they are currently in love. Susan Sprecher of Illinois State University interviewed 1,667 women and men from three different cultures. Seventy-three percent of the Russian women and 61 percent of the Russian men confessed to being currently in love. The comparable figures from Japan were 63 percent for women and 41 percent for men. Americans reported roughly the same levels, with 63 percent of the women and 53 percent of the men admitting that they were currently in love.

Why would love be such a universal emotion—a temporary insanity that drives people to distraction, causes a loss of appetite, and creates obsessional thoughts that crowd out everything else? Why are we all fools for love? The most plausible theory proposes that love evolved in order to solve the related problems of commitment and abandonment. A rational analysis of the mating market tells us that somewhere in this world of billions of people there is someone who might be a better mate than you are—someone who may be smarter, funnier, more exciting, more dependable, more intelligent, or more beautiful to behold. From your persepctive, you risk getting dumped every time your partner meets someone else. This leaves you vulnerable. The odds are that sooner or later your partner will meet someone who might be a bit better than you on the harsh metric of mate value, someone who also wants your partner just as much as you do.

The costs of getting abandoned are severe. We risk losing all of the effort we devoted to searching for and courting a mate. Anyone who's been frustrated, impatient, and bored with the singles scene knows what a drag it is to have to start from scratch to form a new relationship. You need some way to ensure that a partner is unswervingly committed to you and won't leave you when someone new moves to town. It would be foolish to enter a relationship otherwise.

If commitment and the risk of abandonment are the problems, love is the solution, since it's a passion that defies rationality. It tells you that your partner only has eyes for you, that you're the only one. It tells you that your partner is swept away in a sea of emotion that's beyond control.

To test the evolutionary function of love, we asked several hundred women and men to describe the behaviors that signal that a person is in love. A separate sample then rated each of the love acts listed on how much it indicated being in the thrall of love. Signals of commitment emerged as most diagnostic of love, but commitment can take many forms. Lovers commit material resources such as food, shelter, and physical protection to a partner over the long term. Lovers commit sexual resources by remaining sexually faithful and by making love with wild abandon. Lovers commit reproductive resources to their beloved, as in successful conception, pregnancy, and childbirth. And it follows that lovers commit parental resources to their children, the natural result of the love union.

Many of these acts convey self-sacrifice: putting one's own interests aside for the greater needs of the loved one, making significant sacrifices for the partner, and giving up a great deal of time to be with the mate. Other signals involve a sexual openness and trust that may be lacking in lesser relationships: trying out different sexual positions and acting out the lover's deepest sexual fantasies.

Emotional commitment emerged throughout the acts of love, including listening with real attention and interest, giving up fun activities to be with the lover when needed, and showing concern for a partner's problems. Several people described how a partner had gone out of his or her way emotionally when they were in the most desperate psychological state. Several lovers described how their partner provided solace during their darkest hours, reaching down to pull them out of a deep depression when all seemed hopeless.

These findings all support the theory that love is a singular signal of commitment. Acts of love convey that a partner won't leave you when your desirability dips momentarily through sickness or setbacks. We know a partner's love through their actions, but the actions must reveal underlying emotions that defy rationality. One of those emotions is jealousy.

Jealousy is one of the most commonly found correlates of being in love. It evolved to protect love not merely from the threat of loss but from the threat of loss to a *rival*. Consider which of the following scenarios would make you more jealous:

> *Loss due to fate:* Your [partner], with whom you are deeply in love, is killed in an automobile accident.
> *Loss due to partner's destiny:* Your [partner], with whom you are deeply in love, obtains a promotion and moves to a faraway city. You know that you will never see him (her) again.
> *Loss due to rejection:* Your [partner], with whom you are deeply in love, explains that he (she) does not love you anymore and ends the relationship. You know that you will never see him (her) again.
> *Loss due to a rival:* Your [partner], with whom you are deeply in love, falls in love with another and ends his (her) relationship with you. You know that you will never see him (her) again.

In an experiment, Eugene Mathes asked men and women, "If this happened to you, would you feel jealous?" Out of a possible range of 4 to 28, loss of a love due to fate scored only 7 on the jealousy scale; loss due to destiny scored nearly double at 13; loss due to rejection came out at 16;

but loss to a rival provoked the greatest jealousy scored at 22. Because evolution is an inherently competitive process, jealousy evolved not just to protect the loss of love but also to prevent the "double-whammy" of the loss of love to a rival.

In my studies, I discovered that some signs of jealousy are accurately interpreted as acts of love. When a man drops by unexpectedly to see what his partner is doing, this mode of jealous vigilance functions to preserve the safe haven of exclusivity while simultaneously communicating love. When a woman loses sleep thinking about her partner and wondering whether he's with someone else, it indicates simultaneously the depth of her love and the intensity of her jealousy. When a man tells his friends that he is madly in love with a woman, it serves the dual purposes of conveying love and communicating to potential rivals to keep their hands off.

The abysmal failure of most "open marriages" that became popular in the late 1960s and early 1970s is stark testament to the failure of experiments to expunge jealousy from the lives of lovers. Few marriages can endure third-party intruders. One of the positive benefits of jealousy is to preserve that inner sanctum, protecting it from interlopers who have their own hidden agendas. According to Ayala Pines, protecting love is the primary function of jealousy: "jealousy aims to protect romantic relationships. It is not a useless flight of irrationality, but a useful signal people can learn to interpret correctly. . . . Jealousy makes people examine their relationship . . . It teaches couples not to take each other for granted . . . ensures that they continue to value each other and . . . indicates that people value the love relationship it protects."

Safe havens, however, are rarely possible in the modern world. As journalist Judith Viorst noted, "Unfortunately there is an endless supply of women out there in the big world—secretaries and dental assistants and waitresses and women executives . . . And wives with traveling husbands have an even wider selection of potential temptations to get aggravated over—TWA stewardesses, San Francisco topless dancers, old flames in Minneapolis, new models in Detroit."

The maintenance of love, ironically, may hinge on the ever-present threat of rivals and the jealousy they evoke. "On those days when I happen to be feeling mature and secure," Viorst observes, "I'm also going to admit that a man who wasn't attractive to other women, a man who wasn't alive enough to enjoy other women, a man who was incapable of making me jealous, would never be the kind of man I'd love."

Emotional Wisdom

Robert and Anne met in their late 20s. Both were attractive, intelligent, and culturally sophisticated. Anne was a rising star in her field of study. Her professors respected her for her formidable logical powers. Her charisma, cool rationality, and concern for social justice attracted many friends. Robert came from France, was also promising in his field, and radiated an infectious enthusiasm that charmed women and men alike. He knew all the latest musical groups and the best bohemian movies. He impressed Anne with his knowledge of fine wines and cooked exquisite, exotic dishes for her and their friends.

Anne and Robert both had been though several previous affairs, and neither was new to love. In the early months of their relationship, she had the upper hand. She did not want to get hemmed in, and refused to give up her other lovers, so he was forced to see her when she made time for him. On nights when Robert knew that Anne was sleeping with another man, he drank more than a few beers, but she had been above board about that from the start, so he quelled his jealousy.

As the months passed, however, this all changed. She dropped her other relationships, decided that he was the love of her life, and now wanted monogamy and commitment. They spent hours together each day, and he brought out sides of her she never knew existed—a talent for singing, a passion for theater, and a new-found interest in dancing.

Within weeks of this change, however, she started showing signs of jealousy. She grilled him about every woman he talked to and forced him to explain every absence. Robert's casual conversation with another woman at a coffee shop would trigger a three-hour argument, with emotional outbursts and tears, until he was finally able to reassure her that her suspicions were unjustified and his commitment to her unshakable. Her friends could not believe Anne's transformation from the master of reason to a weepy mass of jealous insecurity.

Anne constantly suspected that he flirted with other women in her absence and that he was on the verge of betrayal. Her moody episodes grew worse over time as the cycles of accusations and reassurances became increasingly common. But her rational side struggled to overcome these bouts. Since her most emotional moments came when she became premenstrual, she finally decided to attribute them to her hormones. She convinced herself that her jealousy had been irrational. She overrode the green monster with logic and came to believe that she needed to quell her unreasonable suspicions.

Then he dropped the bomb. He was indeed interested in other women and had no intention of being with her permanently. In fact, he'd already started sleeping with other women. Her jealousy had been perfectly justified and not caused by hormonal fluctuations or premenstrual syndrome. Anne had been picking up on real signals that he dismissed and about which she felt needlessly guilty. She had added months to her misery by failing to listen to the emotional wisdom that evolution had given her. Had she not run roughshod over her internal whisperings with logic and rationality, she could have saved herself the prolonged agony of trying to make work what was doomed from the start.

It's unlikely that love, with the tremendous psychological investment it entails, could have evolved without a defense that shielded it from the constant threat from rivals and the possibility of betrayal from a partner. Jealousy evolved to fill that void, motivating vigilance as the first line of defense and violence as the last. In its extreme forms, this vital shield has been called delusional, morbid, and pathological, a symptom of neurosis and a syndrome of psychosis. Therapists try to expunge it from patients, and individuals try to suppress it in themselves.

It's easy to understand why. The spouse who has been falsely accused of betrayal for the hundredth time by a suspicious partner wants it to stop. The wife who calls her husband incessantly at work to make sure he's not cheating can drive him mad. The wife whose self-esteem is bruised, whose body is battered, and whose survival is endangered by a jealous husband lives a life of misery. And the man whose ex-girlfriend stalks him everywhere may have to resort to the desperate measure of a police restraining order. The rage, shame, depression, humiliation, anxiety, confusion, suspicion, sorrow, injured pride, and fear of abandonment that accompany jealousy make it a passion with peril unrivaled in the human emotional landscape.

The experience of jealousy can be psychologically painful, and for this reason it has been called a negative emotion. But the principle of strategic interference explains why we need these painful experiences. They alert us to real threats by real rivals. They tell us when a partner's sexual indifference might not merely mean that he's distracted by work. They cause us to remember subtle signals that, when properly assembled, portend a real defection. We experience pain because pain motivates us to deal with real strategic interference and solve actual adaptive problems. The painful emotions that alert us to strategic interference help us by forcing us to deal with the sources of the problems.

The principle of error management helps to explain why jealousy sometimes seems so irrational. We live in a world riddled with uncertainty, a booming, buzzing chaos of cues requiring inferences about an unseen reality. Over evolutionary time, some errors of inference were more costly than others. Failing to detect an actual infidelity was more costly than mistakenly accusing an innocent partner of betrayal. Evolution, as a consequence, forged a hypersensitive defense system, designed to sound the alarm not just when an infidelity has been discovered, but also when the circumstances make it slightly more likely. These adaptive biases explain why we sometimes infer a betrayal when none has occurred and why these mistakes may not really be "errors" over the long run.

We live in an age where some people bridle at the suggestion that women and men differ. People worry that discoveries of sex differences will justify discrimination. If evolution has made women and men different, this reasoning goes, it might justify keeping women out of certain jobs or at home barefoot and pregnant. But the findings of sex differences provide no justification for these inferences. Neither sex can be considered superior or inferior to the other, any more than a bird's wings can be considered superior or inferior to a fish's fins.

Time after time, the discoveries of sex differences coming out of our lab have been met with outrage, especially when they have been reported in national publications such as the *New York Times* or on television news magazines such as NBC's *Dateline*. The work disturbs so many people that the field swirls with controversy. But I believe that knowledge of these sex differences is critical if we are to stand any chance of dealing with the evolved demons that lurk within all of us.

Some people worry that information about the evolved foundation of our passions will be misused. Men, for example, might justify sexual infidelity—"I couldn't help it; my evolved psychology made me do it." Although this concern should not be discounted, I've witnessed men use this knowledge, instead, to help them remain faithful. "When I find myself attracted to another woman," one man told me, "I realize it's just my evolved desire for sexual variety; it doesn't mean I don't love my wife; it doesn't mean she doesn't understand me; knowing this helps me to stay faithful."

Men are sometimes disturbed when they discover that a partner has sexual fantasies about other men, but I have yet to interview a woman who hasn't had them. They reflect the fact that no matter how good or loving a current relationship is, ancestral women needed mate insurance because something can always go wrong. Women's fantasies don't reflect a lack of love, or mean that a woman will begin an affair with a colleague as soon as her husband leaves town. Knowledge of the purposes of hidden passions may help to keep our desires in proper perspective.

Evolution has equipped all of us with a rich menu of emotions, including jealousy, envy, fear, rage, joy, humiliation, passion, and love. This constellation has co-evolved in men and women, each changing form and function to respond to novel adaptive challenges created by the others. The knowledge that comes with a deeper understanding of our dangerous passions will not eliminate conflicts between lovers, between rivals, or between lovers who become rivals. But it may, in some small measure, give us the emotional wisdom to deal with them.

Notes

Chapter 1: The Dangerous Passion

Page
3 The gulf between the sexes: Buss et al., 1999.
6 In one study of battered women: Wilson & Daly, 1996.
7 I don't know why I killed the woman: Carlson, 1984, p. 9.
9 Sarah Hrdy of the university of California: Hrdy & Whitten, 1987.
10 Among the chimpanzees: de Waal, 1982.
11 As the psychologist Steven Pinker: Pinker, 1997, p. 418.
11 One key to the mystery of love: Frank, 1988.
12 Consider the case of John W. Hinckley: quoted in Hatfield & Rapson, 1993, pp. 36–37.
13 In a recent survey: Baumeister & Wotman, 1992.
13 One of the great love stories: Baumeister & Wotman, 1992.
16 In one of our recent studies: Schmitt, Shackelford, & Buss, under review; many previous studies have confirmed the same fundamental sex differences; see Buss, 1998, for a review of the evidence.
16 In another study: Ellis & Symons, 1990.
17 Sexual infidelity causes divorce worldwide: Betzig, 1989.
17 Indeed, my colleagues: Baker & Bellis, 1995.
18 For the past seven years, Heidi Greiling and I: Greiling & Buss, in press.
19 Research by Steve Gangestad and Randy Thornhill: Gangestad & Thornhill, 1997.
19 During ancestral times: Diamond, 1992, 1998; Nesse & Williams, 1994; Tooby & DeVore, 1987; Williams & Nesse, 1991. For discussions of these factors affecting tribal or traditional cultures, see Chagnon, 1983; Hill & Hurtado, 1996.
19 The paleontological and cross-cultural records: Walker, 1995.
19 Ancestral women who failed: Buss, 1994; Diamond, 1992; Fisher, 1992; Smith, 1984.
20 American divorce rates: Gottman, 1994.
20 In the most extensive study: Stanislaw & Rice, 1988.
21 A recent survey: Baker & Bellis, 1995.
22 The jealous person: Mowat, 1966; quoted in Sommers, 1988, p. 153.
22 Consider the case: Odegaard, 1968.

23 Jealousy is often triggered: Clanton & Smith, 1998; Tooby & Cosmides, 1990; White, 1980; White, 1981b.

23 The man was 35 years old: Shepherd, 1961, p. 732.

23 Differences in desirability: Clanton & Smith, 1998; Tooby & Cosmides, 1990; White, 1980; White, 1981b.

23 Elaine Hatfield and her colleagues: Walster, Traupmann, & Walster, 1978; Walster, Walster, & Berscheid, 1978.

Chapter 2: The Jealousy Paradox

27 Consider these findings: Mullen & Martin, 1994.

27 St. Augustine noted this link: quoted in Claypool & Sheets, 1996.

27 The psychologist Eugene Mathes: Mathes, 1986.

28 Contrast this with another finding: Riggs, 1993.

28 The paradox was reflected in O. J. Simpson's statement: Newsweek, Dec. 28, 1998, p. 116.

28 The emotion of jealousy: Gillard, quoted in Ellis, 1950. p.

28 The Norwegian psychiatrist Nils Retterstol: Retterstol, 1967.

28 The psychologist Gordon Clanton: Clanton & Smith, 1977.

29 Jealousy is "sexual": Daly, Wilson, & Weghorst, 1982.

29 Some writers fail to distinguish: DeSteno & Salovey, 1995.

30 The husband, however, may be jealous of his beautiful wife: Foster, 1972.

30 According to psychologist Ralph Hupka: Hupka, 1991, pp. 254, 260.

30 The psychiatrist Dinesh Bhugra: Bhugra, 1993.

30 Capitalist society encourages: Bhugra, 1993, p. 272.

31 Third, since "motives for jealousy": Bhugra, 1993, p. 273.

31 Another explanation of jealousy: Bhugra, 1993.

31 Sometimes jealousy is indeed pathological: Johnson, 1969.

31 Among the Ache of Paraguay: Borgerhoff Mulder, 1988; Hill & Hurtado, 1996.

31 Even among the Ammassalik Eskimos: Mirksy, 1937.

31 And contrary to Margaret Mead's assertion: cited in Freeman, 1983, p. 244.

31 To cite one example: Freeman, 1983, pp. 243–244.

32 In one case the husband: Freeman, 1983, p. 244.

32 Cultures in tropical paradises: Brown, 1991; Freeman, 1983.

33 In an important sense, therefore: Symons, 1979; Wilson & Daly, 1996.

34 This is especially true if there are genetic kin: Alexander, 1987.

35 Divorced status and the existence of children: Margo Wilson and Martin Daly, personal communication, 1989.

35 The children suffer: Daly & Wilson, 1996.

37 Charles Darwin expressed the key insight: Darwin, 1877, pp. 285–286.

37 The specific array of human fears: Marks, 1987.

37 Fear of heights and strangers: Scarr & Salapatek, 1970.

37 In one study, 80 percent of infants who had been crawling: Bertenthal, Campos, & Caplovitz, 1983.

37 Fear of strangers in human infants has been documented: Smith, 1979.

37 In fact, the risk of infants being killed by strangers: Daly & Wilson, 1988; Hrdy, 1981; Wrangham & Peterson, 1996.

37 As the Harvard psychologist Jerome Kagan: Kagan, Kearsley, & Zelazo, 1978.

39 Paul Mullen, a psychiatrist at the University of Otago: Mullen, 1990.

39 Don Sharpsteen, a professor of psychology at the University of Missouri: Sharpsteen, 1993.

40 The psychiatrist Mary Seeman: Seeman, 1979.

41 Gregory White and Paul Mullen noted: White & Mullen, 1989, p. 179.

44 At the current moment in time: Hall, 1984.

Chapter 3: Jealousy on Mars and Venus

50 Bram Buunk, a professor at the University of Groningen: Buunk & Hupka, 1987.

50 Dozens of other studies verify the conclusion: White & Mullen, 1989.

51 Only later did she realize: Seeman, 1979, p. 356.

51 His wife was simply standing by the stove: Sommers, 1988, p. 160.

52 In Greece, for example, a man's reputation is threatened: Safilios-Rothschild, 1969, pp. 78–79.

53 People from the United States and Germany: Buss, 1994.

54 The anthropologist John Marshal Townsend: Townsend, 1995.

54 Here is what one woman reported: Townsend, 1998, p. 12.

55 As Townsend concludes: Townsend, 1995, p. 173.

55 On a 7-point scale: Buss, 1989b.

56 In this study of 530 men and women: Shackelford, Buss, & Bennett, 1999.

56 Verbal reports are reasonable sources of data: Buss et al., 1992.

58 So my research collaborators and I conducted four studies: Buss et al., 1999; see also Wiederman & Allgeier, 1993, for studies that confirm the evolutionary explanation when pitted against social learning theory explanations.

59 They concluded that "contrary to the double-shot explanation": Wiederman & Kendall, 1999.

60 These and similar sex differences have now been replicated: Buunk et al., 1996; for the Swedish replication, see Wiederman & Kendall, 1999; for the Chinese studies, see Geary et al., 1995; see also Mills & Catalanotti, 1997, for another empirical refutation of the double-shot hypothesis.

62 "I think the everyday kind of jealousy": Viorst, 1998, p. 21.

62 For committed romantic relationships: see Bringle, 1995, for a summary of the evidence.

63 The evolutionary anthropologist William Jankowiak: Jankowiak, Hill, & Donovan, 1992.

63 One study found that gay men: Blumstein & Schwartz, 1983.

63 One study compared 113 homosexual men: Hawkins, 1990.

63 Robert Bringle of Purdue University in Indianapolis: Bringle, 1995.

64 A team of Dutch psychologists led by Pieternel Dijkstra: Dijkstra et al., 1998.

64 Michael Bailey of Northwestern University: Bailey et al., 1994.

65 On July 30, 1771, a man named Werther: Schmitt, 1988.

66 He seems to have little ill-humor: Goethe, 1970, pp. 29–30.

66 This preference does not diminish: Buss, 1994; Townsend & Levy, 1990; Wiederman & Allgeier, 1992.

66 Furthermore, since violence has been a recurrent problem: Buss, 1994; Ellis, 1992.

67 Pieternel Dijkstra and Bram Buunk conducted a study: Dijkstra & Buunk, in press.

69 To answer this question, my colleagues Jae Choe: Buss et al., in press.

71 One of the most vivid demonstrations: Nelson, 1995.

71 The qualities of dangerous rivals: Nelson, 1995, p. 80.

71 Cars and cellular phones signal status: Nelson, 1995, p. 80.

72 "Lucky's babymother had a grudge feeling": Nelson, 1995, pp. 80–82.

72 In Samoa, a culture: Mead, 1931.

Chapter 4: The Othello Syndrome

73 Larry and his wife, Susan, had been happily married for three years: Sommers, 1988.

73 A man named Paul purchased a trendy new overcoat: Eskapa, 1984; cited in Sommers, 1988, p. 179.

74 Her case was sufficiently interesting: Cobb, 1979, p. 513.

76 Martie Haselton of the University of Texas: Haselton & Buss, in press; Haselton, Buss, & DeKay, 1998; see also Schlager, 1995.

76 To explore just how uncertain people really are: Paul, Foss, & Galloway, 1993.

79 In one study of British men: Moulton, 1975.

79 "A boy, a man, on a date, is in competition": Van den Berghe, 1979, p. 219.

79 In a survey of the so-called Standard Sample: Broude & Greene, 1976, p. 417.

80 Armadillo left his house to wander about through the woods: Gregor, 1985, p. 138.

80 These include *maiyala euti,* which means "the penis is tired": Gregor, 1985, p. 139.

80 These are described with the term *japujate euti:* Gregor, 1985, p. 139.

81 One was due to the loss of sexual desire entirely: Vauhkonen, 1968.

81 One man reported: Todd & Dewhurst, 1955, p. 371.

81 Another case involved a 68-year-old man: Richardson, Malloy, & Grace, 1991.

82 As Jed Diamond, author of the book *Male Menopause,* noted: Diamond, quoted in Warga, 1999, p. 315.

82 The sexologist Krafft-Ebing was the first to report: Krafft-Ebing, 1905.

83 A study in 1968 revealed: Vauhkonen, 1968.

83 Paul Mullen found in 1985 that only 11 percent of his sample of 138 alcoholics: Mullen & Maack, 1985.

83 A 1991 study in Germany of 93 cases of "delusional jealousy": Soyka, Naber, & Volcker, 1991.

83 By far the most systematic study: Shrestha et al., 1985.

83 Alcohol is clearly linked with potency problems: Whalley, 1978.

83 Women may develop an "aversion": Krafft-Ebing, 1905, p. 514.

84 In one case, an aging man started to become concerned: Langfeldt, 1961, p. 33.

85 His psychiatrist was unable to contain the man's jealousy: Retterstol, 1967, p. 99.

85 Treatment was unsuccessful: Langfeldt, 1961, pp. 26–27.

85 The therapist of one couple: Retterstol, 1967, p. 104.

85 In my study of 107 married couples: Buss, 1994.

86 A recurrent thought among men: Shrestha et al., 1985, p. 284.

86 In one case, a married man 43 years old: Todd & Dewhurst, 1955, pp. 367–368.

87 Individuals who differ in desirability: Hatfield, Traupmann, & Walster, 1979.

87 Although they both age chronologically at the same rate: Symons, 1979.

87 Simultaneously, the man's elevated status: Betzig, 1986; Buss, 1994; Holmberg, 1950; Symons, 1979.

87 As Donald Symons notes: Symons, 1979, pp. 238–239.

88 With the approach of the menopause: Todd & Dewhurst, 1955, p. 371.

88 Another woman, age 44: Langfeldt, 1961, pp. 30–31.

88 As Claire Warga, author of *Menopause and the Mind:* Warga, 1999, p. 7.

89 Consider the following case of a woman: Seeman, 1979, p. 351.

89 Oscar Wilde asserted: cited in Enoch & Trethowan, 1979, p. 46.

89 In fact, the theory predicts a counterintuitive result: see Hatfield et al., 1979; Tooby & Cosmides, 1990.

89 This is especially true when the husband experiences professional success: Buss, 1994; Holmberg, 1950.

89 As therapist Mary Seeman noted: Seeman, 1979, p. 354.

89 In these cases, when questioned about the sexual fantasies: Seeman, 1979, p. 355.

91 A married couple initially well matched: Buss, 1987; Buss et al., 1990.

91 Although systematic large-scale studies of illness and jealousy: Breitner & Anderson, 1994.

91 Prior to Parkinson's disease: Breitner & Anderson, 1994, p. 704.

92 In ancestral times, a man's aging and ill health: Buss, 1994; Buss et al., 1990.

92 Those who are lower in desirability: Critelli & Wade, 1980; Hatfield et al., 1979; Kenrick, 1994; Kenrick et al., 1993; Symons, 1979; Thiessen & Gregg, 1980; Tooby & Cosmides, 1990; White, 1980, 1981a, 1981b.

93 The people who believed that they were superior: Hatfield et al., 1979.

93 These circumstances trigger: Tooby & Cosmides, 1990.

93 The less attractive partner, in contrast: Frank, 1988.

93 In one study of 220 married couples: Hansen, 1985.

93 Scenario 1: "Your mate returns from a business trip": Hansen, 1985, p. 267.

94 Scenario 2: "Your mate has developed an ongoing emotional and sexual relationship": Hansen, 1985, p. 267.

94 The overwhelming majority of vivid memories: Thorne, 1998.

95 In the most detailed study, psychiatrists John Docherty and Jean Ellis: Docherty & Ellis, 1976.

96 His jealousy began when his wife: Docherty & Ellis, 1976, p. 681.

96 Each man had developed a heightened sensitivity: Marks, 1987.

96 In one case, a man showed absolutely no indications: Mullen & Maack, 1985, p. 114.

97 She had left him two years earlier because he was unfaithful: Todd & Dewhurst, 1955, p. 370.

98 One study of 36 agoraphobic women explored this: Hafner, 1979.

99 When the therapist recontacted the couple a year later: Hafner, 1979, pp. 99–100.

99 The trouble started when he entered therapy: Turbott, 1981.

99 One morning, she felt "moisture on his penis": Turbott, 1981, p. 167.

100 According to Shirley Glass: Shirley Glass, personal communication, August 15, 1998: Laura Nitzberg, personal communication, 1992.

Chapter 5: If I Can't Have Her, Nobody Can

101 "Confess. You slept with him": Zola, 1956/1890; quoted in Mullen, 1990, p. 24.

101 The first case is told by a woman, age 19: Gelles & Strauss, 1988, p. 132.

102 In a second case, "the wife, confronted with yet another round": White & Mullen, 1989, p. 224.

102 "A lady saw a woman in the street": White & Mullen, 1989, p. 227.

102 Evidence has been cumulating for decades: Daly et al., 1982.

102 In one interview study of 44 battered wives: Miller, 1980.

103 In another study of 150 cases of women who were battered: Roy, 1977.

103 In a third study of 31 battered women in hostels and hospitals: Rounsaville, 1978.

103 In 57 out of the 60 cases, the women reported: Hilberman & Munson, 1978, p. 461.

103 A fifth study found that 87 out of 101 battered women: Church, 1984.

103 More than a dozen studies have examined date violence: Sugarman & Hotaling, 1989.

103 As summarized by Sugarman and Hoteling: Sugarman & Hotaling, 1989, p. 12.

104 "A particularly nasty husband might hit his wife": Chagnon, 1992, p. 147, italics added.

104 "N/ahka, a middle-aged woman, was attacked by her husband": Draper, 1992, p. 54.

105 Paul Mullen of the University of Otago: Mullen & Maack, 1985.

105 The psychologists John Gottman and Neil Jacobson: Jacobson & Gottman, 1998.

106 In a large study of more than 8,000 participants: Wilson & Daly, 1996.

107 The controversy was initiated in 1978: Steinmetz, 1978.

107 The controversy ignited: Gelles & Strauss, 1988, p. 105.

108 Some research on date violence: Bookwala et al., 1992.

108 "When he hits me, I retaliate": Gelles & Strauss, 1988, p. 90.

108 "I know that look he gets when he gets ready to hit me": Gelles & Strauss, 1988, p. 91.

108 A third case involved Francine Hughes: Gelles & Strauss, 1988, p. 133.

109 According to sociologist R. N. Whitehurst: Whitehurst, 1971, p. 686.

110 As Neil Jacobson and John Gottman argue: Jacobson & Gottman, 1998, pp. 55–56.

110 As a result of patriarchy, they continue: Jacobson & Gottman, 1998, pp. 268–269.

110 "Dad could get really mad": Sammons, 1978, p. 43.

111 "Most duels start between two men": Chagnon, 1983, p. 171.

111 Thousands of miles away from the Yanomamö: Hart & Pilling, 1960.

112 Margo Wilson and Martin Daly speculate: Wilson & Daly, 1993a, 1993b.

113 In a study of 100 women at a shelter for battered women: Gayford, 1975, p. 195.

113 Some women respond to a man's violence: Wilson & Daly, 1993a, 1993b.

113 "I had been discussing the roots of wife battering": W. Zimmerman, personal communication, March 26, 1998.

113 One study interviewed a sample of battered women: Shields & Hanneke, 1983.

116 When the definition is broadened: Jason, Reichler, Easton, Neal & Wilson, 1984.

116 According to a research review: Tjaden, 1997.

117 The most extensive study of mate homicides: Wilson, Daly, & Wright, 1993.

118 In a study of 25 spousal homicides: Chimbos, 1978.

118 "She often called me a 'damned mute'": Chimbos, 1978, p. 52.

118 "Her infidelity really bothered me": Chimbos, 1978, p. 52.

118 "She would humiliate me in front of others": Chimbos, 1978, p. 53.

118 "You see, we were always arguing about her extramarital affairs": Chimbos, 1978, p. 54.

118 "We got married on a Saturday": Chimbos, 1978, pp. 54–55.

119 Martin Daly and Margo Wilson compiled evidence: Daly, Wilson, & Weghorst, 1982.

120 Peter Chimbos conducted intensive interviews: Chimbos, 1978.

120 In one study of court records in the Sudan: Lobban, 1972.

120 In a study of Ugandan homicides: Tanner, 1970.

120 The most extensive cross-cultural study: Bohannan, 1960.

120 This is surely an underestimate of jealous homicides: Daly, Wilson, & Weghorst, 1982.

120 The second most extensive non-Western study: Sohier, 1959.

121 "Men . . . strive to control women": Daly & Wilson, 1988, p. 205; italics added.

121 They elaborate in a later publication: Wilson, Daly, & Daniele, 1995; italics added.

121 But sometimes the violence gets out of hand: Wilson & Daly, 1993a, p. 281.

121 Joshua Duntley and I have proposed: Buss & Duntley, 1998, 1999; Duntley & Buss, 1998, 1999.

122 One Australian man, who killed his wife: Wallace, 1986, p. 120.

122 In another case, an Illinois man issued the following threat: Wilson & Daly, 1993b, p. 3.

122 As Daly and Wilson note: Daly, Wilson, & Weghorst, 1982, p. 19.

123 Ironically, Wilson and Daly, the proponents: Wilson, Daly, & Wright, 1993.

123 Research conducted in three separate countries: Wilson & Daly, 1993b.

124 Here is what one Chicago woman declared: Wilson & Daly, 1993b, p. 10.

124 It is clear that the laws on the books: Daly & Wilson, 1988.

124 As Daly and Wilson state: Daly & Wilson, 1988, pp. 193–194.

124 Among the Yapese, for example: Muller, 1917, p. 229.

125 According to the Texas penal code: Daly & Wilson, 1988, p. 194.

125 In New Mexico and Utah until the 1970s: Le Fave & Scott, 1972.

125 The killing of an adulterous wife used to be exempt: Blackstone, 1803, book 4, pp. 191–192.

125 As one legal scholar described this notion: Edwards, 1954, p. 900.

126 In Daly and Wilson's study of spousal homicides: Daly & Wilson, 1988, p. 206.

126 First, women usually want men who are only a few years older: Buss, 1989a.

127 Among the spousal homicides in Miami: Wilbanks, 1984.

127 The largest sample of spousal homicides: Wilson, Daly, & Wright, 1993.

127 A disturbing statistic attests to this conflict: Daly & Wilson, 1988.

127 Daly and his colleagues explored this issue: Daly, Wiseman, & Wilson, 1997.

128 "One woman was slain 4 days after moving out": Daly et al., 1997, p. 68.

Chapter 6: Secrets and Lies

131 On February 28, 1997, Monica Lewinsky entered the Oval Office: *Newsweek*, September 21, 1998, pp. 58–60.

132 Shere Hite put the rates as high as 70 percent: Hite, 1987; Greeley, 1991.

133 One study was particularly revealing: Green, Lee, & Lustig, 1974.

133 Anthony Thompson of Western Australian Institute: Thompson, 1983.

133 Graham Spanier, of the State University of New York: Spanier & Margolis, 1983.

134 A recent example: "Fourth Woman Accuses 'Guru' of Sex": *Austin American Statesman*, June 23, 1999, p. B2.

134 This is one of many studies: Clark & Hatfield, 1989.

134 The journalist Natalie Angier questions these results: Angier, 1999.

135 Russell Clark of the University of North Texas: Clark, 1990.

136 In one study by Ralph Johnson: Johnson, 1970.

136 In a classic older study by Lewis Terman: Terman, 1938.

136 Germans reveal similar tendencies: Sigusch & Schmidt, 1971.

136 More recent studies by David Wyatt Seal: Seal, Agostinelli, & Hannett, 1994.

136 As evolutionary psychologist Donald Symons: Symons, 1979, p. 207.

137 Research conducted in Japan, Great Britain, and the United States: Ellis & Symons, 1990; Wilson, 1987.

137 Here is one sample fantasy: Berkowitz, 1997, pp. 137–138.

138 As Bruce Ellis and Donald Symons: Ellis & Symons, 1990, p. 544.

138 Consider this sexual fantasy: Maltz & Boss, 1997, p. 38.

139 Here is one from Bobbi: Maltz & Boss, 1997, pp. 227–228.

139 As one woman observed: Barclay, 1973, p. 211.

140 When studying the avian species: Burley, 1986a, 1986b.

141 It was as if the less desirable birds: Burley, 1986a, 1986b; Trivers, 1985.

141 The first evidence for the importance: Berscheid, Hatfield, & Bohrnstedt, 1973; Walster, Walster, & Berscheid, 1978.

142 In a more recent study of newlywed couples: Buss & Shackelford, 1997a; Shackelford & Buss, 1997b.

143 These findings have some degree of cross-cultural generality: Prins, Buunk, & van Yperen, 1993.

144 The same logic applies to the time and energy: Alexander, 1979.

144 To find out, David Waynforth at the University of New Mexico: Waynforth, 1999.

146 Shirley Glass and Thomas Wright explored the link: Glass & Wright, 1985.

146 Glass related the following incident: Glass, 1998, p. 36.

147 "Here is a list of reasons": Glass & Wright, 1992, p. 371.

147 One final sex difference: Roscoe, Cavanaugh, & Kennedy, 1988.

148 To answer this question, Todd Shackelford and I: Buss & Shackelford, 1997a.

148 People high on narcissism: Buss & Chiodo, 1991.

149 Good behavioral markers of narcissism include: Buss & Chiodo, 1991.

149 Narcissism proved highly linked with susceptibility to infidelity: Shackelford & Buss, 1997a.

150 The psychoticism scale is something of a misnomer: Eysenck & Eysenck, 1975.

151 On the positive side, emotionally unstable persons: Barron, 1963; Konner, 1990.

151 When emotional instability is linked with another personality characteristic: Buss, 1991.

152 In 1997, Todd Shackelford and I explored an array: Shackelford & Buss, 1997a.

155 Worldwide, infidelity is the leading cause of divorce: Betzig, 1989.

155 In studies of Western cultures: Hunt, 1974; Kelly & Conley, 1987; Levinger, 1976.

156 As part of the study of 107 married couples: Shackelford & Buss, 1997a.

157 Early in the study, each person: Ellis, 1997.

157 "These days, there are many uncertainties": White & Booth, 1991.

Chapter 7: Why Women Have Affairs

159 As noted by the feminist evolutionary Sarah Hrdy: Hrdy, 1981.

160 Women have evolved concealed or cryptic ovulation: Baker & Bellis, 1995.

160 The logic of the mating market dictates: Buss, 1994; Symons, 1979; Wright, 1994.

160 Steve Gangestad and Randy Thornhill proposed one answer: Gangestad & Thornhill, 1997.

161 First, symmetry signals "developmental stability": Gangestad & Thornhill, 1997.

163 As Pamela des Barres observed: des Barres, 1987.

164 Imagine that you are on a camping trip: Orians & Heerwagen, 1992.

165 One solution to all these problems: Fisher, 1992; Greiling, 1995; Greiling & Buss, in press; Smith, 1984.

165 Cultivating a backup mate provides security: Buss, 1994; Fisher, 1992; Hrdy, 1981; Smith, 1984; Smuts, 1985; Hill & Hurtado, 1996.

165 As the biologist Robert Smith notes: Smith, 1984, p. 613.

166 The famous anthropologist Margaret Mead: Fisher, 1992, p. 159.

166 These two anecdotes, of course, do not add up: Buss & Schmitt, 1993.

166 According to Helen Fisher, several ancestral conditions: Fisher, 1992.

167 There are several other circumstances: Betzig, 1989; Buss, 1994; Smith, 1984.

167 Her regular mate might have become: Buss, 1989b.

167 One modern woman described her affair in these terms: Atwater, 1982, p. 75.

167 Some husbands become "slackers" over time: Betzig, 1989.

167 He could prove infertile: Smith, 1984.

167 Our studies of women's perceptions: Greiling & Buss, in press.

168 The affair, by boosting a woman's self-esteem: Thornhill, 1992.

168 "Yes, it built up my confidence": Atwater, 1982, p. 143.

168 "I think I'm more sure of myself": Atwater, 1982, p. 144.

168 After interviewing 50 women who were having affairs: Atwater, 1982, p. 144.

169 One woman reported: Atwater, 1982, p. 145.

169 Our more systematic studies: Greiling & Buss, in press.

169 "Oh, Christ, I could write a book!": Atwater, 1982, p. 110.

170 "Sexually it was really great for me": Atwater, 1982, p. 111.

170 "Our sexual relationship is totally different": Atwater, 1982, pp. 109–110.

170 When we asked women to evaluate which circumstances: Greiling & Buss, in press.

171 Sperm competition occurs: Baker & Bellis, 1995.

171 Averaging across a handful of studies: Baker, 1997; Smith, 1984.

172 Recent work, however, has focused: Baker, 1997.

174 To answer these questions, Heidi Greiling and I contrasted women: Greiling & Buss, in press.

177 As Laura Betzig documented: Betzig, 1989.

177 In one study of 100 battered women: Gayford, 1975, p. 195.

177 Children without an investing father: Hill & Hurtado, 1996.

178 In some Mediterranean cultures: Daly & Wilson, 1988.

178 We often base our evaluations of ourselves: Leary & Downs, 1995; Leary et al., in press; see also Kirkpatrick & Ellis, in press, for discussions of the evolutionary functions of self-esteem.

179 The end result is: Thornhill, 1992.

179 As Robert Frank of Cornell University observes: Frank, 1988, p. 198.

179 My study concerning the psychology of reputation in Zimbabwe: Buss, 1995b.

Chapter 8: Coping Strategies

181 Jonathan used field glasses: Todd & Dewhurst, 1955, p. 369.

181 In Barbados: Lawson, 1988.

182 She sat on her rival's stairs: Lawson, 1988, p. 281.

183 The central coping issue: Pines, 1998.

184 Some researchers: Salovey & Rodin, 1988.

184 And some view violent expressions of jealousy: Salovey & Rodin, 1988, p. 31.

184 In a chapter in the *Clinical Handbook of Couple Therapy:* Pittman & Wagers, 1995, p. 297.

185 In one case, a man could not decide: Pittman & Wagers, 1995, p. 309.

185 "The triangle meeting had been planned": Pittman & Wagers, 1995, p. 309.

186 He "explained to his wife": Pittman & Wagers, 1995, p. 311.

186 In one case, a man diagnosed as irrationally jealous: White & Mullen, 1989, p. 251.

187 "For the first offense": Mantegazza, 1935, p. 195.

187 Among the Baiga: Elwin, 1939.

187 Among the Cumae in Campagna: Mantegazza, 1935, p. 204.

187 In North American Indian tribes: Mantegazza, 1935.

188 Throughout the entire world: Daly & Wilson, 1988.

188 Among the Yap in the Micronesian islands: Hunt et al., 1949.

188 In various groups in Africa: Borgerhoff Mulder, 1988.

188 According to one passage: Num. 5:11–28, quoted in Hartung (n.d.).

188 Clitoridectomy is inflicted: Walker & Parmar, 1993.

188 "Among my people, girls are not excised": Walker & Parmar, 1993, pp. 258–259.

189 French law made it a crime: Daly & Wilson, 1988.

190 Our studies of dating and married couples: Buss, 1988b; Buss & Shackelford, 1997b.

190 Joyce Shettel-Neuber and her colleagues: Shettel-Neuber, Bryson, & Young, 1978.

191 In a follow-up study of this newlywed sample: Buss & Shackelford, 1997b.

191 In one case, a woman who had been married: Grold, 1972, p. 123.

191 Every woman caused her to wonder: Grold, 1972, p. 123.

192 All of these love acts: Buss, 1988a.

192 According to evolutionary theorist Paul Gilbert: Gilbert, 1989.

193 It works in part because crying: Tooby & Cosmides, 1996.

195 In a study of 351 individuals in Dunedin: Mullen & Martin, 1994.

195 The psychologists Peter Salovey and Judith Rodin: Salovey & Rodin, 1988.

196 It becomes all the more puzzling: Sharpsteen & Schmalz, 1988.

197 At this stage in the co-evolutionary arms race: Tooby & Cosmides, 1990.

197 In our studies of mate retention tactics: Buss, 1988b; Buss & Shackelford, 1997b.

197 White asked men and women: White, 1980.

198 If suppressing one's own jealousy: Buss & Dedden, 1990.

198 Then they evaluated their own standing: Schmitt, 1988.

198 After rating their partner's preferences: Schmitt, 1988, p. 377.

199 This interpretation is endorsed: White & Mullen, 1989, p. 50.

199 But the first codified version: Ecclus. 28:17.

199 The psychologists Gordon Allport and Leo Postman: Allport & Postman, 1947, p. 314.

199 Lisa Dedden, David Schmitt, and I tested this idea: Buss & Dedden, 1990; Schmitt & Buss, 1996.

200 Since men's social status is heavily affected: Buss, 1995b.

201 Our actual perceptions of a person's beauty: Graziano et al., 1993.

201 These tactics acquire their effectiveness: Buss et al., 1990.

202 One of Bryson's female respondents said: Bryson, 1991, p. 202.

203 The project was continued after arguments: Dawkins, 1982, p. 48.

203 Yet psychologists have documented: Tversky & Kahneman, 1974.

203 It turns out that even digger wasps: Dawkins, 1982.

204 When Jeff Bryson studied a wide variety of responses: Bryson, 1991.

Chapter 9: Emotional Wisdom

206 In 1931, Margaret Mead disparaged jealousy: Mead, 1931, p. 35–36.

206 Kathy Labriola, a leading advocate of polyamory: Labriola, 1999, p. 1.

206 Social scientist Jan Wagner denounces jealousy: Wagner, 1976.

206 Even Zen Buddhists argue: Clanton & Smith, 1998, p. 178; Orage, n.d., p. 17–19.

206 The husband, a physician in his mid-forties: Pines, 1998, pp. 191–192.

208 All these puzzling phenomena: Zahavi, 1977; Zahavi & Zahavi, 1997.

208 Accurate evaluation of a partner's psychological involvement: Zahavi & Zahavi, 1997.

208 Physical appearance can change: Buss, 1999; Symons, 1995.

209 "The only way to obtain reliable information": Zahavi & Zahavi, 1997, p. 112.

210 In some species of birds: Zahavi & Zahavi, 1997.

210 How do we go about this delicate task: Research has barely begun on this topic, but a variety of research projects are under way and have led to some preliminary answers. See Friedman, Bleske, & Buss, in progress; Tooke, Cline, & Dailey, 1993.

210 If you have done any of these things: Sheets, Fredendall, & Claypool, 1997; Tooke et al., 1993. Intentional evocation of jealousy, however, does not necessarily imply conscious intent; often people are unaware of the strategic functions of their behavior.

211 In one study: White, 1980.

211 They found strong sex differences: Tooke et al., 1997.

212 Antonia Abbey of Wayne State University: Abbey, 1982.

212 Martie Haselton and I have labeled: Haselton & Buss, in press.

212 Gregory White conducted an in-depth: White, 1980.

213 Forty percent of the women: White, 1980.

213 Gregory White confirmed this conclusion: White, 1980.

214 Virgil Sheets and his colleagues: Sheets et al., 1997.

214 After becoming jealous: Sheets et al., 1997, p. 394.

214 Inspiring excessive jealousy: Sheets et al., 1997.

214 Consider one man's report: Fischer, 1999, p. 56.

215 "Let's call him Goatee Boy": Fischer, 1999, p. 56.

215 Or consider the case of Ben and Stacy": Pines, 1998.

216 "You hurt me more than any other woman": Pines, 1998, p. 204.

216 "When we made love afterward": Pines, 1998, p. 204.

216 The passionate nature of the sex: Baker & Bellis, 1995.

217 In one study, Mary Seeman found: Seeman, 1979, p. 358.

217 One woman in Seeman's study: Seeman, 1979, p. 359.

217 The great Russian writer Tolstoi: Tolstoi, 1960, p. 177.

217 One testament to the universality of love: Jankowiak, 1995.

218 Taita women in fact prefer: Jankowiak, 1995.

218 Susan Sprecher of Illinois State University: Sprecher et al., 1994.

218 The most plausible theory: Frank, 1988; Pinker, 1997.

220 Jealousy is one of the most commonly found correlates: Mathes, 1991.

220 Consider which of the following scenarios: Mathes, 1991, pp. 93–94.

221 In my studies: Buss, 1988b.

221 According to Ayala Pines: Pines, 1998, pp. 205–206.

221 As journalist Judith Viorst noted: Viorst, 1998, p. 19.

221 "On those days when I happen to be feeling mature": Viorst, 1998, p. 24.

References

Abbey, A. (1982). Sex differences in attributions for friendly behavior: Do males misperceive females' friendliness? *Journal of Personality and Social Psychology, 32,* 830–838.

Alexander, R. D. (1979). *Darwinism and human affairs.* Seattle: University of Washington Press.

————. (1987). *The biology of moral systems.* Hawthorne, NY: Aldine de Gruyter.

Allport, G. W., & Postman, L. (1947). *The psychology of rumor.* New York: Holt.

Angier, N. (1999). *Woman: An intimate geography.* Boston: Houghton Mifflin.

Atwater, L. (1982). *The extramarital connection.* New York: Irvington Publishers.

Bailey, J. M., Gaulin, S., Agyei, Y., & Gladue, B. A. (1994). Effects of gender and sexual orientation on evolutionary relevant aspects of human mating. *Journal of Personality and Social Psychology, 66,* 1081–1093.

Baker, R. R. (1997). Copulation, masturbation, and infidelity: State of the art. In Schmitt (Ed.), *New aspects of human ethology* (pp. 163–187). New York: Plenum Press.

Baker, R. R., & Bellis, M. (1995). *Human sperm competition.* London: Chapman Hall.

Barclay, A. M (1973). Sexual fantasies in men and women. *Medical Aspects of Human Sexuality, 7,* 205–216.

Barron, F. (1963). *Creativity and psychological health.* Princeton, NJ: Van Nostrand.

Baumeister, R. F., & Wotman, S. R. (1992). *Breaking hearts: the two sides of unrequited love.* New York: The Guilford Press.

Berkowitz, B. (1997). *His secret life: Male sexual fantasies.* New York: Simon & Schuster.

Berscheid, E., Hatfield, E., & Bohrnstedt, G. (1973). The body image report. *Psychology Today, 7,* 119–131.

Bertenthal, B. I., Campos, J. J., & Caplovitz, K. S. (1983). Self-produced locomotion: An organizer of emotional, cognitive, and social development in infancy. In R. N. Emde & R. Harmon (Eds.), *Continuities and discontinuities in development.* New York: Plenum Press.

Betzig, L. L. (1986). *Despotism and differential reproduction: A Darwinian view of history.* Hawthorne, NY: Aldine de Gruyter.

————. (1989). Causes of conjugal dissolution. *Current Anthropology, 30,* 654–676.

Bhugra, D. (1993). Cross-cultural aspects of jealousy. *International Review of Psychiatry, 5,* 271–280.

Blackstone, W. (1803). *Commentaries on the laws of England*. Philadelphia: William Young Birch & Abraham Small.

Blumstein, P., & Schwartz, P. (1983). *American couples*. New York: Morrow.

Bohannan, P. (1960). *African homicide and suicide*. Princeton, NJ: Princeton University Press.

Bookwala, J., Frieze, I. H., Smith, C., & Ryan, K. (1992). Predictors of dating violence: A multivariate analysis. *Violence and Victims, 7*, 297–311.

Borgerhoff Mulder, M. (1988). Kipsigis bridewealth payments. In L. L. Betzig, M. Borgerhoff Mulder, & P. Turke (Eds.), *Human reproductive behavior* (pp. 65–82). New York: Cambridge University Press.

Breitner, B. C. C., & Anderson, D. N. (1994). The organic and psychological antecedents of delusional jealousy in old age. *International Journal of Geriatric Psychiatry, 9*, 703–707.

Bringle, R. G. (1995). Sexual jealousy in the relationships of homosexual and heterosexual men: 1980 and 1992. *Personal Relationships, 2*, 313–325.

Broude, G., & Greene, J. (1976). Cross-cultural codes on twenty sexual attitudes and practices. *Ethnology, 15*, 409–429.

Brown, D. E. (1991). *Human universals*. New York: McGraw-Hill.

Bryson, J. B. (1991). Modes of response to jealousy-evoking situations. In P. Salovey (Ed.), *The psychology of jealousy and envy* (pp. 178–207). New York: Guilford Press.

Burley, N. (1986a). Sexual selection for aesthetic traits in species with biparental care. *American Naturalist, 127*, 415–445.

———. (1986b). Comparison of the band color preferences of two species of estrilid finches. *Animal Behavior, 34*, 1732–1741.

Buss, D. M. (1987). *Personality and the evocation of anger and upset*. Unpublished manuscript, University of Michican, Ann Arbon, Michigan.

———. (1988a). Love acts: The evolutionary biology of love. In R. J. Sternberg & M. L. Barnes (Eds.), *The psychology of love* (pp. 100–118). New Haven, CT: Yale University Press.

———. (1988b). From vigilance to violence: Tactics of mate retention. *Ethology and Sociobiology, 9*, 291–317.

———. (1989a). Sex differences in human mate preferences: Evolutionary hypotheses testing in 37 cultures. *Behavioral and Brain Sciences, 12*, 1–49.

———. (1989b). Conflict between the sexes: Strategic interference and the evocation of anger and upset. *Journal of Personality and Social Psychology, 56*, 735–747.

———. (1991). Conflict in married couples: Personality predictors of anger and upset. *Journal of Personality, 59*, 663–688.

———. (1994). *The evolution of desire: Strategies of human mating*. New York: Basic Books.

———. (1995a). Evolutionary psychology: A new paradigm for psychological science. *Psychological Inquiry, 6*, 1–49.

———. (1995b, June). *Human prestige criteria*. Paper presented at the annual meeting of the Human Behavior and Evolution Society, Santa Barbara, CA.

———. (1998). Sexual strategies theory: Historical origins and current status. *Journal of Sex Research, 34*, 19–31.

———. (1999). *Evolutionary psychology: The new science of the mind*. Boston: Allyn & Bacon.

Buss, D. M., Abbott, M., Angleitner, A., Asherian, A., Biaggio, A., and 45 other co-authors (1990). International preferences in selecting mates: A study of 37 cultures. *Journal of Cross-Cultural Psychology, 21*, 5–47.

Buss, D. M., & Chiodo, L. A. (1991). Narcissistic acts in everyday life. *Journal of Personality, 59,* 179–216.

Buss, D. M., & Dedden, L. A. (1990). Derogation of competitors. *Journal of Social and Personal Relationships, 7,* 395–422.

Buss, D. M., & Duntley, J. (1998, July). *Evolved homicide modules.* Paper presented at the Annual Meeting of the Human Behavior and Evolution Society, Davis, CA.

———. (1999). *Killer psychology: The evolution of intrasexual homicide.* Paper presented by Annual Meeting of the Human Behavior and Evolution Society, Salt Lake City, UT, June 5.

Buss, D. M., Larsen, R., Westen, D., & Semmelroth, J. (1992). Sex differences in jealousy: Evolution, physiology, and psychology. *Psychological Science, 3,* 251–255.

Buss, D. M., & Schmitt, D. P. (1993). Sexual strategies theory: An evolutionary perspective on human mating. *Psychological Review, 100,* 204–232.

Buss, D. M., & Shackelford, T. K. (1997a). Susceptibility to infidelity in the first year of marriage. *Journal of Research in Personality, 31,* 193–221.

———. (1997b). From vigilance to violence: Mate retention tactics in married couples. *Journal of Personality and Social Psychology, 72,* 346–361.

Buss, D. M., Shackelford, T. K., Choe, J., Buunk, B., & Dijkstra, P. (in press). Distress about rivals: Reactions to intrasexual competitors in Korea, the Netherlands, and America. *Personal Relationships.*

Buss, D. M., Shackelford, T. K., Kirkpatrick, L. A., Choe, J., Hasegawa, M., Hasegawa, T., & Bennett, K. (1999). Jealousy and the nature of beliefs about infidelity: Tests of competing hypotheses about sex differences in the United States, Korea, and Japan. *Personal Relationships, 6,* 125–150.

Buunk, A. P., Angleitner, A., Oubaid, V., & Buss, D. M. (1996). Sex differences in jealousy in evolutionary and cultural perspective: Tests from the Netherlands, Germany, and the United States. *Psychological Science, 7,* 359–363.

Buunk, B., & Hupka, R. B. (1987). Cross-cultural differences in the elicitation of jealousy. *Journal of Sex Research, 23,* 12–22.

Carlson, C. A. (1984). *Intrafamilial homicide: A sociobiological perspective.* Unpublished bachelor's thesis, McMaster University. Hamilton, Ont.

Chagnon, N. (1983). *Yanomamö: The fierce people* (3rd ed.). New York: Holt, Rinehart & Winston.

———. (1992). *Yanomamö: The last days of Eden.* San Diego: Harcourt Brace Jovanovich.

Chimbos, P. D. (1978). *Marital violence: A study of interspouse homicide.* San Francisco: R & R Associates.

Church, J. (1984). *Violence against wives: Its causes and effects.* Christchurch, New Zealand: Author.

Clanton, G., & Smith, L. G. (1977). *Jealousy.* New York: Prentice-Hall.

———. (1998). *Jealousy.* (3rd ed.) New York: University Press of America.

Clark, R. D. (1990). The impact of AIDS on gender differences in willingness to engage in casual sex. *Journal of Applied Social Psychology, 20,* 771–782.

Clark, R. D., & Hatfield, E. (1989). Gender differences in receptivity to sexual offers. *Journal of Psychology and Human Sexuality, 2,* 39–55.

Claypool, H., & Sheets, V. (1996, June). *Jealousy: Adaptive or destructive?* Paper presented at the annual meeting of the Human Behavior and Evolution Society, Evanston, IL.

Cobb, J. (1979). Morbid jealousy. *British Journal of Hospital Medicine, 21,* 511–518.

241

Critelli, J. W., & Wade, L. R. (1980). Physical attractiveness, romantic love, and equity restoration in dating relationships. *Journal of Personality Assessment, 44,* 624–629.

Daly, M., & Wilson, M. (1988). *Homicide.* Hawthorn, NY: Aldine de Gruyter.

———. (1996). Violence against stepchildren. *Current Directions in Psychological Science, 5,* 77–81.

Daly, M., Wilson, M., & Weghorst, S. J. (1982). Male sexual jealousy. *Ethology and Sociobiology, 3,* 11–27.

Daly, M., Wiseman, K. A., & Wilson, M. (1997). Women with children sired by previous partners incur excess risk of uxoricide. *Homicide Studies, 1,* 61–71.

Darwin, C. (1871). *The descent of man and selection in relation to sex.* London: Murray.

———. (1877). A biographical sketch of an infant. *Mind, 2,* 285–294.

Dawkins, R. (1982). *The extended phenotype.* Oxford: Oxford University Press.

Deaux, K., & Hanna, R. (1984). Courtship in the personals column: The influence of gender and sexual orientation. *Sex Roles, 11,* 363–375.

des Barres, P. (1987). *I'm with the band: Confessions of a groupie.* New York: Jove Books.

DeSteno, D. A., & Salovey, P. (1995). Jealousy and envy. In A. S. R. Manstead & M. Hewstone (Eds.), *The Blackwell encyclopedia of social psychology.* Oxford: Basic Blackwell.

de Waal, F. (1982). *Chimpanzee politics: Sex and power among apes.* Baltimore: Johns Hopkins University Press.

Diamond, J. (1992). *The third chimpanzee.* New York: HarperCollins.

———. (1998). *Guns, germs, and steal.* New York: Norton.

Diamond, J. (1997). *Male menopause.* Naperville, IL: Sourcebooks.

Dijkstra, P., & Buunk, B. P. (in press). Jealousy as a function of rival characteristics: An evolutionary perspective. *Personality and Social Psychology Bulletin.*

Dijkstra, P., Buunk, B. P., Groothof, H., Poel, G., Lavermans, T., & Schrier, M. (1998). *Sex differences in the events that elicit jealousy among homosexuals.* Unpublished manuscript, University of Groningen, The Netherlands.

Docherty, J. P., & Ellis, J. (1976). A new concept and finding in morbid jealousy. *American Journal of Psychiatry, 133,* 679–683.

Draper, P. (1992). Room to maneuver: !Kung women cope with men. In D. A. Counts, J. K. Brown, & J. C. Campbell (Eds.), *Sanctions and sanctuary: Cultural perspectives on the beating of wives.* Boulder, CO: Westview Press.

Duntley, J. D., & Buss, D. M. (1998, July). *Evolved anti-homicide modules.* Paper presented at the Annual Meeting of the Human Behavior and Evolution Society, Davis, CA.

———. (1999). *Killer psychology: The evolution of mate homicide.* Paper presented at the Annual Meeting of the Human Behavior and Evolution Society, Salt Lake City, UT, June 5.

Edwards, J. (1954). Provocation and the reasonable man: Another view. *Criminal Law Review,* 898–906.

Ellis, B. J. (1992). The evolution of sexual attraction: Evaluative mechanisms in women. In J. Barkow, L. Cosmides, & J. Tooby (Eds.), *The adapted mind* (pp. 267–288). New York: Oxford University Press.

———. (1997). *The dating alternatives questionnaire: An evolutionary approach to relationship dependence.* Unpublished manuscript.

———. (1998). The Partner-Specific Investment Inventory: An evolutionary approach to individual differences in investment. *Journal of Personality, 66,* 383–442.

Ellis, B. J., & Symons, D. (1990). Sex differences in fantasy: An evolutionary psychological approach. *Journal of Sex Research, 27,* 527–556.

Elwin, V. (1939). *The Baiga.* London: John Murray.

Enoch, M. D., & Trethowan, W. H. (1979). *Uncommon psychiatric syndromes.* Bristol: John Wright & Sons.

Eskapa, S. (1984). *Woman versus woman: The extra-marital affair.* Danbury, CT.: Franklin Watts.

Eysenck, H. J., & Eysenck, S. B. G. (1975). *Eysenck Personality Questionnaire Manual.* San Diego; Educational Testing Service.

Figueredo, A. J., & McClosky, L. A. (1993). Sex, money, and paternity: The evolution of domestic violence. *Ethology and Sociobiology, 14,* 353–379.

Fischer, N. (1999, February). Why making me jealous makes me hot. *Cosmopolitan,* p. 56.

Fisher, H. E. (1992). *The anatomy of love.* New York: Norton.

Foster, G. M. (1972). The anatomy of envy: A study in symbolic behavior. *Current Anthropology, 13,* 165–201.

Frank, R. (1988). *Passions within reason.* New York: Norton.

Freeman, D. (1983). *Margaret Mead and Samoa: The making and unmaking of an anthropological myth.* New York: Penguin Books.

Friedman, B. X., Bleske, A., & Buss, D. M. (in progress). Testing the testing of a bond. Research in progress, Department of Psychology, University of Texas, Austin.

Gangestad, S. W., & Thornhill, R. (1997). The evolutionary psychology of extrapair sex: The role of fluctuating asymmetry. *Evolution and Human Behavior, 18,* 69–88.

Gayford, J. J. (1975). Wife battering: A preliminary survey of 100 cases. *British Medical Journal, 1,* 194–197.

Geary, D. C., Rumsey, M., Bow-Thomas, C. C., & Hoard, M. K. (1995). Sexual jealousy as a facultative trait: Evidence from the pattern of sex differences in adults from China and the United States. *Ethology and Sociobiology, 16,* 355–383.

Gelles, R. J., & Strauss, M. A. (1988). *Intimate violence.* New York: Simon & Schuster.

Gilbert, P. (1989). *Human nature and suffering.* Hillsdale, NJ: Erlbaum.

Gillard, E. (1950). Quoted in Ellis, H. *Studies in the psychology of sex* (Vol. 2, chap. 11.) London: Heinemann.

Glass, S. P. (1998 July/August). Voices of infidelity. *Psychology Today,* 36–78.

Glass, S. P., & Wright, T. L. (1985). Sex differences in the type of extramarital involvement and marital dissatisfaction. *Sex Roles, 12,* 1101–1119.

———. (1992). Justifications for extramarital relationships: The association between attitudes, behaviors, and gender. *Journal of Sex Research, 29,* 361–387.

Goethe, J. W. (1970). *The sufferings of young Werther.* New York: Norton.

Gottman, J. (1994). *What Predicts Divorce.* Hillsdale, NJ: Erlbaum.

Gray, J. (1992). *Men are from Mars, women are from Venus.* New York: HarperCollins.

Graziano, W. G., Jensen Campbell, L., Shebilske, L., & Lundgren, S. (1993). Social influence, sex differences, and judgments of beauty: Putting the 'interpersonal' back in interpersonal attraction. *Journal of Personality & Social Psychology, 65,* 522–531.

Greeley, A. M. (1991). *Faithful attraction: Discovering intimacy, love, and fidelity in American marriage.* New York: Tom Doherty.

Green, B. L., Lee, R. R., & Lustig, N. (1974). Conscious and unconscious factors in marital infidelity. *Medical Aspects of Human Sexuality,* 87–105.

Gregor, T. (1985). *Anxious pleasures: The sexual lives of an Amazonian people*. Chicago: University of Chicago Press.

Greiling, H. (1995, June). *Women's mate preferences across contexts*. Paper presented at the Annual Meeting of the Human Behavior and Evolution Society, Santa Barbara, CA.

Greiling, H., & Buss, D. M. (in press). Women's sexual strategies: The hidden dimension of short-term extra-pair mating. *Personality and Individual Differences*.

Grold, L. J. (1972). Patterns of jealousy. *Medical Aspects of Human Sexuality, 6,* 118–126.

Guerrero, L. K., & Reiter, R. L. (1998). Expressing emotion: Sex differences in social skills and communicative responses to anger, sadness, and jealousy. In D. J. Canary & K. Dindia (Eds.), *Sex differences and similarities in communication* (pp. 321–350). Mahwah, NJ: Erlbaum.

Hafner, R. J. (1979). Agoraphobic women married to abnormally jealous men. *British Journal of Medical Psychology, 52,* 99–104.

Hall, J. A. (1984). *Nonverbal sex differences: Communication accuracy and expressive style*. Baltimore: Johns Hopkins University Press.

Hansen, G. L. (1985). Perceived threats and marital jealousy. *Social Psychology Quarterly, 48,* 262–268.

Hart, C. W., & Pilling, A. R. (1960). *The Tiwi of North Australia*. New York: Holt, Rinehart & Winston.

Hartung, J. (n.d.). *Chastity and fidelity: Biblical roots of the short leash on women*. Unpublished manuscript.

Haselton, M. G., & Buss, D. M. (in press). Biases in cross-sex mind-reading: Errors in design or errors by design? *Journal of Personality and Social Psychology*.

Haselton, M. G., Buss, D. M., & DeKay, W. T. (1998, July). *A theory of errors in cross-sex mind-reading*. Paper presented at the Annual Meeting of the Human Behavior and Evolution Society, Davis, CA.

Hatfield, E., & Rapson, R. L. (1993). *Love, sex, and intimacy*. New York: HarperCollins.

———. (1996). *Love and sex: Cross-cultural perspectives*. Boston: Allyn & Bacon.

Hatfield, E., Traupmann, J., & Walster, G. W. (1979). Equity and extramarital sex. In M. Cook & G. Wilson (Eds.), *Love and attraction* (pp. 232–324). Oxford: Pergamon.

Hawkins, R. O. (1990). The relationship between culture, personality, and sexual jealousy in men in heterosexual and homosexual relationships. *Journal of Homosexuality, 19,* 67–84.

Hilberman, E., & Munson, K. (1978). Sixty battered women. *Victimology, 2,* 460–470.

Hill, K., & Hurtado, A. M. (1996). *Ache life history*. Hawthorne, NY: Aldine de Gruyter.

Hite, S. (1987). *Women and love: A cultural revolution in progress*. New York: Knopf.

Holmberg, A. R. (1950). *Nomads of the long bow: The Siriono of Eastern Bolivia*. Washington DC: U.S. Government Printing Office.

Hrdy, S. B. (1981). *The woman that never evolved*. Cambridge: Harvard University Press.

Hrdy, S. B., & Whitten, P. P. (1987). Patterning of sexual activity. In B. Smuts, D. L. Cheney, R. M. Seyfarth, R. W. Wrangham, & T. T. Struhsaker (Eds.), *Primate Societies* (pp. 370–384). Chicago: University of Chicago Press.

Hunt, E. E., Schneider, D. M., Kidder, N. R., & Stevens, W. D. (1949). *The Micronesians of Yap and their depopulation*. Washington, DC: Pacific Science Board, National Research Council.

Hunt, M. (1974). *Sexual behavior in the 1970's*. Chicago: Playboy Press.

Hupka, R. B. (1991). The motive for arousal of romantic jealousy: Its cultural origin. In P. Salovey (Ed.), *The psychology of jealousy and envy* (pp. 252–270). New York: Guilford Press.

Jacobson, N., & Gottman, J. (1998). *When men batter women*. New York: Simon & Schuster.

Jankowiak, W. (Ed.). (1995). *Romantic passion: A universal experience?* New York: Columbia University Press.

Jankowiak, W. R., Hill, E. M., & Donovan, J. M. (1992). The effects of sex and sexual orientation on attractiveness judgments. *Ethology and Sociobiology, 13,* 73–85.

Jason, L. A., Reichler, A., Easton, J., Neal, A., & Wilson, M. (1984). Female harassment after ending a relationship: A preliminary study. *Alternative Lifestyles, 6,* 259–269.

Johnson, J. (1969). Organic psychosyndromes due to boxing. *British Journal of Psychiatry, 115,* 45–53.

Johnson, R. E. (1970). Some correlates of extramarital coitus. *Journal of Marriage and the Family, 32,* 449–456.

Kagan, J., Kearsley, R. B., & Zelazo, P. R. (1978). *Infancy: Its place in human development.* Cambridge: Harvard University Press.

Kelly, E. L., & Conley, J. J. (1987). Personality and compatibility: A prospective study of marital stability and marital satisfaction. *Journal of Personality and Social Psychology, 52,* 27–40.

Kenrick, D. T. (1994). Evolutionary social psychology: From sexual selection to social cognition. *Advances in Experimental Social Psychology, 26,* 75–121.

Kenrick, D. T., Groth, G. E., Trost, M. R., & Sadalla, E. K. (1993). Integrating evolutionary and social exchange perspectives on relationships: Effects of gender, self-appraisal, and involvement level on mate selection criteria. *Journal of Personality and Social Psychology, 64,* 951–969.

Kirkpatrick, L. A., & Ellis, B. J. (in press). Evolutionary perspectives on self-evaluation and self-esteem. In M. Clark & G. Fletcher (Eds.), *The Blackwell handbook in social psychology, Vol. 2: Interpersonal Processes.* Oxford: Blackwell Publishers.

Kitzinger, C., & Powell, D. (1995). Engendering infidelity: Essentialist and social constructionist readings of a story completion task. *Feminism & Psychology, 5,* 345–372.

Konner, M. (1990). *Why the reckless survive.* New York: Viking.

Krafft-Ebing, R. von. (1905). *Textbook of insanity* (C. G. Chaddock, Trans.). Philadelphia: S. A. Davis.

Labriola, K. (1999). *Unmasking the green-eyed monster: Managing jealousy in open relationships.* Unpublished manuscript.

Langfeldt, G. (1961). The erotic jealousy syndrome: A clinical study. *Acta Psychiatrica Scandinavica, 36* (suppl. 151), 7–68.

Lawson, A. (1988). *Adultery: An analysis of love and betrayal.* New York: Basic Books.

Leary, M. R., & Downs, D. L. (1995). Interpersonal functions of the self-esteem motive: The self-esteem system as a sociometer. In M. H. Kernis (Ed.), *Efficacy, agency, and self-esteem* (pp. 123–144). New York: Plenum Press.

Leary, M. R., Haupt, A. L., Strausser, K. S., & Chokel, J. T. (in press). Calibrating the sociometer: The relationship between interpersonal appraisals and self-esteem. *Journal of Personality and Social Psychology.*

Le Fave, W. R., & Scott, A. W. (1972). *Handbook of criminal law.* New York: West Publishing.

Levinger, G. (1976). A social psychological perspective on marital dissolution. *Journal of Social Issues, 32,* 21–47.

Lobban, C. F. (1972). *Law and anthropology in the Sudan (an analysis of homicide cases in Sudan)*. African Studies Seminar Series No. 13, Sudan Research Unit, Khartoum University.

Maltz, W., & Boss, S. (1997). *In the garden of desire: The intimate world of women's sexual fantasies*. New York: Broadway Books.

Mantegazza, P. (1935). *The sexual relations of mankind*. New York: Eugenics Publishing.

Marks, I. (1987). *Fears, phobias, and rituals: Panic, anxiety, and their disorders*. New York: Oxford University Press.

Mathes, E. W. (1986). Jealousy and romantic love: A longitudinal study. *Psychological Reports, 58*, 885–886.

———. (1991). *Jealousy: The psychological data*. New York: University Press of America.

Mead, M. (1931). Jealousy: Primitive and civilized. In S. D. Schmalhausen & V. F. Calverton (Eds.), *Women's coming of age* (pp. 35–48). New York: Horace Liveright.

Miller, D. J. (1980). *Battered women: Perspectives of their problems and their perception of community response*. Unpublished masters thesis, University of Windsor, Ont.

Mills, M. E., & Catalanotti, R. (1997, June). *Are sex differences in jealousy better explained by evolutionary theory or the "double shot" hypothesis?* Paper presented at the Annual Meeting of the Human Behavior and Evolution Society, Tuscon, AZ.

Mirksy, J. (1937). The Eskimo of Greenland. In M. Mead (Ed.), *Cooperation and competition among primitive peoples*. New York: McGraw-Hill.

Moulten, J. (1975). Sex and reference. In R. Baker & F. Elliston (Eds.), *Philosophy and Sex* (pp. 34–44). Buffalo: Prometheus Books.

Mowat, R. R. (1966). *Morbid jealousy and murder: A psychiatric study of morbidly jealous murderers at Broadmour*. London: Tavistock.

Mullen, P. E. (1990). A phenomenology of jealousy. *New Zealand Journal of Psychiatry, 24*, 17–28.

Mullen, P. E., & Maack, L. H. (1985). Jealousy, pathological jealousy, and aggression. In D. P. Farrington & J. Gunn (Eds.), *Aggression and dangerousness* (pp. 103–126). New York: Wiley.

Mullen, P. E., & Martin, J. (1994). Jealousy: A community study. *British Journal of Psychiatry, 164*, 35–43.

Muller, W. (1917). *Yap*. Band 2, Halbband 1 (as translated in HRAF). Hamburg: Friederichsen.

Nelson, J. (1995, August). Babymothers. *Elle*, pp. 79–84.

Nesse, R. M., & Williams, G. C. (1994). *Why we get sick*. New York: Times Books.

Odegaard, J. (1968). Interaksjonen Mellom Prnerne ved de Patolhiske Sjalusireaksjoner. *Nordisk Psykiatrisk Tidsskrift, 22*, 314–319.

Orage, A. R. (n.d.). *On love*. New York: Weiser.

Orians, G. H., & Heerwagen, J. H. (1992). Evolved responses to landscapes. In J. Barkow, L. Cosmides, & J. Tooby (Eds.), *The adapted mind* (pp. 555–579). New York: Oxford University Press.

Paul, L., Foss, M. A., & Galloway, J. (1993). Sexual jealousy in young women and men: Aggressive responsiveness to partner and rival. *Aggressive Behavior, 19*, 401–420.

Pines, A. M. (1998). *Romantic jealousy: Causes, symptoms, cures*. New York: Routledge.

Pinker, S. (1997). *How the mind works*. New York: Norton.

Pittman, F. S. III, & Wagers, T. P. (1995). Crises of infidelity. In N. S. Jacobson & A. S. Gurman (Eds.), *Clinical handbook of couple therapy* (pp. 295–316). New York: Guilford Press.

Prins, K. S., Buunk, B. P., & VanYperen, N. W. (1993). Equity, normative disapproval and extramarital relationships. *Journal of Social and Personal Relationships, 10,* 39–53.

Retterstol, N. (1967). Jealousy-paranoiac psychoses. *Acta Psychiatric Scandinavica, 43,* 75–107.

Richardson, E. D., Malloy, P. F., & Grace, J. (1991). Othello Syndrome secondary to right cerebrovascular infarction. *Journal of Geriatric Psychiatry and Neurology, 4,* 160–165.

Riggs, D. S. (1993). Relationship problems and dating aggression: A potential treatment target. *Journal of Interpersonal Violence, 8,* 18–35.

Roscoe, B., Cavanaugh, L. E., & Kennedy, D. R. (1988). Dating infidelity: Behaviors, reasons, and consequences. *Adolescence, 23,* 35–43.

Rounsaville, B. J. (1978). Theories in marital violence: Evidence from a study of battered women. *Victimology, 3,* 11–31.

Roy, M. (1977). A current survey of 150 cases. In M. Roy (Ed.), *Battered women: A psychoso-ciological study of domestic violence.* New York: Van Nostrand Reinhold.

Safilios-Rothschild, C. (1969). 'Honor' crimes in contemporary Greece. *British Journal of Sociology, 20,* 205–218.

Salovey, P., & Rodin, J. (1988). Coping with envy and jealousy. *Journal of Social and Clinical Psychology, 7,* 15–33.

Sammons, R. (1978). *Ache Texts.* Asuncion, Paraguay: New Tribes Mission.

Scarr, S., & Salapatek, P. (1970). Patterns of fear development during infancy. *Merrill-Palmer Quarterly, 16,* 53–90.

Schlager, D. (1995). Evolutionary perspectives on paranoid disorder. *Delusional Disorders, 18,* 263–279.

Schmitt, B. H. (1988). Social comparison in romantic jealousy. *Personality and Social Psychology Bulletin, 14,* 374–387.

Schmitt, D. P., & Buss, D. M. (1996). Strategic self-promotion and competitor derogation: Sex and context effects on perceived effectiveness of mate attraction tactics. *Journal of Personality and Social Psychology, 70,* 1185–1204.

Schmitt, D. P., Shackelford, T. K., & Buss, D. M. (1999). Sex differences in desire for sexual variety. Manuscript submitted for publication.

Seal, D. W., Agosinelli, G., & Hannett, C. A. (1994). Extradyadic romantic involvement: Moderating effects of sociosexuality and gender. *Sex Roles, 31,* 1–22.

Seeman, M. V. (1979). Pathological jealousy. *Psychiatry, 42,* 351–361.

Shackelford, T. K., & Buss, D. M. (1997a). Cues to infidelity. *Personality and Social Psychology Bulletin, 23,* 1034–1045.

———. (1997b). Anticipation of marital dissolution as a consequence of spousal infidelity. *Journal of Social and Personal Relationships, 14,* 793–808.

Shackelford, T. K., Buss, D. M., & Bennett, K. (1999). Sex differences in responses to a partner's infidelity. Manuscript submitted for publicatiion.

Sharpsteen, D. J. (1993). Romantic jealousy as an emotion concept: A prototype analysis. *Journal of Social and Personal Relationships, 10,* 69–82.

Sharpsteen, D. J., & Schmalz, C. M. (1988). *Romantic jealousy as a blended emotion.* Unpublished manuscript, University of Denver.

Sheets, V. L., Fredendall, L. L., & Claypool, H. M. (1997). Jealousy evocation, partner reassurance, and relationship stability: An exploration of the potential benefits of jealousy. *Evolution and Human Behavior, 18,* 387–402.

Shepherd, M. (1961). Morbid jealousy: Some clinical and social aspects of a psychiatric symptom. *Journal of Medical Science, 107,* 687–753.

Shettel-Neuber, J., Bryson, J. B., & Young, C. E. (1978). Physical attractiveness of the "other person" and jealousy. *Personality and Social Psychology Bulletin, 4,* 612–615.

Shields, N. M., & Hanneke, C. R. (1983). Battered wives' reactions to marital rape. In D. Finkelhor, R. J. Gelles, G. T. Hotaling, & M. A. Straus (Eds.), *The dark side of families* (pp. 131–148). Beverly Hills, CA: Sage.

Shrestha, K., Rees, D. W., Rix, K. J. B., Hore, B. D., & Faragher, E. B. (1985). Sexual jealousy in alcoholics. *Acta Psychiatrica Scandinavica, 72,* 283–290.

Sigusch, V., & Schmidt, G. (1971). Lower-class sexuality: Some emotional and social aspects in West German males and females. *Archives of Sexual Behavior, 1,* 29–44.

Smith, P. K. (1979). The ontogeny of fear in children. In W. Sluckin (Ed.), *Fear in animals and man* (pp. 164–168). London: Van Nostrand.

Smith, R. L. (1984). Human sperm competition. In R. L. Smith (Ed.), *Sperm competition and the evolution of animal mating systems* (pp. 601–659). New York: Academic Press.

Smuts, B. B. (1985). *Sex and friendship in baboons.* Hawthorne, NY: Aldine de Gruyter.

Sohier, J. (1959). *Essai sur la criminalite dans la province de Leopoldville.* Brussels: J. Duculot.

Sokoloff, B. (1948). *Jealousy: A psychological study.* London: Carroll and Nicholson.

Sommers, P. V. (1988). *Jealousy.* New York: Penguin Books.

Soyka, M., Naber, G., & Volcker, A. (1991). Prevalence of delusional jealousy in different psychiatric disorders: An analysis of 93 cases. *British Journal of Psychiatry, 158,* 549–553.

Spanier, G. B., & Margolis, R. L. (1983). Marital separation and extramarital sexual behavior. *Journal of Sex Research, 19,* 23–48.

Sprecher, S., Aron, A., Hatfield, E., Cortese, A., Potapova, E., & Levitskaya, A. (1994). Love: American style, Russian style, and Japanese style. *Personal Relationships, 1,* 349–369.

Stanislaw, H., & Rice, F. J. (1988). Correlation between sexual desire and menstrual cycle characteristics. *Archives of Sexual Behavior, 17,* 499–508.

Steinmetz, S. K. (1978). The battered husband syndrome. *Victimology, 2,* 449–509.

Stekel, W. (1921). *The depths of the soul* (S. A. Tannenbaum, Trans.). London: Kegan Paul.

Sugarman, D. B., & Hotaling, G. T. (1989). Dating violence: Prevalence, context, and risk markers. In M. A. Pirog-Good & J. E. Stets (Eds.), *Violence in dating relationships* (pp. 3–32). New York: Praeger.

Symons, D. (1979). *The evolution of human sexuality.* New York: Oxford University Press.

Symons, D. (1995). Beauty is in the adaptations of the beholder: The evolutionary psychology of human female sexual attractiveness. In P. R. Abramson & S. D. Pinkerton (Eds.), *Sexual nature, sexual culture* (pp. 80–118). Chicago: University of Chicago Press.

Tanner, R. E. S. (1970). *Homicide in Uganda, 1964: Crime in East Africa.* Uppsala: The Scandinavian Institute of African Studies.

Terman, L. M. (1938). *Psychological factors in marital happiness.* New York: McGraw Hill.

Thiessen, D. D., & Gregg, B. (1980). Human assortative mating and genetic equilibrium: An evolutionary perspective. *Ethology and Sociobiology, 1,* 111–140.

Thompson, A. P. (1983). Extramarital sex: A review of the literature. *Journal of Sex Research, 19,* 1–22.

Thorne, A. (1998, August). *Interpersonal memories as building blocks for social identity and the life story.* Paper presented at the annual meeting of the American Psychological Association, San Francisco.

Thornhill, N. (1992). *Female short-term sexual strategies: The self-esteem hypothesis.* Paper presented at the Annual Meeting of the Human Behavior and Evolution Society, Albuquerque, NM.

Tjaden, P. (1997, November). The crime of stalking: How big is the problem? *National Institute of Justice Research Review.*

Todd, J., & Dewhurst, K. (1955). The Othello Syndrome: A study in the psychopathology of sexual jealousy. *Journal of Nervous and Mental Disease, 122,* 367–376.

Tolstoi, L. (1960). *La Sonate à Kreutzer.* Paris: Gallimard.

Tooby, J., & Cosmides, L. (1990). On the universality of human nature and the uniqueness of the individual: The role of genetics and adaptation. *Journal of Personality, 58,* 17–68.

———. (1996). Friendship and the banker's paradox: Other pathways to the evolution of adaptations for altruism. *Proceedings of the British Academy, 88,* 119–143.

Tooby, J., & DeVore, I. (1987). The reconstruction of hominid behavioral evolution through strategic modeling. In W. G. Kinzey (Ed.), *The evolution of human behavior* (pp. 183–237). New York: State University of New York Press.

Tooke, W., Cline, K., & Daily, J. (1993, August). *The coevolution of jealousy and strategic jealousy induction: An evolutionary psychological approach.* Paper presented at the Annual Meeting of the Human Behavior and Evolution Society, Binghamton, NY.

Townsend, J. M. (1995). Sex without emotional involvement: An evolutionary interpretation of sex differences. *Archives of Sexual Behavior, 24,* 173–206.

———. (1998). *What women want—what men want.* New York: Oxford University Press.

Townsend, J. M., & Levy, G. D. (1990). Effects of potential partners' physical attractiveness and socioeconomic status on sexuality and partner selection. *Archives of Sexual Behavior, 19,* 149–164.

Trivers, R. (1985). *Social evolution.* Menlo Park, CA: Benjamin-Cummings.

Turbott, J. (1981). Morbid jealousy—an unusual presentation with the reciprocal appearance of psychopathology in either spouse. *Australian and New Zealand Journal of Psychiatry, 15,* 164–167.

Tversky, A., & Kahneman, D. (1974). Judgment under uncertainty: Heuristics and biases. *Science, 185,* 1124–1131.

Van den Berghe, P. (1979). *Human family systems: An evolutionary view.* New York: Elsevier.

Vauhkonen, K. (1968). *Acta psychiatrica Scandinavica* (Suppl. 202), 1.

Viorst, J. (1998). Confessions of a jealous wife. In G. Clanton & L. G. Smith (Eds.), *Jealousy* (3rd ed.), (pp. 17–24). New York: University Press of America.

Wagner, J. (1976). Jealousy, extended intimacies, and sexual affirmation. *ETC, 33,* 269–288.

Walker, A., & Parmar, P. (1993). *Warrior marks: Female genital mutilation and the sexual blinding of women.* New York: Harcourt Brace.

Walker, P. (1995, July). *Documenting patterns of violence in earlier societies: The problems and promise of using bioarchaeological data for testing evolutionary theories.* Paper presented at the Annual Meeting of the Human Behavior and Evolution Society, Santa Barbara, CA.

Wallace, A. (1986). *Homicide: The social reality.* Sydney: New South Wales Bureau of Crime Statistics and Research.

Walster, E., Traupmann, J., & Walster, G. W. (1978). Equity and extramarital sexuality. *Archives of Sexual Behavior, 7,* 127–176.

Walster, E., Walster, G. W., & Berscheid, E. (1978). *Equity: Theory and research.* Boston: Allyn & Bacon.

Warga, C. (1999). *Menopause and the mind.* New York: Free Press.

Waynforth, D. (1999). Differences in time use for mating and nepotistic effort as a function of male attractiveness in rural Belize. *Evolution and Human Behavior, 20,* 19–28.

Whalley, L. J. (1978). Sexual adjustment of male alcoholics. *Acta Psychiatriac Scandinavica, 58,* 281-298.

White, G. L. (1980). Inducing jealousy: A power perspective. *Personality and Social Psychology Bulletin, 6,* 222–227.

———. (1981a). Jealousy and partner's perceived motives for attraction to a rival. *Social Psychology Quarterly, 44,* 24–30.

———. (1981b). Relative involvement, inadequacy, and jealousy. *Alternative Lifestyles, 4,* 291–309.

White, G. L., & Mullen, P. E. (1989). *Jealousy: Theory, research, and clinical strategies.* New York: The Guilford Press.

White, L. K., & Booth, A. (1991). Divorce over the life course: The role of marital happiness. *Journal of Family Issues, 12,* 5–21.

Whitehurst, R. N. (1971). Violence potential in extramarital sexual responses. *Journal of Marriage and the Family, 33,* 683–691.

Wiederman, M. W., & Allgeier, E. R. (1992). Gender differences in mate selection criteria: Sociobiological or socioeconomic explanation? *Ethology and Sociobiology, 13,* 115–124.

———. (1993). Gender differences in sexual jealousy: Adaptationist or social learning explanation? *Ethology and Sociobiology, 14,* 115–140.

Wiederman, M. W., & Kendall, E. (1999). Evolution, gender, and sexual jealousy: Investigation with a sample from Sweden. *Evolution and Human Behavior, 20,* 121–128.

Wilbanks, W. (1984). *Murder in Miami.* Lanham, MD: University Press of America.

Williams, G. C., & Nesse, R. M. (1991). The dawn of Darwinian medicine. *Quarterly Review of Biology, 66,* 1–22.

Wilson, G. D. (1987). Male-female differences in sexual activity, enjoyment, and fantasies. *Personality and Individual Differences, 8,* 125–126.

Wilson, M., & Daly, M. (1993a). An evolutionary perspective on male sexual proprietariness and violence against wives. *Violence and Victims, 8,* 271-294.

———. (1993b). Spousal homicide risk and estrangement. *Violence and Victims, 8,* 3–16.

———. (1996). Male sexual proprietariness and violence against wives. *Current Directions in Psychological Science, 5,* 2–7.

Wilson, M., Daly, M., & Daniele, A. (1995) Familicide: The killing of spouse and children. *Aggressive Behavior 21,* 275–291.

Wilson, M., Daly, M., & Wright, C. (1993). Uxoricide in Canada: Demographic risk patterns. *Canadian Journal of Criminology, 35,* 263–291.

Wrangham, R., & Peterson, D. (1996). *Demonic males.* Boston: Houghton Mifflin.

Wright, R. (1994). *The moral animal.* New York: Vintage Books.

Zahavi, A. (1977). The testing of a bond. *Animal Behavior, 25,* 246–247.

Zahavi, A., & Zahavi, A. (1997). *The handicap principle.* New York: Oxford University Press.

Zola, E. (1956). *The beast in man.* London: Elk Books. (Original work published in 1890).

Index

BF
575
J4
B87
2011